RELIGION, ECONOMICS, AND CULTURE IN CONFLICT AND CONVERSATION

RELIGION, ECONOMICS, AND CULTURE IN CONFLICT AND CONVERSATION

Laurie Cassidy and Maureen H. O'Connell,
Editors

THE ANNUAL PUBLICATION
OF THE COLLEGE THEOLOGY SOCIETY
2010
VOLUME 56

ORBIS BOOKS
Maryknoll, New York 10545

Founded in 1970, Orbis Books endeavors to publish works that enlighten the mind, nourish the spirit, and challenge the conscience. The publishing arm of the Maryknoll Fathers and Brothers, Orbis seeks to explore the global dimensions of the Christian faith and mission, to invite dialogue with diverse cultures and religious traditions, and to serve the cause of reconciliation and peace. The books published reflect the views of their authors and do not represent the official position of the Maryknoll Society. To learn more about Maryknoll and Orbis Books, please visit our website at www.maryknollsociety.org.

Published by Orbis Books, Maryknoll, New York 10545-0302.
Manufactured in the United States of America.

Library of Congress Cataloging-in-Publication Data

Religion, economics, and culture in conflict and conversation / Laurie Cassidy and Maureen H. O'Connell, editors.
    p. cm. -- (The annual publication of the College Theology Society ; 2010, v. 56)
Includes bibliographical references.
ISBN 978-1-57075-913-0 (pbk.)
1. Globalization—Religious aspects—Christianity. 2. Economics—Religious aspects—Christianity. 3. Christianity and culture. 4. Theology. I. Cassidy, Laurie M. II. O'Connell, Maureen H. III. Title. IV. Series.

BR115.G59R46 2010
261.8—dc22

                              2010050073

Contents

PART II
EMBODIED CONFLICTS AND CONVERSATIONS

PART III
EXPANDING THE BOUNDARIES OF CONVERSATION

Introduction

Laurie Cassidy and Maureen H. O'Connell

"With my ear to the ground I heard tomorrow pass by."[1]

This embodied image of listening, one's ear pressed to the ground, is reminiscent of Vatican II's call for Christians to read the signs of the times.[2] Could the architects of that council have imagined the times we are living in as theologians of the third millennium? Living in the shadows of the Holocaust and the scourge of European colonialism, participants of Vatican II had fresh memories of the horrors of inhumanity. For them the past imposed responsibilities to create a new future for the church and for humanity. For us, it is the specter of humanity's endangered future that makes the present moment urgent.

The unprecedented scale of current global events appears to endanger humanity's very future. The present that envelops us demands that we listen to the conflicts and conversations among religion, economics, and culture in order to interpret theologically the time in which we live; this is essential if we are to participate in the possibility of a future. The 2010 annual meeting of the College Theology Society at the University of Portland was a moment to do just that, to collectively press our theological ears to the ground.

Although Vatican II's call to "read the signs of the times" is a profound challenge, has the phrase itself become no more than a well-worn trope that no longer empowers the activity of interpretation? This phrase, once turned into a cipher, no longer communicates the urgent activity required of Christians. The interconnected nature of world events calls forth more of us, both personally and collectively.

1

The metaphor of reading the signs of the times implies activities such as seeing, hearing, and feeling the world as a dramatically performative text. Critics of this metaphor point out that it suggests that theologians are spectators who view and interpret history from a privileged distance.[3] Yet, listening with one's ear to the ground demands a whole other set of activities. Our whole body is required for listening; it must be connected to events by being on the ground, a position that is vulnerable, dirty, and close to the earth. But such full-bodied theological interpretation allows us to hear root connections and causes below the surface of events.

Deepwater Horizon: A Sign of the Times

One event taking place during June 2010 while we were gathered in Portland demonstrates the urgency of this new theological posture. On Louisiana's coast between 2.4 and 2.9 million gallons of oil were spilling into the gulf waters each day of our meeting.[4] The scale of this ecological event has been compared to events in Bhopal and Chernobyl.[5] For residents in the Gulf, in the advent of Katrina's fifth anniversary, the spill not only desecrated an ecosystem, it also called into question whole ways of life dependent on oil. Using the image of a snaking network of oil pipelines, Monique Harden explains that this system both literally and metaphorically illustrates the economic, cultural, and political complexity of the region's oil dependence.[6] This web of oil pipelines is an underground system of interconnection trod upon everyday, yet it remains unseen and below the level of everyday consciousness.[7] For Harden, the oil spill brings to the surface the inextricably linked cultural, economic, and political systems that go far beyond an environmental disaster.

The oil spill has devastated diverse fishing communities composed of Vietnamese, Cambodian, Laotian, Croatian, African American, and Cajun and Creole Americans.[8] In addition, the oil slick has not only scarred Louisiana but also caused harm to Mississippi, Alabama, and other coastal states. The "cost" of this event far exceeds what can be estimated by economic means, and ongoing monetary calculations defy comprehension.[9] The cost and consequence of the spill is also cultural. Some observers fear that some coastal communities, particularly those founded by freed slaves, will become extinct, with whole patterns of life being lost, and their histories erased.[10] The event has also called into question the faith of local people, who ask: "Why is God punishing us—again?" Some Christians are also interpreting the spill as a heralding event of the apocalypse.[11]

While the oil spill in the Gulf has been reported world wide, other environmental disasters go unnoticed. Nigerian environmental activists, aware of events in the Gulf, describe that in their own country 1.5 million tons of oil have been spilled in the last fifty years yet oil companies and governments have remained silent.[12] We theologians must face up to these staggering statistics. We must also face up to the knowledge that the network of pipelines that supplies fuel does more than that—it also entraps us in a way of life that at present is not self-sustaining. As theologians we must make every effort to adequately understand and effectively respond to our current global and interconnected reality.

It is tempting to view the Gulf oil spill only through the lens of social ethics. However, the "Deepwater Horizon" event is also a theological locus that challenges us to make intelligible many concepts in our North American context. This "unprecedented disaster" in an already vulnerable region of the country presents questions to contemporary Catholic theologies from cosmology and theodicy to eschatology and soteriology. Is it time to name our consumption of non-reusable sources of energy as a sin? Of whom should we ask forgiveness, and what does repentance entail? Human destruction of the natural world is indeed a desecration of God's creation, the very medium of sacramentality.[13] What does baptism mean in a world of toxic water? The far-reaching ramifications of this ecological catastrophe demonstrate the immediate need to "read the signs of the times" with our ears to the ground, listening for what is going on in the pipelines just below the surface of reality.

Hearing through Conversation

Is it naïve to claim that conversation is a possible way of putting our ear to the ground to examine contemporary religious, cultural, and economic conflicts? Amid the polarizing conflicts in American society, the theme of "Religion, Economics, and Culture in Conflict and Conversation" raises questions about the possibility of conversation as a public practice in theology. In contemporary North American culture, conversation appears to be an endangered activity in public and private discourse. Conversation as genuine encounter seems threatened by both our method and our manner of communication.

With our personal and collective reliance on email, texting, and "tweets" to relay information, the virtual has replaced the personal, affective, and embodied forms of encounter. For Christians the embodied encounter of conversation holds the possibility of personal and social transformation. Indeed, Mary Elizabeth Hobgood maintains that responding to world events will not be through appeal to concepts, but on embodied experiences of the world and relationships that empower us to change.[14] Peter Hans Kolvenbach, S.J., in speaking about "well-educated solidarity," claims that "solidarity is learned through 'contact' rather than 'concepts.' "[15]

It is not only the means but also the manner of our communication that threatens conversation. Public discourse in America today reveals a heartbreaking and embarrassing portrait of a society in moral decay. Whether in our preoccupation with trivial and vapid celebrity spectacle or the cruelty of political punditry, we are at a collective loss to turn to one another and communicate meaningfully in public about our deepest values. The manipulative rhetoric of "talk radio" and the cynicism of political spin have relegated meaningful conversation to the realm of the private, making it almost impossible for authentic public inquiry into our shared human reality. This lack of meaningful public speech reveals a deeper collective wound of hopelessness, despair, and "*deadening nihilisms.*"[16]

To listen deeply to the signs of the times is to see that conversation is an urgent imperative for American Catholic theologians. This theme invites reflection on the necessity of interdisciplinary conversation and also discernment about our collective capacity to engage in conversation as theologians—publicly and with each other. In his insightful book *In Over Our Heads*, Robert Kegan contends that education in our times is not about accumulating more information; rather education requires developing the capacity to see, understand, and respond to the connections in our experience.[17] For Kegan, understanding the connections among discrete areas of information empowers agency in responding to reality.

Reflecting on events such as the Gulf oil spill and Kegan's observation about contemporary education strongly suggests that exploring the "pipelines" of reality is an imperative for theology. But the question is, How shall we do this together? Conversation is a moral practice that depends on the intentional relationship among persons. As Christians, it is within this matrix of relationality that God's grace is discovered amid the chaos and crisis of our times.[18] From the Christian perspective, conversation can be a praxis that offers the hope of finding God and of creating meaning amid the seeming fragmentary and disconnected experiences of our suffering world.

The commitment to intentional and public conversation is a praxis of hope. Based on its Latin roots, conversation means turning to one another.[19] To turn to each other is an act of faith that presupposes another person who is also turning to speak and to listen. As theologians we must engage in conversation for deeper theoretical insight, and our relationships with each other should help deepen our theoretical insights. As William Lynch reminds us, without hope, "we do not act or function. There is no energy."[20] Commitment to the practice of public conversation with each other as a work of theology nurtures us in the struggle of "faith seeking understanding" in a world of crisis, suffering, and despair.[21] The theme of "Religion, Economics, and Culture in Conflict and Conversation" implies an integral relationship between conversation as a metaphor for theological method and conversation as an integral human activity for contemporary American Catholic theologians.[22] The way in which members of the College Theology Society engage with one another embodies this understanding.

Map of the Volume

This collection of essays examines the dynamic relationship among religion, economics, and culture—three spheres of distinctly human activity whose increasing overlap is a result of globalization and the very essence of what it means to live in a globalized world. As we have demonstrated, we can no longer isolate the economic causes and implications of the Gulf spill, for example, from its catastrophic environmental and cultural dimensions.

In addition to situating themselves intentionally in the complexity of our times, the authors in this volume embrace the critical and yet optimistic tone of its theme. After the difficult task of naming and theologically engaging the conflict inherent in religion, economics, and culture, most authors do not conclude their essays; rather, they identify new possibilities that emerge when we attune theological sensibilities to the fact that we are all being inculturated by globalization. As such, the essays engage a variety of familiar theological concepts and themes, but often with unexpected twists. In part, this results from engaging with less familiar conversation partners. For example, Anselm K. Min speaks of the *flesh* of Christ and not simply the Body of Christ. Timothy Gabrielli negotiates identity in the multi-dimensional space of globalization and not simply the space of historical context. Daniel P. Scheid calls for ecological solidarity and not simply human solidarity.

Their individual contributions almost naturally arranged themselves into three parts. The six essays in the first section, "Conflicts Inherent in Conversation," unearth the tensions of conversation. If, as we have noted, conversation is a praxis of hope for theologians, then we must become conscious of what often goes unnoticed and undetected when we speak with and listen to each other as theologians. Identifying these tensions is a pivotal task in building relationships of solidarity, which many of our authors propose as both a primary principle and virtue in a global age.

Mary Ann Zimmer illuminates the power dynamics in the "ostensibly innocuous metaphor" of conversation that mask "relations of power and inequality that distort our theology" and dictate the structure, content, and practice of theological discourse. Zimmer suggests an asceticism to enact the mutuality of an authentic Christian practice of conversation. Andrew Prevot and María Teresa Morgan recapture and elaborate upon their real time conversation in Portland about "aporia" in creating adequate speech about race and ethnicity. As Prevot explains, aporia signifies that language about race is at an impasse, both determining and unable to determine the reality it struggles to communicate.

Rebecca Todd Peters acknowledges the emotional impasses that privileged Christians face in responding to globalization's seeming tsunami of suffering and she teases out four components of an ethic of solidarity. Most notable among these is "honoring difference," which requires deep listening and creating space for new voices that cultivate "more practical, more realistic, and more egalitarian solutions to our collective social problems." It is in these very relationships of solidarity, however, that Traci C. West calls us to be wary of the absence of conflict, particularly among ourselves as theologians. If "assisting the poor with their poverty" becomes the primary motivation for solidarity, then West worries that we will fail to perceive "the nature of our shared broken socio-economic system," which, perhaps more so than voluntary relationships of solidarity, binds us to suffering persons around the world.

The ways in which we converse about these broken systems are also critical. Elizabeth Lee recommends the virtues of humility and magnanimity as necessary for increasing our focus on how we engage each other on issues of religion, economics, and culture in the public square. She suggests that humility "encourages us to let go: to acknowledge that we do not have as much control as we think we do, and that we do not know as much as we think we know," while the magnanimity "encourages us to be confident in our gifts and abilities—our greatness—even in the face of oppression, and to affirm that greatness of soul not only in ourselves but in all people."

Returning to the image of the dynamic connection among religion, economics, and culture as a system of pipelines snaking throughout various dimensions of our social reality, then we might also imagine the human body—both individual and collective—as the space where these pipelines converge. The conflicts among religion, economics, and culture exact a destructive toll and whisper a creative promise in the embodied space of the person. These dynamic relationships are not "out there" in the globalized world but manifest themselves in our own flesh and blood, and in the spaces of our everyday life. The five essays in the volume's middle section, "Embodied Conflicts and Conversations," theologically reflect on the body in the matrix of religion, economics, and culture.

Anselm K. Min explores what would happen to the five marks of the church if we were to use "the *Flesh* of Christ," rather than "the Body of Christ," as our central ecclesial metaphor. "Flesh," according to Min, not only reminds us of the "basic materiality, sexuality, sociality, and historicity of human existence," but also of the "fragility, vulnerability, mortality, and sinfulness" of humanity and the church itself. Vincent Miller considers the bodily impact of "globally sourced consumption" on the distinctively human capability for imagination. Johann M. Vento poses a provocative question: "If we are addicted and dependent (and anaesthetized) as never before—if we are formed to avoid suffering, our own and others, we might ask, what set of practices can form us differently—what can allow us to engage suffering?" Utilizing political theology Vento suggests lament "as a formative practice to remain present to suffering, to wake up in this prison in which we have fallen asleep."

Timothy Gabrielli explores the potential of symbolic corporeality and gift exchange in Louis-Marie Chauvet's spirituality to undercut "piecemeal" approaches to constructing Christian identity that either quarantine individuals from the globalized space in which they live or put them in ideological opposition to it. Particularly in Chauvet's work on the relational exchange in the Eucharist, Gabrielli contends, we discover "not only that we are continually coming to be as Christian subjects, but also that there is not a pure and simple identity to project." Ryan Stander examines how HGTV and the Travel Channel create an alternative consumer liturgy forming desire in relationship to space and place. Drawing upon visual artists and theologians Stander creatively offers an alternative proposal that makes "significant contributions toward unmasking consumerism's disorienting tactics and ultimately the re-making of place."

A focus on bodies in the context of globalization makes us aware of boundaries and borders between persons as well as among communities, cultures, and countries. These borders and boundaries may be physical, emotional, cultural, or economic. As the lines between religion, economics, and culture are increasingly blurred, borders between the "center" and the "periphery" or between the "civilized" and the "non-civilized" are increasingly dangerous places. This is particularly evident as fear of the collapse of borders becomes increasingly palpable. Roberto S. Goizueta names these borders, propped up for so long by Euro-American values, as the "myth of the frontier." Even as we were preparing this volume for publication, we witnessed frequently violent dramas of the sort that come with border crossing: at the site of a proposed Islamic cultural center in lower Manhattan, in the painful passage of homosexual, bisexual, or transgendered adolescence, and along the nation's southern border.

And yet the average American is not the only one retreating to the security of rigid boundaries of religious, economic, or political fundamentalism. Distrust and polarization within the academy and between theologians and the institutional church suggest that theologians are as well. Essays in the last section, "Expanding the Boundaries of Conversation," implicitly provide what Gerald Arbuckle calls "anthropological reflexivity" that can liberate us to be self-critical enough to name our own fears of "the other."[23] Those "others" may be other methods, other interpretations of texts, other emphases in the tradition, or other colleagues in our profession. It is these fears that form and prop up our own impenetrable boundaries. These boundaries may be in our self-understandings, in our theological categories, or in our ethical principles. They may keep us from transformative encounters with difference and ambiguity that are inherent in authentic conversation.

In his essay, Goizueta turns to the *mestizo* history of Latin America as well as the Christological significance of Jesus as an inhabitant of a borderland to propose borders as life-giving spaces that can be the "birthplace of a new, reconciled human community." The authors in this final section write from various contested borders in theological discourse and turn them into the "seedbed" of new possibilities. Daniel P. Scheid challenges the anthropocentric boundaries of the principle of solidarity in arguing for a deep and persevering commitment to the earth. Charles C. Camosy traverses the passionately defended border between the "culture of life" and the "culture of death" by identifying potential common ground between the cultural icons of Benedict XVI and the secular utilitarian Peter Singer in their concern for the poor and the environment. In finding a passage for conversation between the Catholic and Anglican traditions, Christine Fletcher suggests "middle axioms," a distinctively Anglican method of ethical reflection, as an approach to the signs of the times with the potential to create dialogue among various constituents of the church with particular ties to religion, politics, or culture. Karen Teel authors the volume's only essay in interreligious dialogue and pushes the boundaries of a "closed monotheism." Creatively drawing on the work of Kelly Douglas, she argues that "closed monotheism"—the idea that the Christian God is the only god and that, for those who know this to be the case, refusing to worship this god is a grave sin that prevents their salvation—has led, deplorably, to extreme violence in God's name. Teel offers a proposal for the ordinary lay person to engage in interreligious dialogue from the context of a God who transcends all definition.

Ears to the Ground

With the tumultuous first decade of the third millennium behind us, the 2010 conference theme and the essays included in this volume present a challenge to the members of the College Theology Society: Are we willing to press our collective ear to the ground in order to listen more closely to the future before it passes us by? To accept this challenge requires that we read the signs of the times in a new way, not simply with a well-trained theological eye for the convergences of religion, economics, and culture in an increasingly globalized social reality, but rather with an incarnational corporeality that makes embodied encounters with others—and all of the personal and social transformation that can come with such encounters—possible at a time when the possibilities for meaningful change appear to be waning. It is our hope that these essays will spark new conversations among us as a society of North American theologians, and inspire in us the courage to risk conversation with less familiar dialogue partners beyond the academy.

Acknowledgments

There are many who contributed to this volume and who deserve our thanks. First, nearly eighty members and friends of the College Theology Society invested significant time in July and August in reviewing the submissions and offering feedback to each author. The essays included here bear the marks of these reviewers' critical and constructive insights, and their generosity of intellect and spirit is a witness to the collegiality of the CTS. We are grateful for the enthusiasm and passionate intellect of our plenary speakers whose various approaches to the conference theme provided the blueprint for this volume. We are also indebted to Alex Mikulich of the Jesuit Social Research Institute of Loyola University in New Orleans for offering key insights about the impact of the Gulf oil spill on his new home of New Orleans. For many years now, Susan Perry at Orbis Books has been the ideal project manager for the annual volume of the CTS, given her intuitive ability to strike a balance for CTS editors between creative liberty and the tight parameters of publishing a project with fast and firm deadlines. We are particularly grateful to Sue for the guidance she provided us as junior scholars.

Notes

[1] This quote of the poet and politician Aimé Césaire appears in the last frame of the 2006 film *Bamako* directed by Abderrahmane Sissako. Set in Bamako, Mali's capital, the film illustrates the conflicts and conversations of religion, economics, and culture that are conditions of everyday life in a globalized world.

[2] "[T]he Church has always had the duty of scrutinizing the signs of the times and of interpreting them in light of the gospel" (*Gaudium et Spes*, 4).

[3] See Roger Berman, *Catholic Social Learning: Educating the Faith That Does Justice* (New York: Fordham University Press, 2011).

[4] See http://www.pbs.org/newshour/rundown/2010/09/latest-oil-flow-estimate-tops-government-numbers.html; and Alex Mikulich, "Gulf Oil Spill: An Unprecedented Disaster for the Environment, the Economy, and the Livelihood of Gulf-coast Fishing Communities," *Just South: An Enewsletter from the Jesuit Social Research Institute* (May 2010), accessed October 11, 2010 at http://www.loyno.edu/jsri/e-newsletter/May-2010/0510-GulfOilSpill-jse.htm.

[5] A number of articles explore this comparison. One example is Ryan Tracy, "Four Environmental Disasters Worse than the Deepwater Horizon Spill," *Newsweek* (June 10, 2010), www.newsweek.com/.../four-environmental-disasters-worse-than-the-deepwater-horizon-spill.html, accessed October 11, 2010.

[6] Monique Harden is a Roman Catholic attorney and co-director of Advocates for Environmental Rights, a New Orleans-based public interest law firm. Her research and work interrogates the oil spill as an issue of human rights, based on the dignity of the human person.

[7] See Monique Harden, "Oil Spill Puts People of Color on Slippery Slope,"

http://www.ehumanrights.org/news_release_apr30-10_slippery_slope.html.

[8]See Mikulich, "Gulf Oil Spill."

[9]One source details BP spending of $11.2 billion to contend with the oil spill. See http://www.huffintonpost.com/2010/10/01/bp-spill-cost-rises-t_n_746562.html. $11.2 billion, accessed October 26, 2010. Some people are seeking compensation of $20 billion from BP. See the ongoing report on the Gulf oil spill by the *New York Times*, http://topics.nytimes.com/top/reference/timestopics/subjects/o/oil_spills/gulf_of_mexico_2010/imdex.html?emc=eta2.

[10]Jordan Flaherty, "Cultural Extinction: Louisiana's Coastal Communities Fear They May Never Recover" in *Black Agenda Report*, http://www.blackagendareport.com, accessed October 26, 2010.

[11]See Lisa Miller, "Blood in the Water," *Newsweek* (June 4, 2010), http://www.newsweek.com/2010/06/04/blood-in-the-water, accessed October 26, 2010.

[12]John Vidal, "Nigeria's Agony Dwarfs the Gulf Oil Spill: The U.S. and Europe Ignore It," *The Guardian* (May 30, 2010), http://www.guardian.co.uk/world/2010/may/30/oil-spills-nigeria-niger-delta-shell, accessed October 11, 2010.

[13]For more on the notion of environmental problems as theological issues, see Sallie McFague, *New Climate for Theology: God, the World and Global Warming* (Minneapolis: Fortress Press, 2008), 30-40.

[14]Mary Elizabeth Hobgood, *Dismantling Privilege: An Ethic of Accountability* (Cleveland: Pilgrim Press, 2009), 117-18.

[15]See Peter Hans Kolvenbach's speech at http://www.scu.edu/news/attachments/kolvenbach_speech.html.

[16]Cornel West, *Democracy Matters* (New York: Penguin Books, 2004), 26. Emphasis in original.

[17]Robert Kegan, *In Over Our Heads: The Mental Demands of Modern Life* (Cambridge: Harvard University Press, 1994).

[18]Catherine Mowry LaCugna, *God for Us: The Trinity and Christian Life* (San Fransisco: Harper Collins, 1997), 288.

[19]See Margaret Wheatley, *Turning to One Another: Simple Conversations to Restore Hope to the Future* (San Francisco: Berrett-Koehler Publishers, 2002).

[20]William Lynch, *Images of Hope: Imagination as Healer of the Hopeless* (Notre Dame: Notre Dame University Press, 1974), 32.

[21]"To live by hope is to believe that it is worth taking the next step: that our actions, our families, our cultures and societies have meaning and are worth living and dying for" (Mary Grey, *The Outrageous Pursuit of Hope: Prophetic Dreams for the Twenty-First Century* [New York: Crossroad Publishing, 2001], 6).

[22]See David Tracy, *Plurality and Ambiguity: Hermeneutics, Religion, Hope* (Chicago: University of Chicago Press, 1987).

[23]Gerald Arbuckle, *Culture, Inculturation and Theologians: A Post-Modern Critique* (Collegeville, MN: The Liturgical Press, 2010), 14.

Part I

CONFLICTS INHERENT
IN CONVERSATION

Interrupting the Conversation

Attending to Concrete Acts
as Mystical-Political Asceticism

Mary Ann Zimmer

In his first chapter of *A Passion for God: The Mystical-Political Dimension of Christianity*, Johannes Metz describes political theology as a fundamental theology committed to saying "farewell to every theology that closes itself off idealistically" in order to include a conscious accounting for the connections between knowledge, freedom, and justice. It must remember the suffering of the other and Christian moral complicity in that suffering: what Metz calls theology "after Auschwitz." It is conscious of and responsible to the "irruption" of the global world into European (first world) awareness. This irruption brings one face to face with "conditions that are absolutely contrary to the Gospel—the degradation of peoples, oppression, racism." Such a theology, Metz warns, will lead one into "pain over the contradictions in creation" and to the doorstep of an unsatisfying theodicy, a "helpless discourse with God" that must finally turn to eschatological hope.[1]

Metz's challenge to consciously account for the connections between knowledge, freedom, and justice applies to the connections that operate in the profession of theology. As Rebecca Chopp observes, "Metz forces us to understand that what is needed is not just more generosity on the part of the bourgeoisie, not just increased production or better understanding, but a total conversion of who we are and how we live in history."[2] The possibility that our work "closes itself off idealistically" can apply to how we define and justify our discipline, admit or limit its participants, and reward or discount its varied sources, methods, and conclusions. In order to respond to Metz's challenge to connect knowledge, freedom, and justice in a conscious manner we must be willing to question our most basic assumptions.

This essay argues that in the North American situation, where the majority of academics are generally able to insulate themselves from the realities that Metz describes, political theology requires a theologian to make a conscious commitment to self-correction. Evidence of the necessity of self-correction can be found in many places. It confronts us sharply in Bryan Massingale's description of a black Catholic theologian's "dark night" of depression, despair, and fear, where the temptation is great to " 'go along to get along' by not raising the pointed question, making the pertinent (though imprudent) observation, or conducting the needed research."[3] I recall my own experience when colleagues asked about my dissertation topic, and I replied, "I am looking at what lay people in a local parish might contribute to academic theology." By far the most frequent follow-up question was, "What if you don't find anything?"

In the face of these realities Metz calls for a theology that is alert to potential problems underlying the generally unquestioned, seemingly harmless habit of referring to theology as a "conversation." This ostensibly innocuous metaphor masks relations of power and inequality that distort our theology. This essay examines the metaphor of conversation that has become so integrated into our profession, using a social-linguistic analysis to indicate the range of concrete experiences that underlie the metaphor and control its concrete effects. Finally, I propose conversion to an ascetical practice of theological conversation that responds to the problematic nature of current practices.

Some questions can ground the discussion that follows: How does one give new space to those whose turns in the conversation have commonly been overrun by dominant assumptions about method, topic, and style of thinking, writing, and speaking? If some people are going to get more turns to speak or participate, how capable are dominant group members of seeing their own listening and facilitation as participation in the conversation? How prepared are dominant group members to question their own cultural commitments, as Ada María Isasi-Díaz does when she speaks of the commitment of *mujerista* theology to ask at each point, "Who benefits from this?" as part of "a hermeneutics of suspicion [applied] to our constructive proposals, to our narratives, to our whole theological enterprise."[4] What losses would one have to experience in order to make a commitment to becoming bi-cultural without taking on a dominant role in a second culture? How prepared are members of dominant groups to experience themselves as learners and as implicated in racist, sexist, heterosexist practices?

Rather than leaning most heavily on the more usual philosophical analysis of metaphor, I use a socio-linguistic analysis to ask about the *actual, concrete experience* behind the metaphor of conversation that figures prominently in theology today.[5] Contemporary theology uses the metaphor of conversation in a way that does not include Metz's requirements for a conscious political theology but, rather, in a way that separates the dominant theological enterprise from awareness of its actual practice. It seems that a metaphor needs to be rooted in the concrete if it is not to work as an aid to amnesia—a form of amnesia that comes into play when the metaphor-user loses track of the concrete experience to which the metaphor refers, or when the user assumes a narrow range of possible experiences. Jacquelyn Grant calls attention to this kind of assumption when Christian preachers and theologians use servanthood as a metaphor for the ideal Christian aspiration. Does this mean, she asks, that "God condone[s] the fact that Black women are systematically relegated to being 'servants of servants?' "[6] At this point the opportunity for distortion enters in.

The remainder of this essay tracks the consequences of this problem by examining the experience that lies behind the use of "conversation." What do we know about the human experience of conversation? What issues does this raise for the practice of a theology that calls itself "conversation?" Entry into this question begins with the work of David Tracy, whose influence on contemporary theological method is unrivaled.

Conversation in Theology

David Tracy's use of "conversation" in his discussion of theological method has been absorbed into the contemporary self-understanding of theology, which takes it for granted that conversation serves as a foundational metaphor.[7] What Tracy means by conversation is an event of communication that takes place in the public sphere. Tracy relies on Jürgen Habermas's ideal speech situation as a background theory.[8] Tracy recommends conversation as a better term than the frequently used "argument," apparently because it allows for a wider range of communication forms, such as "art, myth, and religion."[9]

The influence of Habermas is also evident in traces of the notion of the "ideal speech situation" that can be detected underlying Tracy's vocabulary. The ideal speech situation is Habermas's formulation of the conditions necessary for a public discourse that can yield justifiable claims to truth or to valid norms. For Habermas four conditions are necessary in order to carry discourse to a successful conclusion:

> that the bracketed validity claims of assertions, recommendations, or warrants are the exclusive object of discussion; that participants, themes and contributions are not restricted except with reference to the goal of testing the validity claims in question; that no force except that of the better argument is exercised; and that, as a result, all motives except that of the cooperative search for truth are excluded.[10]

While a theologian, as described by Tracy, is presumed to need these conditions in order to carry out his/her responsibility in public discourse, Tracy, along with Habermas and those who depend on his theory, readily acknowledges that the ideal speech situation is "counterfactual."[11] What he means by this is that the conditions described above never actually exist—"this is what ideal speech would be *if* it ever existed."[12] The question that must be asked of contemporary theology is whether this counterfactual characteristic of Tracy's method is given full weight when the metaphor of "conversation" is adopted for a variety of theological enterprises. If not, a failure to account for the intrinsically counterfactual nature of the ideal speech situation can effectively provide cover for bias and for the covert exercise of power. Examining the concrete functioning of the metaphor can expose this danger.

Conversation—The Experiential Reality

We turn now from the theoretical setting for Tracy's use of "conversation" and approach this term from a different direction, that is, the concrete experience that underlies conversation. The effect of a metaphor is not solely determined by how the user of the linguistic comparison *intends* it to operate. Rather, a metaphor is more widely governed by the actual experience of the reality upon which the comparison draws. For this reason the actual functioning of conversation in everyday life has direct resonance for how the metaphor "conversation" operates in theology. This means that different hearers of the same metaphor may have radically different interpretations of its meaning. What follows are two analyses of the experience of conversation in daily life.

Candace West and Don Zimmerman have examined how ordinary daily conversation establishes and maintains hierarchy by focusing on the mechanism of interruption in conversation.[13] Among acquainted couples in social settings, they found that 96 percent of interruptions were by males of females. In a second study of unacquainted pairs the same was true of about 75 percent of the interruptions. The researchers explore some common explanations for this finding and cite research to show that it cannot be attributed to a greater tolerance of women for interruption or greater amounts of time taken up by women's speech. The authors interpret this pattern not simply as an expression of power differences between men and women but as part of the social patterns that create this difference.[14]

In another study, Pamela Fishman examined samples of naturally occurring conversations between women and men.[15] Citing the social constructionists Berger and Luckmann, who hold that reality is defined by whoever is most powerful,[16] Fishman shows, through analysis of taped conversations, how "verbal interaction helps to construct and maintain the hierarchical relations between men and women."[17] Through the "work" of interaction/conversation, people "produce their relationship to one another, their relationship to the world, and those patterns normally referred to as social structure."[18]

Fishman studied the daily at-home conversations of three

white, college-educated heterosexual couples, all self-described as feminist or sympathetic to the women's movement. She found that women asked two and a half times more questions than men did, while men made twice as many statements as women. Women raised 47 of the 76 topics initiated while men raised 29. However only 17 (38 percent) of the women's topics succeeded in engendering conversation, while 28 of the 29 topics initiated by men were successful. Fishman also observed a significantly greater number of instances when women engaged in what she described as *support* of the conversation through words or sounds indicating interest.

Fishman concludes that men control conversation while women do the majority of the "work" of initiating and maintaining it. Men can rely on women to respond supportively to male-initiated topics. Men determine through their responses or lack of them what topics initiated by women will continue on to become conversation. She points out the importance of this unequal conversational power in defining "normal" feminine gender. She also points out similarities between the approach of women to conversation and that of children—for example, initiating a topic by asking a question. She terms these similarities the strategies of the less powerful.

One survey of the research on women's conversation among themselves has shown that women tend to use collaborative patterns such as "drawing out other speakers, supportive listening and head nods, mutual sharing of emotions and personal knowledge, respect for one another's conversational space."[19] This is in contrast to men's patterns, which tend to focus more on "monopoly of turn space, interruptions, [and] topic control."[20]

Similar analyses show that some of these patterns vary with particular situations, group composition, social class, and racial identity. The conclusions above are merely markers in an extremely broad and complex field that are intended to raise one question: Is everyone having the same experience of "conversation"? These analyses reveal the struggle inherent in the experience of conversation, a struggle that is not generally acknowledged in the use of the term. Conversation is a particular kind of work for non-dominant participants, work that bears the major burden of carrying the conversation forward. While these analyses refer specifically to gender, they are not framed as gender-specific behaviors or genetic differences. They presume habits and self-identities that are culturally produced and have been found to be gender-related in some contexts. However, gender is not the only example that can be cited, since race, class, and education also yield differences in practices of conversational exchange.[21]

The above studies show some of the ways in which conversation is not a univocal experience but rather a different reality for subordinate persons than for dominant ones. This is a difference of power with the consequence that the concerns of subordinates are less often the object of the conversation even when they are present and have opportunities to speak. The greater power of dominant persons is directed toward speaking and topic control rather than to facilitating participation.

It is even possible that dominant members do not recognize forms of participation other than by being the speaker. In my experience of teaching feminist theology to seminary students, men in the class have not infrequently described themselves as "excluded" from a theological conversation that focuses on the self-expression of feminist women because of the students' assumption that what *constitutes* conversation is their own act of speaking. Listening, encouraging, or facilitating the speech of others are not recognized as elements of participation in the conversation.

Non-dominant-group members must learn and exercise special skills to gain some place in the conversation. They also do a vast amount of unacknowledged work that underlies and carries the conversation. The oppressive difference of power in conversation often continues without critique inasmuch as it seems normal to persons who are otherwise aware of issues of domination, which, in the studies cited, was sexism.[22]

These studies have relevance for theological method because they expose the concrete shape of the experience of conversation. To the extent that conversation is not the same experience for all people, it cannot be said to function as a single metaphor. The examination of the concrete dynamics of conversation raises questions about what may be going on when "conversation" is used to describe the process of the construction of theology. As Sallie McFague argues in her work on metaphors for God, metaphors create imaginative constructs that have real effects on behavior.[23] We turn now to the implications of these effects.

Theology as Conversation Revisited

We turn again to theology to attend to the repercussions of the unacknowledged tensions inherent in conversation. Without an analysis of concrete reality, the metaphor "conversation," as currently employed, actually prevents a fruitful interface between the practitioners of academic theology from dominant social, cultural, and economic locations and their "conversation partners"—local and global—who occupy subordinate positions. Rather, "theology as usual" continues to reinforce existing unequal power relations. For this reason the reality that conversation is *struggle* for non-dominant groups and individuals demands new practices from mainstream theologians and their disciplines. The absence of acknowledgment of this fact in Tracy's theology is therefore problematic.

If concrete experiences of conversation shape the way the metaphor operates, there are problems with the way Tracy lays out his theological method. Three difficulties stem from the tendency to gloss over the fact that the ideal speech situation is counterfactual. This becomes evident in the way he handles relations of power, in his treatment of the tradition, and in his descriptions of social location.

To put it a little differently than I have above, the ideal speech situation is one in which "there is mutual understanding between participants' equal chances to select and employ speech acts, recognition of the legitimacy of each to participate in the dialogue as 'an autonomous and equal partner' and where the resulting consensus is due simply 'to the force of the better argument.' "[24] These are the requirements for coming to justifiable claims.

Using conversation as the metaphor for theology without paying attention to the concrete tensions involved in ordinary, power-laden conversation obscures the fact that forces other than "the better argument" are *inherent in the metaphor itself*. The hidden oppressive power of conversation operates in Tracy's proposed method for theology because he does not have an explicit critique of the present structures of power and social interaction inherent in it. If there is no clear role for the critique of power structures, an implicit affirmation of the status quo will operate. Tracy recognizes the possibility of conflictual moments within an ongoing conversation but does not seem to recognize the conflictual and inherently unequal nature of conversation as such.[25]

Furthermore, the ideal speech situation is problematically assumed in speaking as Tracy does of the classics of "a tradition" with no acknowledgment of counter-traditions. James Scott has called these *hidden transcripts*.[26] Scott's term comes from his anthropological work among Malaysian peasants in which he describes "everyday forms of resistance" or "infrapolitics" as hidden transcripts. These are indirect or disguised activities that resist material, status, or ideological domination in situations where direct resistance would be impossible or unwise. Some of the activities he classifies as everyday resistance are poaching, squatting, evasion, foot-dragging, gossip, rumor, myths, folktales, folk religion, and the creation and use of autonomous social space. These practices are the "the hidden transcript," a resistant discourse of practices underlying apparent cooperation or passivity. Because these practices are necessarily subtle, Scott cautions against assuming that they are absent just because they are not overt. Infrapolitics have the specific purpose of achieving some level of resistance without provoking a repressive reaction. The hidden transcript is most likely to develop where dominated groups have no political rights and, therefore, no legitimate avenues for contesting power. From my own field work in a small Roman Catholic parish I know that hidden transcripts exist among ordinary Catholic laypeople.

For the most part, academic theology too easily considers popular religion as merely a site of resistance to theological wisdom and clear thinking that is the domain of the academic.[27] As one of the non-dominant members of the theological conversation, the popular practitioner of a religion operates from the location of infrapolitics. In the meantime, the academic theologian can presume to speak for the faith of the whole community. The everyday faith life of the ordinary church member is absorbed into this "adequate" description of the tradition or is judged by the norms of this description. In this case there is a failure to recognize the tradition that is not represented and has little chance to participate. In the United States there seems to be some concession to the possibility that the popular faith of identifiable ethnic groups will have value. See for only one example the work of Orlando

Espín.[28] There is less of a tendency to concede this about groups most like the dominant theologian.

Finally, the problematic assumption of the ideal speech situation manifests itself in the way that Tracy describes social location. While he uses "social location" as a factor in his description of the theologian, he means by this whether one is doing theology "in a seminary, in a church-related university, in a pastoral setting, in a program for religious education, in a small community, in the secular academy, in an involvement in a particular cultural, political or societal movement."[29] Elsewhere he describes the theologian as "an individual with a particular temperament, history, needs, hopes, desires and fears."[30] Missing in both of these descriptions are gender, race, class, and status in the church. The effect of Tracy's generalization is to mask the reality of the aspects of social location that yield discrepancies of power in the conversation.

These limitations in Tracy may well be attributed, at least partially, to his reliance on Habermas or to the reliance of both of them on an inadequate ideal. As David Held points out,

> the ideal speech situation itself is not a sufficient condition for a fully open discourse, nor, by extension, for the critical assessment of barriers to this type of discourse in society. The conditions of the ideal speech situation fail to cover a range of phenomena, from the nature (content) of cultural traditions to the distribution of material resources, which are obviously important determinants of the possibility of discourse. . . .[31]

While like critiques of the ideal speech situation have been offered from a number of points of view, it is important to spell it out here because of the consistent disconnect between the habit of referring to theologizing as conversation and keeping a critical eye on the implications of the metaphor. This disconnect is most likely those who usually or sometimes already have access to the conversation since their (our) own experience does little to help with this critical awareness. In this situation dominant participants are left in what, taking our clue from Metz, we might describe as idealistic amnesia. This is where attending to concrete acts offers a needed asceticism.

Asceticism: Toward a Self-Correcting Conversation

I claim the concrete as a kind of critical theory in the face of the amnesia Metz warns us about. This is so because suffering and domination take part in the concrete. When we are committed to growing awareness of and responsibility for our concrete structures, relationships, and privileges, we construct a countermovement to the forgetfulness that privilege constructs. This is what I mean by an asceticism.

Margaret Miles's careful examination of the Christian tradition of asceticism provides us with some creative direction for responding to the challenge of the concrete reality of domination within much of theological conversation.[32] Miles distinguishes between the "old asceticism," which most contemporary Christians and many scholars assume to be the nature of the historical Christian asceticism. The "old asceticism" is founded on the assumption that attention to the body can only result in diminishment of the spirit. In this competitive anthropology, spiritual progress depends on suppressing the threat of the body. As Miles points out, this approach is clearly inadequate to a Christian appreciation of the goodness of the body established in such central Christian teachings as creation, incarnation, and resurrection.[33] She finds the "old asceticism" to be, in many cases, a caricature of early Christian understandings of the goal and functioning of asceticism. At the same time, however, the stereotype is firmly in place and easily lends its weight to a historically real tendency to dualism.

In contrast, Miles proposes a "new asceticism" with two distinguishing characteristics. First, a Christian asceticism worthy of the name recognizes the body as the soul's "intimate companion" and affirms "the permanent *connectedness* of body and soul."[34] Second, this asceticism asks what aspects of contemporary life call for ascetical attention in the best spirit of Christian self-reform. The positive function of asceticism is to institute particular, individually appropriate practices that free the Christian from culturally imposed habits that are damaging to the unitary person.[35]

Miles's later work is somewhat more pessimistic about the possibility of a "new asceticism." This pessimism stems from two problematic tendencies. The first is the entrenched popularized view of the history of Christian asceticism and its language as intrinsically negative and dualistic.[36] For this reason Miles is doubtful about the utility of continuing to use this language. The second is the awareness that the practices and language of asceticism, directed as much of it is to denying the body, can be dangerous for members of oppressed groups. Women and subjugated peoples have been identified with the presumably problematic body and suffered a displaced contempt.[37] These cautions are certainly well-founded. They follow both from a long tradition of abuse of those designated as connected with the body and from the violation of the principle that every asceticism is to be particular to an individual's specific challenges.

The tradition insists that any ascetic practice be individually prescribed for the mitigation of a particular habit.[38] What is helpful for one person or group may be damaging for another. As we have seen above, Jacquelyn Grant rejects for black women the spiritual prescription that Christians practice servanthood in imitation of Jesus. She asks, "how does one justify teaching a people that they are called to a life of service when they have been imprisoned by the most exploitive forms of service?"[39] Very early in the formulation of feminist systematic theology Valerie Saiving questioned the appropriateness of recommending sacrificial love and complete self-giving as the antidotes to sin since pride and self-isolation are not the paradigmatic experience of sin for all Christians.[40] With these cautions, we turn now to considering asceticism as a turn to the concrete.

Practices of Dehabituation[41]

While waiting for a plenary session to begin at the annual meeting, a junior scholar strikes up a conversation with someone unfamiliar to her. She asks about her neighbor's area of specialization and receives an answer that is cold and somewhat amused. She later finds out that this is a person who expects to be well known.

An African-American doctoral student finds all the readings by people of color grouped at the end of the syllabus in the last week of class.

An Anglo theologian finds herself irritated by the fact that, after all her efforts to learn Spanish and absorb the literature and culture, she is not treated as an equal participant in the construction of Latina theology.

What Miles calls dehabituation refers to ancient ascetical practices that worked through the body to shift the consciousness.[42] An ascetical, freeing, theological practice will be different for each person in the struggle to converse. This is because persons in different subject positions and positions of privilege or disadvantage will have been habituated differently by our general and professional culture. Recommendations for practices that reorient one's habits depend in large part on one's material and subject positions. It is likely that one will occupy more than one subject position in relation to domination and oppression. In some settings one may be the dominant race but vulnerable by virtue of gender, academic standing, or sexual orientation.

At times my most salient position will be as a member of the dominant culture. My concrete practice might be to willingly put myself in settings where I am not an expert or in which the process of theologizing is not going on in my preferred style. In this setting I need to avoid overburdening the group with the task of helping me understand or translating the process to fit my needs. I need to be modest about how much I speak and accepting of the fact that the group may need to interact chiefly among themselves. I need to exercise patience with myself in the face of the fact that I am not totally competent in this mode and cannot assert expertise at the level I am accustomed to in order to build my professional identity. I need to recognize that not everyone in this setting will know me or be familiar with the work with which I identify my "position" in the profession. If my position or relative social power can be useful to someone in the group, I might offer it carefully without taking over the exchange.

At times I act out of my position as a woman who works in practical theology. I need practices by which I can continue to value and develop my own voice in fidelity to my experience. I need to put time into support networks that offer me respectful critiques, and the resources to be aware of and have access to aspects of the tradition or interdisciplinary material that can be useful in my interdisciplinary work. I need to find suitable mentors and have the courage to take the initiative to ask them for their help.

The cultural habit of shunning any suggestion that we might be prejudiced makes us vulnerable to hiding from the reality of our own racism, sexism, and heterosexism, not to mention ableism and cultural imperialism. It would be easy if there were some fool-proof formula for correct behavior in all circumstances. However, as Seyla Benhabib argues, "It is only in the course of the moral conversation that we can learn those aspects of the otherness of the other which the other wants us to respect and/or take into account in our deliberations. *The concreteness of the concrete other is established through first person self-descriptions.*"[43] The asceticism is the humility to enter the fray, willing to lose our prized sense of ideal, tolerant purity.

Conclusion: Hearing to Speech

Nelle Morton famously notes, "hearing to speech is political."[44] As scholars we are well habituated to producing speech in its varying forms and being rewarded for its production. This has always been political in the sense that it involves the acquisition and use of power. What is needed are thoughtful experiments to treat the mental, emotional, and systemic blockages that impede the distribution of that power.[45]

It should be a source of respect and reward if a senior scholar uses his position to promote the work of junior scholars who are not in his followership. Such a scholar might offer an edited volume of varied viewpoints by scholars in little known or traditionally neglected fields or institutions.

Scholarly credit could be given for being part of a learning community in a local church. Learning the thought forms, concerns, culture, sufferings, and joys of the community would be rewarded as a scholarly activity. Graduate seminars and scholarly meetings could explicitly reward acquiring and exercising skills of facilitating the exchange of ideas as well as respectful critique. Graduate programs could require facility in a second culture for dominant culture students. This would lead to a careful consideration of what constitutes a dominant culture as well as personal cultural mapping for each student.

Gustavo Gutiérrez writes poignantly about the practical and psychological difficulties of scholarly work when one is committed to close collaboration with the local Christian community in their everyday world. It is a collaboration that he argues is "the necessary condition for the creation of a serious, scientific and responsible theology." At the same time, "theology understood thus is not free from tensions. For example, how to reconcile belonging to a community with its daily demands with intellectual work which also has its laws and requires its own space and time? How can one undertake a laborious effort to understand the faith when the poor face immediate needs necessary to their physical survival, with all that this implies for their lives as Christians? These questions arise and must be coped with every day."[46] The asceticism of conversation he describes is not a rote habit of self-denial but the daily, unsettling meeting of abstract reflection and concrete suffering.

When Metz founds theology on the basis of an ability to take into account the connections between knowledge, freedom, and justice, he is clear that this will result in exposure to painful realities that one would naturally like to escape: the suffering of others; one's own moral complicity; pressing, intolerable global conditions. He points to eschatological hope as the force that makes it possible to stay in this reality. Despite its difficulties, theology consciously enacted as a struggling conversation can be a source of eschatological hope. It substitutes for the numbness of denial an awakening pain that is reality. It substitutes healing asceticism for dependence on an impossible desire for perfection. Attention to the concrete subjects in conversation will reveal them to be the "spiritual director" prescribing the specifically needed ascetic discipline.

Notes

[1] Johannes Baptist Metz, *A Passion for God: The Mystical-Political Dimension of Christianity* (Mahwah, NJ: Paulist Press, 1998), 25-29. Note: this chapter was written for the fifth edition and is dated by Metz 1991/92.

[2] Rebecca Chopp, *The Praxis of Suffering: An Interpretation of Liberation and Political Theologies* (Maryknoll, NY: Orbis Books, 1986), 80-81.

[3] Bryan N. Massingale, *Racial Justice and the Catholic Church* (Maryknoll, NY: Orbis Books, 2010), 167-68.

[4]Ada María Isasi-Díaz, *Mujerista Theology* (Maryknoll, NY: Orbis Books, 1996), 76.

[5]See the studies and discussion in *Language, Gender, and Society*, ed. Barrie Thorne, Cheris Kramarae, and Nancy Henley (Cambridge: Newbury House, 1983), and Robin Tolmach Lakoff, *Language and Woman's Place: Text and Commentaries*, 2nd ed., ed. Mary Bucholtz (Oxford: Oxford University Press, 2004).

[6]Jacquelyn Grant, "The Sin of Servanthood and the Deliverance of Discipleship," in *A Troubling in My Soul: Womanist Perspectives on Evil and Suffering*, ed. Emilie M. Townes (Maryknoll, NY: Orbis Books, 1993), 201.

[7]David Tracy, *The Analogical Imagination: Christian Theology and the Culture of Pluralism* (New York: Crossroad, 1981), 101, 447.

[8]Tracy notes, "I understand my summary [on conversation] in the text to be in basic harmony with the position on the implicit validity claims in all communication defended by Karl-Otto Apel and Jürgen Habermas" (David Tracy, *Plurality and Ambiguity: Hermeneutics, Religion, and Hope* [San Francisco: Harper and Row, 1987], 118n28).

[9]Ibid.

[10]Jürgen Habermas, *Legitimation Crisis*, trans. Thomas McCarthy (Boston: Beacon Press, 1975), 107-8.

[11]Tracy, *Plurality and Ambiguity*, 26.

[12]Ibid. Emphasis added.

[13]Candace West and Don H. Zimmerman, "Small Insults: A Study of Interruptions in Cross-Sex Conversations between Unacquainted Persons," in *Language, Gender, and Society*, ed. Barrie Thorne, Cheris Kramarae, and Nancy Henley (Cambridge: Newbury House, 1983), 103-17.

[14]For an overview of extensive research on this issue see Elizabeth Aries, *Men and Women in Interaction: Reconsidering the Differences* (New York: Oxford University Press, 1996), 79-101.

[15]Pamela M. Fishman, "Interaction: The Work Women Do," in *Language, Gender, and Society*, ed. Barrie Thorne, Cheris Kramarae, and Nancy Henley (Cambridge: Newbury House, 1983), 89-101.

[16]Peter L. Berger and Thomas Luckmann, *The Social Construction of Reality: A Treatise in the Sociology of Knowledge* (Garden City, NY: Doubleday, Anchor, 1967).

[17]Fishman, "Interaction," 89.

[18]Ibid., 90.

[19]Barrie Thorne, "Language, Gender, and Society: Opening a Second Decade of Research," in *Language, Gender, and Society*, ed. Barrie Thorne, Cheris Kramarae, and Nancy Henley (Cambridge: Newbury House, 1983), 18. See also the extensive annotated bibliography in this volume.

[20]Ibid., 19.

[21]See the annotated bibliography on race and social class in Thorne et al., *Language, Gender, and Society*, 326-27.

[22]Fishman, "Interaction," 91. No claim is made here that sexism is the only source of unequal power.

[23]Sallie McFague, *Models of God: Theology for an Ecological, Nuclear Age* (Philadelphia: Fortress Press, 1987), 3.

[24]David Held, *Introduction to Critical Theory: Horkheimer to Habermas* (Berkeley: University of California Press, 1980), 343.

[25]Tracy, *The Analogical Imagination*, 447. In this work Tracy does clarify in his initial extended discussion of the theologian's location that he has chosen to begin with a sociology of knowledge rather than a critical theory approach (32n1).

[26]James C. Scott, *Domination and the Arts of Resistance: Hidden Transcripts* (New Haven: Yale University Press, 1990), 198-99.

[27]On this topic see the discussion by Metz, "Church and People: The Forgotten Subject of Faith," in his *Faith in History and Society* (New York: Seabury Press, 1980), 136-53.

[28]Orlando O. Espín, *The Faith of the People: Theological Reflections on Popular Catholicism* (Maryknoll, NY: Orbis Books, 1997).

[29]Tracy, *The Analogical Imagination*, 5.

[30]Ibid., 167.

[31]Held, *Introduction to Critical Theory*, 396.

[32]See Margaret R. Miles, *Fullness of Life: Historical Foundations for a New Asceticism* (Philadelphia: Westminster Press, 1981), and *Practicing Christianity* (New York: Crossroad, 1988).

[33]Miles, *Fullness of Life*, 156.

[34]Ibid., 134.

[35]Miles, *Practicing Christianity*, 94.

[36]Ibid., 104.

[37]Ibid., 100.

[38]Miles, *Fullness of Life*, 160.

[39]Jacquelyn Grant, "The Sin of Servanthood and the Deliverance of Discipleship," 209.

[40]Valerie Saiving, "The Human Situation: A Feminine View," in *Womanspirit Rising: A Feminist Reader in Religion*, ed. Carol P. Christ and Judith Plaskow (New York: Harper & Row, 1979), 25-42.

[41]This term is that of Miles. See *Practicing Christianity*, 94.

[42]Ibid., 95.

[43]Seyla Benhabib, "In Defense of Universalism—Yet Again! A Response to Critics of *Situating the Self*," *New German Critique* 92 (1994): 180.

[44]Nelle Morton, *The Journey Is Home* (Boston: Beacon Press, 1985), 210.

[45]For practical and theoretical arguments toward this end, see Elisabeth Schüssler Fiorenza, *Democratizing Biblical Studies: Toward an Emancipatory Educational Space* (Louisville: Westminster John Knox Press, 2009).

[46]Gustavo Gutiérrez, "The Task of Theology and Ecclesial Experience," in *The People of God Amidst the Poor*, ed. Leonardo Boff and Virgil Elizondo, *Concilium* (Edinburgh: T&T Clark, 1984), 63.

The Virtues of Humility and Magnanimity and the Church's Responses to the Health Care and Gay Marriage Debates

Elizabeth Lee

In the past few years, several issues have become contentious, even divisive, in American politics. The political sphere seems increasingly polarized, and there seems to be more name-calling—socialist, racist, fascist, the antichrist—than there is discussion. Among the more litigious issues have been healthcare reform and same-sex marriage, which have affected not only the political sphere but also the church. Lay Catholics are divided on these tricky issues, and some priests and bishops have been outspoken in their support for or opposition to them.[1] With healthcare, the U.S. bishops outlined several priorities for reform, among which were quality affordable care for all, access to health care for immigrants, and not using federal funds for abortions.[2] Despite this platform of multiple concerns, the healthcare reform debate seemed to come down mainly to abortion. The bishops spoke out against any reform bill that uses federal funds for elective abortions, and many of their letters to Congress focused on this issue.[3]

The issue of gay marriage, and of homosexuality more generally, has also been contentious. Documents from the Vatican and the U.S. bishops have repeatedly emphasized the "naturalness" of heterosexual marriage and the "unnaturalness" of homosexual acts.[4] During the 2008 presidential election, individual dioceses in states with ballot initiatives to legalize gay marriage, such as California, contributed hundreds of thousands of dollars to counter such initiatives. Further, dioceses such as that of Portland, Maine, actually received contributions from dozens of other dioceses across the country to defeat measures that supported same-sex marriage.[5] Such efforts, it could be argued, have reinforced the perception, both within and outside the church, that the Catholic Church is obsessed with sex.

For the most part, people on both sides of these issues speak about them sincerely and respectfully, yet the church is not immune to the polarization of the wider American political landscape. In both the healthcare/abortion and the same-sex marriage debates, some church leaders, in an attempt to strengthen their own positions, have failed to acknowledge the complexity of the issues, and have been vocal about the universality and truthfulness of their own views and the errors of others.

This essay examines some of the responses to the healthcare and same-sex marriage debates through the lens of virtue ethics. As a review of news articles and bishops' statements on these two issues uncovered an abundance of material, far too much for one essay, the focus here is on two specific instances in which Catholic officials have spoken about or acted upon their opinions on healthcare reform or same-sex marriage: first, the response of the U.S. nuns and the U.S. Catholic bishops to the healthcare bill, and, second, the ways in which Catholic grade schools in two dioceses—Denver and Boston—have recently dealt with children of lesbian parents.[6]

Particular attention is given to the ways in which two somewhat neglected virtues, humility and magnanimity, have been practiced (or not practiced) in each of these cases. I begin with a brief overview of virtue ethics and then examine the virtues of humility and magnanimity. I then apply these virtues to the two instances of Catholic responses to the same-sex marriage or healthcare debates noted above. It is not my intention to argue *about* the merits of either public policy or ecclesial positions on healthcare or same-sex marriage, but rather to examine the ways in which humility and magnanimity have been practiced in the debates concerning these issues, and the ways in which these virtues could be better cultivated. In other words, the focus of my analysis is more the public presentation of an argument, rather than the argument itself, though both are addressed.

Virtue Ethics

Joseph Kotva defines virtue ethics as that which "deals with the transition from who we are to who we could be."[7] That is, virtue ethics aims to help us become a certain sort of person. A virtue ethic framework can be said to consist of three parts—a picture of who we are now, a picture of who we want to become, and a set of dispositions and habituated actions that will help us get from one to the other. Because of its teleological focus, virtue ethics recognizes that as we grow physically and emotionally, we will also grow in virtue; becoming virtuous is necessarily a gradual process. Thomas Aquinas notes that a virtue is "a good habit, productive of good works;"[8] acquiring virtues means practicing them, so every moment of our lives is a chance to get better at being virtuous. As James Keenan puts it, virtue ethics sees "the ordinary as the terrain on which the moral life moves."[9] Virtue ethics is, in short, a practical, person-centered approach to good living.

Contemporary Christian virtue ethicists draw heavily from scripture and theology to offer a distinctively Christian account of the virtues.[10] Some have also begun to think through the ways in which a virtue approach can contribute to social ethics, and not simply personal ethics, as well as the relationship between virtue and our vision of the common good. Kotva argues, for example, that Christian virtues call us to concern for others while at the same time helping us to become our truest selves: "true human excellence, the true human good, includes loving service to God and others."[11]

Christopher Vogt has suggested that Catholic social teaching is best presented in terms of virtues rather than principles: "Instead of understanding its primary social mission to be the proclamation of a social doctrine to the world, the Church should see its role primarily in terms of the conscious, public practice of specific virtues and intentional efforts at the formation of those virtues among its membership."[12] Thus, virtue ethics can be applied both in small instances in our daily personal lives and as we begin to think through Christian visions of social life and the common good. In this essay, I contend that virtue ethics can help inform Christian responses to political issues. The virtues of humility and magnanimity in particular can help guide the public presentation of religious views on social and political topics.

Humility

Humility, according to Thomas Aquinas, includes knowledge of one's deficiency and prevents one from aiming at great things against right reason. Like most virtues, humility is the mean between two extremes. Practicing this virtue guards us against too much pride on one end, and too much obsequiousness on the other.[13] Lisa Fullam has noted three popular incorrect interpretations of humility. The first misinterpretation is that humility entails lying about ourselves, the second is that it entails actively putting oneself down and belittling our gifts and talents, and the third is that humility requires accepting humiliation or subjugation as good for us.[14] Though it has often been interpreted negatively as a quality that encourages unnecessary self-effacement or subservience, the virtue of humility does not in fact encourage such subjugating qualities. Indeed, a humility that is degrading is a false humility; true humility simply encourages a person to know where his or her weaknesses lie. It is the virtue of being honest with one's self, or, as Fullam puts it, "the habitual practice of seeking self-knowledge."[15]

Like most virtues, humility is relational. Thomas argues that "humility makes us honor others and esteem them better than ourselves, insofar as we see some of God's gifts in them."[16] Acquiring the virtue of humility, therefore, enables us to be honest about our own limitations and to appreciate the strengths of others.

In addition to a relational aspect that encourages us to recognize our limitations and see the good in others, the virtue of humility can also have an epistemic aspect. In cultivating epistemic humility, we may come to realize that, in Judith Butler's words, "it may be that what is right and what is good consist in staying open to the tensions that beset the most fundamental categories we require, in knowing unknowingness at the core of what we know, and what we need, and in recognizing the sign of life in what we undergo without certainty about what will come."[17]

Practicing the virtue of humility thus encourages us to let go: to acknowledge that we do not have as much control as we think we do, and that we do not know as much as we think we know. This virtue opens a space for new ideas and perspectives to be heard. Drawing again from Judith Butler, the virtue of humility might allow us to learn "to feel the surety of one's epistemological and ontological anchor go,"[18] to acknowledge that our point of view is not the only one, and to be willing to deal with complex and confusing issues honestly.

The virtue of humility is also related to what Margaret Farley has called the "grace of self-doubt," which is "a grace for recognizing the contingencies of moral knowledge when we stretch toward the particular and the concrete. It allows us to listen to the experience of others, take seriously reasons that are alternative to our own, rethink our own last word."[19] For Farley, this grace of self-doubt is what allows for epistemic humility. In short, the virtue of humility encourages us to be honest about our shortcomings (but not to exaggerate them), to recognize the strengths of others, and to let go of our desire for order, control, and easy answers.

In the practice of virtues, one relies on role models; we imitate those further along in virtue. For Christians, we find many of these role models in the saints and, of course, in Jesus. Aspects of Jesus' life and teachings can serve as models of humility. For example, Jesus tells the parable of the wedding feast as a lesson in humility, encouraging his listeners to sit at a lower place at a wedding feast and not the place of honor (Lk 14:7-12). Further, the washing of the disciples' feet is a concrete act of humility. In this scene, Jesus, the Teacher, washes the feet of his disciples, urging them to follow his example and to wash one another's feet (Jn 13:1-20). Both of these instances remind us that practicing humility means putting others before ourselves (without degrading ourselves).

In the area of epistemic humility, we can turn, interestingly enough, to former Secretary of Defense Donald Rumsfeld. At a press conference about the Iraq War in 2002, Mr. Rumsfeld noted the following: "there are known knowns; there are things we know we know. We also know there are known unknowns; that is to say we know there are some things we do not know. But there are also unknown unknowns—the ones we don't know we don't know."[20] Those of us wishing to better practice epistemic humility could benefit from this statement and remember that, in most situations, we have a limited perspective and we do not have all the facts.

Magnanimity

The virtue of magnanimity complements humility, according to Thomas Aquinas, by encouraging a person to aim for great things according to right reason. Whereas humility entails being honest about one's weaknesses, magnanimity entails being honest about one's strengths. It is the virtue of not selling oneself short.

Rebecca DeYoung notes that without magnanimity "we become habitual self-underestimators, we believe our self-disparaging comments about our worth and abilities, and as a result, we fail to live up to all we are called to be."[21] Thomas Aquinas suggests that magnanimity is an aspect of fortitude, noting that this virtue is "about the hope of something difficult."[22] He categorizes magnanimity as an aspect of fortitude because it confirms the mind in hoping for or obtaining the greatest goods. The virtue of magnanimity trains us to work toward greatness, even though this may be difficult at times; it does not get sidetracked by lesser, more immediate possibilities, nor is it discouraged in the face of obstacles. Magnanimity, coming from the Latin word for "greatness," calls a person to greatness of soul and to use his or her unique gifts confidently and generously. Further, Thomas argues that a magnanimous person has confidence not only in his or herself, but also in others. This virtue thus enables us to see the greatness in ourselves and in others.

Paul Wadell, a contemporary Christian ethicist, reiterates Thomas's understanding of magnanimity, defining it as "the virtue that trains us to reach for what is best in every dimension of our lives."[23] Wadell, with Thomas, contrasts magnanimity with pusillanimity, which allows a person to become comfortable with mediocrity by taking the easy way out. Wadell argues "a pusillanimous life asks nothing of us," whereas a life of magnanimity constantly calls us to have the courage to strive for excellence and to accept "the greatness to which God has called us."[24] Pusillanimity is the vice on one side of magnanimity that claims too little for the self. The vice on the other side is presumption, which claims too much.[25]

Elizabeth Johnson's understanding of conversion offers an insightful feminist interpretation of magnanimity. For Johnson, women's experiences and awareness of oppression eventually lead them to resist that oppression. Women's "no" to subjection and "yes" to their own worth take place in a process of conversion. Johnson notes that her understanding of "conversion" differs from its traditional usage. Traditionally, she argues, conversion has been understood as a process of disowning oneself or making oneself lesser and God greater. Because women have historically been relegated to the margins as the "lesser sex," this type of conversion would be harmful to women rather than spiritually enriching.

Johnson argues that the type of conversion women are called to undergo is not conversion as loss of self but rather conversion as "discovery of self and affirmation of one's strength, giftedness, and responsibility . . . turning away from demeaning female identity toward new ownership of the female self as God's good gift."[26] Thus, based on women's experiences of oppression, Johnson redefines conversion as self-affirmation rather than self-abnegation.

Johnson's understanding of conversion can be seen as an aspect of magnanimity. Sometimes it is difficult to see the greatness in oneself if we have experienced oppression or if we have been told somehow that we are not great, or are less than that. Magnanimity can be a difficult virtue to put into practice because it requires people to "lay hold of their genuine human dignity and value,"[27] often in the face of systems of oppression that tell certain people—because of gender, race, class, sexual preference, disability, age—that they are not called to greatness.

Magnanimity, in these situations, is a difficult but prophetic self-affirmation. Just because I am different from you does not mean that I am not also called to greatness. Farley's "grace of self-doubt" is helpful here. Farley notes that the grace of self-doubt does not extend to doubts about our basic worth: "It is not a grace for anyone to doubt fundamentally his or her own self-worth, or the value of her experience and the possibility of his insight. There are forms of insecurity that require transformation into strength."[28] The virtue of magnanimity, as I interpret it, enables this transformation into strength. In short, the virtue of magnanimity encourages us to be confident in our gifts and abilities—our greatness—even in the face of oppression, and to affirm that greatness of soul not only in ourselves but in all people.

Just as Jesus offered us a model of humility, so too can he offer a model of magnanimity. We can look, for example, to his reading in the synagogue at Nazareth. After reading the passage from Isaiah proclaiming good news to the poor, release to the captives, and recovery of sight to the blind, Jesus remarks, "Today this scripture has been fulfilled in your hearing" (Lk 4:21). The virtue of magnanimity enables to be who God has called us to be. In this passage Jesus announces his own calling as God's prophet. In this case, his magnanimity got him thrown out of town, which is why this virtue is annexed to fortitude; it takes courage to proclaim who we are. We also see in Jesus the relational aspect of magnanimity that asks us to promote the greatness of others. Jesus, "friend of tax collectors and sinners" (Lk 7:34), consistently stood on the side of the oppressed and marginalized.

Applying the Virtues of Humility and Magnanimity

Humility and magnanimity are often described as complementary virtues because we cannot really have one without the other. The two virtues work together to enable us to have a realistic understanding of ourselves and our capabilities: humility keeps us from aiming too high and magnanimity from aiming too low. The goal of practicing the virtues of humility and magnanimity is perhaps best expressed in Jesus' articulation of the second great commandment: "Love your neighbor as yourself" (Mt 22:39). That is, these two virtues work together to enable us to value both ourselves and other people: "humility opens one's eyes to see and appreciate the gifts of others, just as magnanimity does for one's own."[29]

How have these two virtues of humility and magnanimity been practiced in the debates about gay marriage and healthcare reform within the Catholic Church? I focus below on two cases, the first dealing with debates around healthcare reform and the second with children of same-sex parents in parochial schools. In both instances, I ask how the virtues of magnanimity and humility were practiced, and how they could have been practiced more effectively. When applying the virtues, I tend to focus on (1) the relational aspect of magnanimity—do the arguments or actions promote the greatness of *all* people (especially the most marginalized and vulnerable)?; and (2) the epistemic aspect of humility—do the actions or arguments acknowledge their limitations and respect other points of view? There are, of course, other ways to apply these virtues, and other virtues to use, so this analysis is not intended to be definitive.

Case #1: Healthy Debate

On March 17, 2010, more than seventy-five heads of women's religious orders in the United States signed a letter to members of Congress urging them to pass the Senate healthcare reform bill. The letter notes that, in their various ministries, including running hospitals and free clinics, the nuns have "witnessed firsthand the impact of our national healthcare crisis, particularly its impact on women, children and people who are poor."[30] They note that although it is an imperfect measure, the bill will make crucial investments in community health centers and expand coverage to over thirty million people. The nuns further argue that, as they interpret it, the Senate bill will not provide taxpayer funding for elective abortions. They note that the bill will make "historic new investments" in pregnant women, which "is the REAL pro-life stance."[31] The nuns' letter takes a stand for the vulnerable, privileging the poor, women, and children and it interprets the Senate bill to mean that there will be no federal funding for abortion.

Two days before the nuns' letter was released, the U.S. bishops wrote a letter urging Congress *not* to pass the Senate bill. Like the nuns, they note that the bill has its shortcomings, but, unlike the nuns, the bishops argue that "the flaws are so fundamental that they vitiate the good that the bill intends to promote."[32] The bishops note that two principles have shaped their concerns: first, that health care means taking care of the health of all people, from very young to very old, and second, that the expansion of health care should not involve the expansion of abortion funding. The bishops interpret the bill to mean that there will be increased funding for abortion, thus arguing that the bill is not in accord with their second principle.

Where do we see humility and magnanimity at work here, and where do we see them lacking? Both the religious women and the bishops are confident that they have interpreted the bill correctly. The former think supporting the bill is the most pro-life stance, while the latter think opposing it is more pro-life.

The nuns do tend to point more to the poor and vulnerable in their reasoning, while the bishops tend to point more to their two principles. If part of magnanimity means promoting the greatness of others—especially the most vulnerable—the nuns appear to fare better than the bishops. This is particularly true in light of Bishop Thomas Olmsted of Phoenix who announced in May 2010 that Sister Margaret McBride, a hospital administrator there, had excommunicated herself by approving an abortion to save a mother's life.[33] Thus, Catholic healthcare professionals, in addition to Catholic politicians, can apparently run the risk of excommunication when they make difficult decisions that run counter to a particular interpretation of church teaching.

The editors of *Commonweal*, a Catholic weekly magazine, wrote an editorial about the hard line many bishops have drawn on the abortion issue, from opposing the healthcare bill to excommunicating pro-choice politicians.[34] The *Commonweal* editorial notes that these kinds of stances on abortion admit of no complexity: "Instead of addressing the legitimate concerns of those who oppose the church's teaching on abortion—such as concerns for the health of women—American bishops too often seem to fear that any acknowledgment of the complexity of this issue would weaken their own position."[35] Part of the epistemic practice of humility entails acknowledging complexity and grey areas; the bishops could stand to put it into better practice in their public statements, at least according to *Commonweal*.

Archbishop Charles Chaput of Denver took a harder line on healthcare reform than either U.S. bishops as a whole or American religious women. In an editorial he wrote in *First Things* in March 2010, he argued that "the Senate version of healthcare reform currently being forced ahead by congressional leaders and the White House is a bad bill that will result in bad law. It does not deserve, nor does it have, the support of the Catholic bishops of our country. Nor does the American public want it."[36] He further chastises other Catholic groups that have been in favor of the bill: "The most painful feature [of the process] has been those 'Catholic' groups that by their eagerness for some kind of deal undercut the witness of the Catholic community and help advance a bad bill into a bad law. Their flawed judgment could now have damaging consequences for all of us."[37] Here we see neither respect for the opinions of others on a complicated issue, nor any acknowledgment that the issue is, in fact, complicated. Bishop Chaput's letter gives a distinct sense of epistemic over-confidence, rather than humility.

Both the bishops as a group, and Archbishop Chaput (and probably most of us, too), could learn how to better acknowledge and deal with the complexities of healthcare reform, especially with the issues surrounding abortion funding. The statements of both the U.S. bishops and American women religious indicate two major complexities with regard to abortion provisions in the healthcare bill. The first has to do with the public funding of abortion—does the bill provide such funding? Should it? The second issue is larger and has to do with finding the most effective ways of reducing the number of abortions. Is it better to invest in pregnant women and mothers, as the nuns suggest, or is it better to outlaw abortion, as the bishops seem to suggest? Should we pursue both courses of action? Engaging these questions will begin to address some of the complexities of the abortion provisions in the healthcare bill and general discussions about women's health.

That there are complexities, however, does not mean that the bishops need to embrace a pro-choice position. After all, if the prophetic aspect of magnanimity does require standing up for the greatness of all people, especially the most vulnerable, this presumably entails witnessing to the unborn. A balance of humility—listening to other points of view, and magnanimity—promoting the greatness of all people, might allow the bishops to present their views confidently, but perhaps not absolutely. It might allow them to acknowledge the complexity of the abortion issue and to listen to other views on it while still maintaining a general pro-life stance.

The religious women, perhaps because so many of them work directly in healthcare and are confronted daily with its complexities (as we have seen in the case of Sister McBride), seem to be doing a better job of balancing these virtues. In general, practicing the virtue of humility when discussing healthcare reform or abortion could entail the following: the skills to listen to other points of view, a willingness to acknowledge complexity, and an awareness of the limits of one's own knowledge or perspective. Practicing the virtue of magnanimity might entail: clarity of thought regarding one's own position, the courage of conviction, and a willingness to promote the greatness of all people. When combined, these virtues enable a person to stand up for his or her own beliefs and to articulate them clearly while also respecting and learning from the perspectives of others.

Case #2: "Out" Parents Out of Luck?

A second case in which the virtues of humility and magnanimity can be applied is the manner in which the archdioceses of Denver and Boston have dealt with same-sex parents of children in parochial schools. In March of 2010, a school in the Denver archdiocese announced that it planned to expel a child because her parents were lesbians. The child would be allowed to complete kindergarten but would be asked to find a new school for first grade. The pastor of the parish argued, "To allow children in these circumstances to continue in our school would be a cause of confusion for the student, in that what they are being taught in school conflicts with what they experience in the home."[38] Archbishop Charles Chaput supported the school's decision, and the archdiocese now has a policy excluding children of same-sex parents from parochial schools: "To preserve the mission of our schools, and to respect the faith of the wider Catholic community, we expect all families who enroll students to live in accord with Catholic teaching. Parents living in open discord with Catholic teaching in areas of faith and morals unfortunately choose by their actions to disqualify their children from enrollment."[39]

A school in Boston faced a similar situation in May of 2010. The school principal and the parish pastor decided that an eight-year-old boy would not be allowed to enroll because his parents are lesbians. Unlike the Denver case, though, neither the superintendent of schools nor Boston Archbishop Sean O'Malley issued a definitive statement about the case. Cardinal O'Malley wrote on his blog that Catholic schools have had a history of accepting students from all kinds of backgrounds, noting, "We have never had categories of people who were excluded."[40] At the same time, he defended the pastor of the church, Fr. James Rafferty, for his decision, arguing that Fr. Rafferty would not exclude a child in order to chastise the parents and that he made the decision based on what he thought was best for the child. Cardinal O'Malley does not, however, issue a definitive statement on a diocese-wide policy on accepting children of same-sex parents. He notes that the central question is:

The essence of what we are looking at is the question of how do we make Catholic schools available to children who come from diverse, often unconventional households, while ensuring the moral theology and teachings of the Church are not compromised? It is true that we welcome people from all walks of life. But we recognize that, regardless of the circumstances involved, we maintain our responsibility to teach the truths of our faith, including those concerning sexual morality and marriage. We need to present the Church's teachings courageously and yet in a way that is compassionate and persuasive.[41]

Unlike Archbishop Chaput, it seems like Cardinal O'Malley is ready to acknowledge and deal with the complexity of the situation. The major issue here is how to balance the duty of Catholic schools to uphold Catholic teachings while also offering hospitality to children from all kinds of families, including those with single, divorced, or same-sex parents.

Where, in these two instances, do we see humility and magnanimity at work, and where could we see them used more effectively? Archbishop Chaput and the archdiocese of Denver opt for an unambiguous policy: children of same-sex parents cannot attend parochial schools. Cardinal O'Malley, on the other hand, appears to be more willing to wrestle with some complex issues—thus demonstrating the virtue of humility. In attempting to discern how to present the church's teachings courageously, while also acknowledging the complexities of people's lives and families, Cardinal O'Malley's public response is a good example of balance between humility and magnanimity. This kind of nuanced and thoughtful response could be held as a model for other bishops and church leaders; it is hoped that further statements and policies that come out of the Boston archdiocese are equally as nuanced and thoughtful.

Humility and Magnanimity as Virtues of "Public Relations"

Bishops and other religious leaders or public figures who take public stands on contentious social or political issues face a difficult task. By practicing the virtues of humility and magnanimity as individual Christians, and by encouraging church leaders to do the same, we will be better equipped to speak publicly as people of faith in a spirit of openness and generosity while also remaining true to our core convictions. Envisioning the role of church leaders through a framework of virtue ethics can help form their public personas in ways that demonstrate a sensitivity to multiple perspectives, a willingness to admit the complexity of many issues, and the courage to articulate basic theological and ethical beliefs.

Humility and magnanimity can be understood as the virtues of "public relations," in the sense that they are both public and relational. First, these, and perhaps other virtues as well, can help guide church leaders as they discern the most fitting way to speak publicly about issues facing the church, the country, and the world. As public virtues, they can enable communications that offer a clear statement of one's own position while also acknowledging the validity of other points of view. As relational, these virtues can enable both church leaders and the laity to relate to others, even those with whom we disagree, in a spirit of openness and honesty. The virtue of magnanimity encourages self-respect and the courage to make our opinions heard, and the virtue of humility encourages respect for other persons, allowing them the space to articulate their own perspectives.

The complementary virtues of humility and magnanimity can help the church find balance in its public response to pressing contemporary issues. Magnanimity calls the church to a prophetic stance, promoting the greatness of all people, and to articulate its values clearly. Humility calls for a greater awareness of the church's limitations and a letting go of the certainty with which it pronounces many of its teachings. In cultivating these two virtues, individual Catholics and church leaders might find that they become more comfortable with ambiguity and that their public stances on contemporary political issues will be more credible.

As noted earlier, virtue ethics helps us transition from who we are to who we want to become. So the question is, what does the Catholic Church want to become? Another way to ask this is, what is the purpose of the church? What is it here to do? When oriented by the virtues of humility and magnanimity, we might come to understand the church's purpose less in terms of being an "epistemic authority" or avoiding ambiguity and complexity by insisting that complicated issues are black and white, and more in terms of following Jesus and embodying the virtues that he himself practiced.

Indeed, if the incarnation teaches us anything it is that God is not afraid of getting a little messy and not afraid to take on and participate in the messiness of our human lives. Perhaps this, then, may be one purpose of the church: to incarnate God's loving and compassionate presence in the world without being afraid of a little "messiness." And perhaps the virtues of humility and magnanimity—the virtues of truly knowing ourselves, of becoming more comfortable with complexity and ambiguity, of recognizing our greatness and calling others to that same greatness—perhaps these virtues can help move the church and its leaders from the church it is now to the church it can become.

Notes

[1] A 2009 Gallup Poll indicated that American Catholics are divided on a number of moral issues. For example, 40 percent of those surveyed believed abortion is morally acceptable, 67 percent believed premarital sexual relations are morally acceptable, and 53 percent believed that homosexuality is morally acceptable; http://politics.usnews.com/news/blogs/god-and-country/2009/03/30/gallup-poll [accessed 9/26/2010].

[2] See the letters and statements on the U.S. bishops website: http://www.usccb.org, especially "Letter to the U.S. Senate on Healthcare" (September 2009) and "Letter to Congress on Eve of Healthcare Summit" (February 2010), which outline the bishops' three priorities [accessed 9/23/2010].

[3] Though the U.S. bishops emphasized each of their three priorities in some letters to Congress, a look at other letters and at their action alerts and fact sheets reveals a heavier emphasis on abortion. See, for example, "Nationwide Bulletin Insert" and "Pulpit Announcement and Prayer Petition" (January 2010), "Joint Letter on Healthcare to US Senate" (December 2009), the fact sheet on the Stupak Amendment (November 2009), and the action alert urging support of the Nelson-Hatch-Casey amendment (December 2009), all of which deal exclusively or almost exclusively with abortion. All documents are available on the USCCB website.

[4] Several official church documents over the past thirty years have dealt with the issue of homosexuality. See, for example, two documents from the Vatican: *On the Pastoral Care of Homosexual Persons*, 1986, and *Considerations Regarding Proposals to Give Legal Recognition to Unions between Homosexual Persons*, 2003; available at http://www.vatican.va/. See also the document from the U.S. bishops, *Ministry to Persons with a Homosexual Inclination*, www.nccbussc.org/. Each of these documents, while advising respect and compassion for homosexual persons, upholds the unnaturalness or objective disorder of homosexual acts because they violate the procreative function of sexual intercourse and the complementarity of man and woman. Pope John Paul II's series of lectures on "The Theology of the Body" emphasizes the naturalness of heterosexual marital relationships and implicitly critiques homosexual sexual relationships. Perhaps the pope's most important point is that, in their original unity, the first man and woman were spontaneously aware of the meaning of their bodies. The pope calls this the body's "nuptial" meaning, which is bound up with our ability to express our love for another person through self-gift. The nuptial meaning of the body, in essence, suggests

that the man exists as a gift for the woman, and the woman for the man, and that in the mutual acceptance of the gift of the other, the two become one flesh and "submit their whole humanity to the blessing of fertility." The person, the pope argues, essentially through a process of self-discovery in which he or she comes to realize the body's nuptial meaning, discovers at the same time the objective moral norms drawn from the principles of the natural law. Because the nuptial meaning of the body relies on a complementarity between men and women and leads to procreation, homosexual relationships are excluded. See John Paul II, *The Theology of the Body: Human Love in the Divine Plan* (Boston: Pauline Books and Media, 1997), 46.

[5]Chuck Colbert, "Dioceses Major Contributors to Repeal Same-Sex Marriage," *National Catholic Reporter*, November 25, 2009.

[6]I cite the specific sources as I introduce them. On the healthcare issue, I draw mostly from the U.S. bishops' letters to Congress, statements from women religious, and news articles or editorials. On the issue of children of same-sex parents, I generally draw from news articles and official statements from bishops and dioceses.

[7]Joseph Kotva, *The Christian Case for Virtue Ethics* (Washington, DC: Georgetown University Press, 1996), 17.

[8]Thomas Aquinas, *Summa Theologiae*, trans. Fathers of the English Dominican Province (New York: Benziger, 1947).

[9]James Keenan, "Virtue Ethics," in *Christian Ethics: An Introduction*, ed. Bernard Hoose (Collegeville, MN: Liturgical Press, 1998), 89.

[10]See, for example, James Keenan and Daniel Harrington, *Jesus and Virtue Ethics: Building Bridges between New Testament Studies and Moral Theology* (Oxford: Sheed and Ward, 2002); William Spohn, *Go and Do Likewise: Jesus and Ethics* (New York: Continuum Publishing Group, 2000); Paul Wadell, *Happiness and the Christian Moral Life: An Introduction to Christian Ethics* (New York: Sheed & Ward, 2008).

[11]Kotva, *The Christian Case for Virtue Ethics*, 145.

[12]Christopher Vogt, "Fostering a Catholic Commitment to the Common Good: An Approach Rooted in Virtue Ethics," *Theological Studies* 68 (2007): 399.

[13]Thomas Aquinas, *Summa Theologiae* II.ii 161.2-3.

[14]Lisa Fullam, "Humility: A Pilgrim's Virtue," *New Theology Review* 19, no. 2 (May 2006): 47.

[15]Ibid., 48.

[16]Thomas Aquinas, *Summa Theologiae* II.ii 129.3.

[17]Judith Butler, "Beside Oneself: On the Limits of Sexual Autonomy," in *Undoing Gender* (New York: Routledge, 2004), 39.

[18]Ibid., 35.

[19]Margaret Farley, "Ethics, Ecclesiology, and the Grace of Self-Doubt," in *A Call to Fidelity: On the Moral Theology of Charles E. Curran*, ed. James Walter, Timothy O'Connell, and Thomas Shannon (Washington, DC: Georgetown University Press, 2002), 68-69.

[20]Department of Defense News Briefing—Secretary Rumsfeld and

Gen. Myers, Feb 12, 2002, http://www.defense.gov/transcripts/transcript. aspx?transcriptid=2636 [accessed 9/25/10].

[21]Rebecca DeYoung, "Aquinas' Virtues of Acknowledged Dependence: A New Measure of Greatness," *Faith and Philosophy* 21 (April 2004): 215.

[22]Thomas Aquinas, *Summa Theologiae* II.ii 129.6. For more on magnanimity's relation to courage, see R. E. Houser, "The Virtue of Courage (IIa IIae, qq. 123-140) in *The Ethics of Aquinas*, ed. Stephen J. Pope (Washington, DC: Georgetown University Press, 2002).

[23]Wadell, *Happiness and the Christian Moral Life*, 57.

[24]Ibid.

[25]See Thomas Aquinas, *Summa Theologiae* II.ii 133.2.

[26]Elizabeth Johnson, *She Who Is: The Mystery of God in Feminist Theological Discourse* (New York: Crossroad, 1994), 64.

[27]Ibid.

[28]Farley, "Ethics, Ecclesiology, and the Grace of Self-Doubt," 68.

[29]David Horner, "What It Takes to Be Great: Aristotle and Aquinas on Magnanimity," *Faith and Philosophy* 15, no. 4 (October 1998): 434.

[30]U.S. Nuns' Letter to Congress, http://www.networklobby.org/press/3-17-10HealthcareSistersLetter.htm [accessed 6/1/2010].

[31]Ibid.

[32]USCCB News Release, http://www.usccb.org/comm/archives/2010/10-043. shtml [accessed 6/1/2010].

[33]Several Catholic news outlets ran this story. See, for example, "Nun excommunicated, loses hospital post over decision on abortion" (http://www. catholicnews.com/data/stories/cns/1002085.htm), and Michael Clancy, "Nun Excommunicated for Allowing Abortion," May 18, 2010, http://ncronline. org/news/justice/nun-excommunicated-allowing-abortion. The news also found its way into secular news organizations, such as National Public Radio. See Barbara Hagerty, "Nun Excommunicated for Allowing Abortion," May 19, 2010, http://www.npr.org/templates/story/story.php?storyId=126985072 [all accessed 9/26/2010].

[34]"A Pattern of Missteps," Editors of *Commonweal*, http://www.common-wealmagazine.org/pattern-missteps [accessed 6/1/2010].

[35]Ibid.

[36]Charles Chaput, "Catholics, Health Care, and the Senate's Bad Bill," http://www.firstthings.com/onthesquare/2010/03/catholics-health-care-and-the-senatersquos-bad-bil [accessed 6/1/2010].

[37]Ibid.

[38]"Catholic School Rejects Children of Lesbian Parents, Sparking Faith Debate," Lauren Green, http://www.foxnews.com/us/2010/03/12/catholic-school-rejects-children-lesbian-parents-sparking-faith-debate/ [accessed 6/1/2010].

[39]Ibid.

[40]Cardinal Sean's Blog, http://www.cardinalseansblog.org/2010/05/19/on-the-hingham-school-situation/ [accessed 6/1/2010].

[41]Ibid.

The Aporia of Race and Identity

J. Kameron Carter and the Future of Black Liberation Theology

Andrew Prevot

> What would a path be without aporia?
> —Jacques Derrida[1]

> More often than not, they accounted for their perseverance on the basis of their faith in God who helped them "make a way out of no way."
> —Delores S. Williams[2]

In discourses of race and identity, indeterminate and determinate speech present themselves, in distinct ways, as simultaneously dangerous, necessary, and incompatible. Such is the aporetic condition this essay seeks to clarify. An additional goal is to show how this paradoxical discursive situation comes to light in J. Kameron Carter's critical intervention within the tradition of black liberation theology.

Carter proposes Christ as the most definitive and liberating paradigm of identity. He contends, moreover, that this theologically incarnate paradigm partially incorporates but also destabilizes other features of human particularity, which have been treated as focal points of racial and other sorts of identification. In the end, Carter's theological account of race radically subordinates raciology and all other identity discourses to a "catholic" mode of Christian theology and in this way moves the tradition of black liberation theology forward in a very promising direction.

At the same time, however, Carter's proposal remains somewhat aporetic, insofar as it is not immune to the threat of re-inscribing something structurally similar to racial exclusion, precisely in the form of Christian identity. Before considering Carter in more detail, I shall offer a few initial remarks regarding the aporetic state of the question of race and identity in general.

Delineating the Aporia

Although its precise meaning remains up for dispute, racial reference has found a foothold not only in "common sense" ways of thinking and acting, but also within an ethically charged academic lexicon, in which it names one of the many particularities (along with gender, class, culture, and so on) that make up identity. To insist upon the socially constructed nature of identity discourse, as many do, does not cancel out its concrete expressions or effects. The creative license afforded by such historicization seems, in fact, only to embolden the pragmatically minded, such as David Theo Goldberg and Cornel West, to speak determinately about race and its analogous identity-markers, provided that the appropriate political ends are in view.[3]

At the same time, the widespread account of race as a specific and inescapable feature of identity has been destabilized by an urgent question concerning identity as such. Identity discourse cannot help but negate, both conceptually and practically, at least some measure of the untold diversity and vitality that characterize human experience. Accordingly, a postmodern embrace of the indeterminate, the hybrid, the unknowable excess, or the other as such should not be dismissed too quickly as mere linguistic play. In some cases, it also functions as a prophetic warning against the very real destructive potential inherent in categorical designation. Jacques Derrida's writings remain perhaps the most radical example of this deconstructive mode of the prophetic, but one also sees it represented in Paul Gilroy's arguments against race, as well as in Victor Anderson's early critique of ontological blackness.[4]

By tracking these divergent trends one could argue that historical struggles for liberation tend to oscillate between advocating determinate identities, on the one hand, and striving to transcend them through a rhetoric of indeterminacy, on the other. The aporia that defines this oscillation is precisely that the pragmatically determinate use of race and the indeterminacy of a postmodern aesthetic have both come to light as dangerous but necessary conditions of liberation that are, at the same time, apparently incompatible.

The determinate and the indeterminate are dangerous because both modes of discourse have the potential to support or shelter violent structures of inhumanity. For instance, Goldberg shows that the indeterminate can facilitate color-blind or "born again" racism, whereas Gilroy demonstrates that the determinate can further entrench divisive stereotypes in the power dynamics of contemporary culture.[5] The necessity of both modes of discourse stems primarily from the hope for a historically conditioned liberation in which the determinate structures of humanity's historical existence are transcended in some respects but retained in others. This general goal of liberation (which, no doubt, has many variants)[6] demands that the concrete not be left behind. And yet, to the extent that the concrete becomes ossified into restrictive structures of identity, liberation in a postmodern age also requires that these structures be overcome. In order to sustain any hope of approaching the embodied, social, fully alive and inclusive freedom that is typically associated with liberation, it seems that each mode of speech must be employed to counterbalance the excesses of the other.

And yet, the problem attains its highest intensity in the recognition that the two do not seem compatible. At least in some cases decisions must be made regarding how to proceed, whether more nearly determinately or indeterminately—for example, do I assert myself as black in this circumstance, or not?—and in such cases the failure to embody a clear decision risks a paralyzing, contradictory, and potentially offensive form of double-speak or double-consciousness.[7] But, in another sense, the conflict is something that cannot be avoided simply by choosing one route or another. For the modes of determinate and indeterminate speech are never pure: to some extent, they are always given together, as mutually dependent oppositional aspects of the polyvalent, dynamic, mysterious, and never perfectly adequate reality of human language (which includes "body language" and an endless variety of cultural media, aside from the written word).[8]

In short, it seems that the struggle for liberation must somehow be both racial and post-racial, both formed by and against identity, and yet there is no obvious way to make sense of this pairing, especially in concrete moments of decision, which are themselves never totally decisive, and there are perils at every turn. This situation imposes itself as something that feels inescapable, hence as an aporia in its precise etymological sense: a predicament from which there is no way out. In naming this predicament, my intention is to be realistic but not despairing. There is still much to be gained in the ongoing pursuit of liberation, and yet whatever progress is possible must be achieved precisely through the apparent contradictions of this aporia, and not through their neglect. My properly theological purpose in this essay is to suggest that the future of black liberation theology in particular, and to some extent theology in general, depends on how carefully it confronts this aporetic condition.

Carter's Theological Proposal

J. Kameron Carter, author of *Race: A Theological Account*,[9] has already contributed a great deal to this endeavor. Carter discloses our aporetic condition as a problem that is deeply theological, and he does so in a manner that is as yet unparalleled.[10] Before considering the details of this disclosure, it will be helpful to present, briefly, the basic contours of Carter's theological proposal. Although Carter fashions his theological account of race as a movement beyond black liberation theology,[11] his work also takes some inspiration from this tradition. As in James Cone's project, so too in Carter's it is not enough to do theology in abstraction. Rather, one must do it from within the "crises of life and death" that, in modernity, have afflicted people of color in a particularly devastating way.[12] And this means doing theology in solidarity with these subjugated peoples and in support of their struggles for liberation.[13]

However, Carter also moves the conversation forward in at least two ways. First, he demonstrates a greater awareness of the aporetic condition of race and identity. Then he engages this condition by developing a theology that is intentionally more catholic, with a small "c," in the sense that it lets itself be shaped by a broader (ancient and yet contemporary) theological tradi-tion.[14] In contrast to many others working at the intersection of racial and religious discourse, Carter's work is in close contact with normative patristic sources such as Irenaeus, Gregory of Nyssa, Maximus the Confessor, and Augustine, on the one hand, and contemporary figures of orthodoxy such as Karl Barth, Hans Urs von Balthasar, and John Milbank, on the other; they help him approach the aporia of race and identity in a theological way.

The basic structure of Carter's Christology is composed of ele-ments drawn from these theological interlocutors. Carter presents Christ as a concrete universal whose embodied existence reveals the triune love of God and counter-culturally shapes both self and society in kenotic or ecstatic relation with the other. From Irenaeus's critique of the protoracial mythology of the Gnostics,[15] Carter gleans the idea that Christology needs to situate itself within the covenantal salvation history of Israel, recounted in scripture; it therefore cannot forget Jesus' Jewishness, nor his particular embodiment within a specific history that is not initially that of the West.[16] This concentration on Christ's Jewish, covenantal, historical, scriptural, bodily, and non-Western concreteness is counterbalanced by a concern for the universality that is expressed in Irenaeus's account of Christ's recapitulation of the whole of creation.[17] By recapitulating all things in himself, Christ is able to open the divine communion between the Father, Son, and Spirit to all human beings.[18]

This basic concrete-universal paradigm is retained but recon-figured in Gregory and Maximus. Gregory's uncompromising abolitionism, which was singular in his time,[19] presupposes an understanding of the concreteness of Christ, as crystallized by the paschal mystery,[20] and of the universality of Christ, as conveyed by the doctrine that all human beings are created in Christ and participate analogically in his divine image.[21] Maximus, for his part, expresses the concrete universality of Christ in his discussion of Pentecost, in which the diverse *logoi* of humanity—an abundant variety of languages, cultures, peoples, and bodies—are united by the Spirit in the one *Logos* who was made flesh in fulfillment of Israel's covenantal history.[22]

The counter-cultural, ecstatic, and kenotic aspects of Carter's Christology are an index of resistance to various sorts of oppression, including in particular those oppressions that stem from a false view of one's personal or communal being as though it were absolute or self-constituting. This is the central danger of a determinate discourse of race and identity in the present,[23] but it has also appeared in various forms in the past. Irenaeus, Gregory, and Maximus each disclose Christ's existence as a counter-cultural norm that subverts Gnostic proto-raciology, dehumanizing slavery, and the colonialist annihilation of difference, respectively, by means of radical ecstasis toward both God and neighbor.[24] Likewise, Carter's interpretation of Augustine's *Confessions*, as a theological autobiography inscribed in the Son and written against the prevailing culture of Roman imperial pride, provides another important example of Christology as a counter-cultural narration of self and society.[25]

Carter's patristic retrieval forms the positive background against which he articulates a genealogy of modern decline. Although Carter critiques Milbank for neglecting race and failing to acknowledge the extent to which claims to orthodoxy have been implicated in the socio-political order of whiteness,[26] he nevertheless adopts the basic structure of Milbank's genealogical project (with supplements from Michel Foucault and Cornel West) by arguing that secularity is a falsification of an ancient Christian discourse that it parasitically mimics.[27]

Immanuel Kant constitutes one of the clearest examples of the fall into secular pseudo-theology. In *Religion within the Limits of Reason Alone*, Christ loses his concreteness and becomes, if anything, an abstract universal, an archetype of good will. But in light of Kant's earlier writings on anthropology and race, it becomes clear that this ostensible universality is also counterfeit, inasmuch as it ultimately refers only to a white European quasi-racial community that allegedly possesses universal reason but is still marked off by particular characteristics.[28] This community is meant to exert control over the other three supposedly inferior races—the "American Indian," the "Negro," and the "Hindu,"[29] which are each characterized by a geographically, climatologically, and dermatologically correlated incapacity for rational self-rule.[30] Thus for Kant (and for the modern intellectuals who follow him), Christ is no longer truly concrete or universal and, moreover, is used ideologically to prop up a self-constituting identity rather than embraced as a counter-cultural form of kenosis or ecstasis deeply revelatory of the Trinity's superabundant love.

When Carter turns to an analysis of African American religious scholars (including Albert Raboteau, James Cone, and Charles Long), on the one hand, and New World Afro-Christian narratives (by Briton Hammon, Frederick Douglass, and Jarena Lee), on the other, his evaluations are mixed. The exact proportion of the mixture in each case depends on the relative degree to which these texts reflect the normative patristic Christology that Carter has retrieved or its modern, Kantian, racialized distortion. For instance, Carter praises the early Cone's Barthian emphasis on Christ's concrete universality[31] but critiques Cone's later formulation of ontological blackness, insofar as this formulation is influenced by Paul Tillich's existential ontology, which is tied, genealogically, to the Kantian project.[32] Carter's assessments of other Afro-Christian or black religious writings follow a similar pattern, insofar as they employ a theologically catholic hermeneutic in order to avoid various post-Kantian dangers, but a detailed reading of these analyses will have to be reserved for another occasion.

Carter's Two-stage Theological Disclosure of the Aporia

With this all too brief summary, we can begin to see how the theological dimension of the aporia of race and identity is disclosed in Carter's work. This disclosure happens in two stages. The first brings together Carter's movement beyond race (indeterminacy) and his abiding, quasi-racial mode of reference (determinacy). The second juxtaposes his bold affirmation of Christian identity (determinacy) with his welcoming of abundant human diversity (indeterminacy).

The first stage of the aporia comes to light initially in Carter's genealogy. In order to overcome the Kantian distortion of Christian theology into a religious and sociopolitical order of self-constituting whiteness, Carter promotes a certain amount of indeterminacy regarding questions of race and other comparable modes of identity. Although Carter argues that Gilroy's cosmopolitanism remains embedded in the Kantian project of modern identity, insofar as it is insufficiently theological,[33] Carter nevertheless appropriates as his own the indeterminacy of Gilroy's stance "against race" and against all analogous reifications of the self.[34] And yet, Carter reveals the other side of the aporia by retaining various ways of referring to race, as it were, without race—speaking, for instance, of "dark flesh" and the "Afro-Christian." Carter employs this quasi-racial mode of reference in order to claim a place for a geographically, culturally, or phenotypically distinctive segment of humanity, which others have preferred to call "black," within the body of Christ. Ultimately, then, although Carter explicitly endorses a post-racial imaginary in keeping with the postmodern aesthetic of indeterminacy, as represented by Gilroy, he nevertheless makes use of a select terminology that has an approximately racial function in order to locate the significance of his discourse for a particular people.

Carter's emphasis, however, is on destabilizing racial determinacy. This emphasis has a warrant that is not only genealogical but also, and more importantly, theological. For Carter, no distinctive, historically manifest form constitutes the humanity of any individual or community absolutely *except* the concrete universal form of Christ. Because racial identity and other modes of categorization pretend this absoluteness, or mimic it, they must be conceived indeterminately (which is to say, relationally, openly, provisionally, perhaps even reluctantly) lest they begin to function as idols that conceal the theological understanding of Christ as the most authentic paradigm of personal and political embodiment.

This has been the problem of modern identity discourse, which much of the tradition of black liberation theology has only partially overcome. But a residual degree of quasi-racial determinacy is also important in light of the catholic theological doctrines of creation, recapitulation, analogy, and Pentecost, which affirm the relative goodness of the diverse human forms (cultures, languages, peoples, bodies, and so on) as contingent, yet authentic, participations in Christ, and thereby in God's triune life.[35]

The second stage of the aporia stems from Carter's theological navigation of the first. It can be expressed in this way: on the one hand, Carter's theology is quite determinate on one point—namely, Christ, as the truest form of both self and society, is a form that counter-culturally resists and denounces its alternatives as pseudo-theological imitations. On the other hand, however, Carter seeks to render his Christology as hospitable to the other as possible, by acknowledging a somewhat indeterminate plurality of human forms (cultures, languages, peoples, bodies) through which one can participate in Christ.

Yet, one may question, especially from the perspective of the non-Christian other, whether Carter has made conditions for authentic selfhood or inclusion within society sufficiently indeterminate. But this means questioning the extent to which what is essentially problematic about race as a determinate discourse—namely, the categorical positing of identity, which has the potential to exclude or negate large swaths of lived human experience—is mirrored or re-inscribed in Carter's theological movement beyond race. In response to this question, one must admit that the danger of such re-inscription is historically and theoretically evident, and yet nevertheless maintain that Carter's theological arguments regarding the first stage of the aporia are, from a Christian perspective, irreversible.

That Carter's Christologically determined openness is limited is confirmed initially in the recognition that pre-modern Gnostics and modern Kantians are not the only supersessionists. Rather, as R. Kendall Soulen demonstrates, for instance, Irenaeus's Christological doctrine of recapitulation affirms biblical Judaism only at the expense of all post-biblical forms of Judaism that are not contained within the church.[36] But the problem persists when one considers the possible implications of Carter's theological proposal for other modes of religious belonging, besides Judaism, that are also jeopardized by the conditional inclusivity of Christian identity. For instance, Goldberg's analysis of the perception of Muslims in Israel and Europe as possessing an overlapping racial and religious identity, which is, as such, doubly unwelcome, compels one to ask how we can insist upon the covenantally Jewish flesh of Christ as a paradigm for humanity today without investing in a discourse that functions quasi-racially with respect to Islam?[37] One may also wonder about the potential impact of Carter's proposal on secular societies that have, according to Charles Taylor (who differs from Milbank considerably in this respect), achieved various social goods that were not realizable in a dominantly Christian milieu.[38]

Derrida's perceptive comments regarding the paradoxical theme of hospitality shed light on the general structure of the second stage of the aporia in Carter's thought. Derrida notes that there is a contradiction between hospitality conceived as a determinate "invitation" to the other, which conditions or limits what is to be welcomed, and hospitality understood as a radical indeterminacy, which does not preclude any unpredictable "visitation."[39] Carter's Christology seems, at best, to satisfy the second condition of hospitality only partially or selectively, to the extent that it discounts any personal or communal being that situates itself (whether for cultural, religious, or any other reasons) outside the concrete universal of Christ.

One could be tempted to think, therefore, that Derrida's performance of the most radical indeterminacy—in the nameless name of the *khōra*—is the most promising direction to be taken by culture, the one most likely to secure hospitality in the purest sense.[40] In Plato's *Timaeus*, the *khōra* is the pure matter that receives the creative forms of the demiurge; it is, therefore, in some sense, the most abstract place of openness or possibility imaginable. In Derrida's writings, the *khōra* retains this significance but also comes to function as a sign of hope for a maximally inclusive democratic society that is capable of receiving whatever forms may come.

And yet, one must be careful not to overlook the first condition of hospitality that Derrida illuminates, that is, its unavoidable determinacy, which inevitably limits or circumscribes its potential—and, by the same token, threatens to exclude those who do not meet its requirements. This applies to the *khōra* as well: insofar as it takes place, becomes actual, closes out some possibilities and realizes others, it acquires determinate content that is, as such, potentially perilous to others. Ultimately, the Christian lives within the promises of God, as these are communicated through scripture and the ecclesial tradition, whereas Derrida performatively commits himself to the impossible promise of a deconstructive intellectual discourse whose openness to concrete others in the world (especially those with specific religious beliefs and practices) is certainly not absolute. The divergent commitments between Carter and Derrida decide only the locations at which the aporia becomes most intense—namely, Christ and the *khōra*, respectively—but neither offers liberation simply, safely, or non-aporetically.

Conclusion

Carter's engagement with the first stage of the aporia positions the tradition of black liberation theology in a theologically catholic mode of proclamation, in which the concrete universal of Christ is praised as inclusive of innumerable human forms that are neither wholly determinate nor wholly indeterminate, neither absolute nor insignificant. In this way he moves beyond the problematic account of blackness as a mode of being that is (almost) on equal footing with Christ, or as a performance occurring within the pseudo-theological fabrication of whiteness as self-posited identity. The remaining, and indeed to some extent inescapable, difficulty, which constitutes the second stage of the aporia, is something with which Christians must continually struggle. Any hope in the triumph of Christian identity, even in its inclusivity, risks repeating one of the most problematic effects of race, to the extent that the promised universality of Christ remains determinate and thus exclusionary of other forms of lived human experience. And yet, one cannot avoid *some version* of this danger. Even Derrida is not immune to it. The question is how to approach it.

In short, Carter's recommendation, and mine as well, would be to strive to live out a kenotic and ecstatic existence in Christ. The scripturally and ecclesially given concreteness of Jesus' life, death, and resurrection reveals God's love for a diversely beautiful and yet destructively bellicose humanity, a humanity that cries out with many tongues and in countless ways for the fullness of liberation. The *khōra* does not; it cannot. For this reason, it seems necessary to say more than Derrida—and, in fact, to proclaim in many respects precisely what Carter proclaims about Christ—but without forgetting the aporia, which Derrida and other interlocutors have helped us to identify, and the unanswered questions with which it confronts even the most authentic and magnanimous Christian praxis. To forget this could prove disastrous (as it has historically).

Finally, as the conflicts and tensions between determinate and indeterminate identity continue to intensify and proliferate, let us remember with Delores Williams those generations of Afro-Christian women and men who have placed their trust in God, as the one who alone has the power "to help [us] make a way out of no way," to lead us through the dark night of aporia into the dawn of liberation.

Notes

¹Jacques Derrida, "Sauf le nom," in *On the Name*, ed. Thomas Dutoit (Stanford: Stanford University Press, 1995), 83.

²Delores Williams, *Sisters in the Wilderness: The Challenge of Womanist God-Talk* (Maryknoll, NY: Orbis Books, 1993), xi.

³David Theo Goldberg has defended the claims that racial reference is indispensable for the necessarily specific analysis of racism and that a pragmatic use of it is compatible with its historicization. His argument develops through his major monographs: *Racist Culture: Philosophy and the Politics of Meaning* (Cambridge, MA: Blackwell, 1993); *The Racial State* (Malden, MA: Blackwell, 2002); and *The Threat of Race* (Malden, MA: Wiley-Blackwell, 2009). For a religious version of this pragmatic use of race, see Victor Anderson, *Creative Exchange: A Constructive Theology of African American Religious Experience* (Minneapolis: Fortress Press, 2008) and Cornel West, *Prophecy Deliverance! An Afro-American Revolutionary Christianity* (Louisville: Westminster John Knox, 2002).

⁴Derrida's use of the *khōra* (discussed in the third section of this essay) is perhaps the limit-case of this postmodern, prophetic gesture. Other thinkers exhibit an analogous preference for indeterminacy, with particular reference to race. See especially Paul Gilroy, *Between Camps: Nations, Cultures and the Allure of Race* (London: Routledge, 2004), originally published in 2000 under the title *Against Race*, and Victor Anderson's early work, *Beyond Ontological Blackness: An Essay on African-American Religious and Cultural Criticism* (New York: Continuum, 1995).

⁵Goldberg defines "born again racism" as a "racism without race, racism gone private, racism without the categories to name it as such," and in this way gives a name to the danger of indeterminacy (*The Threat of Race*, 23). By contrast, Gilroy's discussion of the "crisis of raciology" clarifies what is perilous about determinate identity discourse during the genome era and within a globalizing market economy (*Between Camps*, 11-32).

⁶The claim that liberation is historically conditioned may indicate, on the one hand, that liberation includes incremental or partial aspirations, such as those that Williams associates with her survival/quality-of-life hermeneutic (*Sisters in the Wilderness*, 196). Although Williams contrasts survival/quality-of-life and liberation as proximate and ultimate goals, both are integral to the pursuit of human freedom. On the other hand, it may indicate that the eschaton has historical significance. James Cone clarifies that an "eschatological perspective must be grounded in the historical present, thereby forcing the oppressed community to say no to unjust treatment, because its present humiliation is inconsistent with its promised future" (see *A Black Theology of Liberation* [Maryknoll, NY: Orbis Books, 1990], 137).

[7]Note that this is not the double-consciousness of a black man living in a white world, as one finds in W. E. B. DuBois or Frantz Fanon. Rather, what is envisioned here is the danger of an aporetic consciousness that affirms racial ascriptions only insofar as it also denies them, but which nevertheless asserts this "yes" and "no" simultaneously, and thus contradictorily, out of a real sense of ethical and intellectual obligation. Liberation itself appears to demand such duplicity. Yet, in concrete situations, it has the feel of being illogical or impractical, and sometimes even reprehensible. Gilroy discloses the potential for offense in his discussion of the case of Constable Lesley Turner, a black officer policing a protest who was attacked by black protestors for betraying his race (*Between Camps*, 51). In this specific case, Turner's blackness seemed to be at once affirmed by his phenomenality and negated by his actions, with the result that he had the appearance (wrongly or rightly is difficult to judge) of being a traitor, a double-agent.

[8]See Jacques Derrida, "*Différence*," in *Speech and Phenomena: And Other Essays on Husserl's Theory of Signs*, trans. David B. Allison and Newton Garver (Evanston, IL: Northwestern University Press, 1973).

[9]J. Kameron Carter, *Race: A Theological Account* (New York: Oxford University Press, 2008).

[10]Carter's disclosure of this aporia is only partially given in the individual statements that he makes and hence also partially dependent on another level of interpretation in which one tracks the logic that both follows from the statements and implicates them in the dynamics of a much larger conversation.

[11]Ibid., 192.

[12]Ibid., 377.

[13]Ibid., 192.

[14]Carter makes this point about the need for catholicity in his "Contemporary Black Theology: A Review Essay," *Modern Theology* 19, no. 1 (January 2003): 117-38. Carter argues that the work of Dwight Hopkins represents a larger refusal within black liberation theology as a whole "to let its considerations of Afro-Christianity . . . overflow their banks to acquire 'catholic' significance" (ibid., 118). Because it is enclosed within the limits of American Protestantism (ibid., 131), "black faith and its contribution to the wider enterprise of speculative theology and philosophy—how it is a measure within, and is thus measured by, the musical score that is the eternal Word, Jesus the Liberator—are themselves lost to view" (ibid., 118).

[15]Carter, *Race*, 20.

[16]Ibid., 31.

[17]Ibid., 24.

[18]Ibid., 30.

[19]Ibid., 232.

[20]Ibid., 242, 250.

[21]Ibid., 237, 240, 248.

[22]Ibid., 364-65.

[23]Ibid., 353.

[24]Ibid., 234.

[25]Ibid., 264.

[26]Carter argues that "whiteness" needs to be understood "not merely and banally as pigment but as a structural-aesthetic order and as a sociopolitical arrangement" (ibid., 89).

[27]Carter, *Race*, 387, n. 5.

[28]Ibid., 82, 88.

[29]Ibid., 91.

[30]Ibid., 105.

[31]Ibid., 158.

[32]Ibid., 187-91. Carter's critique of Cone's "ontological blackness" is closely connected with Anderson's work but is also meant to go "beyond" it (ibid., 159).

[33]Gilroy might respond to Carter's critique by noting that he (Gilroy) proposes a form of cosmopolitanism that is in many ways importantly different from Kant's: it is more inclusive, embodied, indeterminate, open, and what one might call "horizontally" ecstatic (*Between Camps*, 16-17, 30). But Carter seems right to suggest that it lacks a necessary mode of "vertical," properly theological ecstasis toward God in Christ.

[34]Ibid., 346, 458, n. 6.

[35]Carter gives poignant expression to this point in his discussion of Jarena Lee, who, he argues, makes visible her despised, dark, female flesh within Christ through a prayerful participation in the paschal mystery (ibid., 336ff.). In this context, Carter suggests something similar to M. Shawn Copeland's turn to "exploited, despised, poor women of color" as "the new anthropological subject" of theology, a view that she articulates most recently in *Enfleshing Freedom: Body, Race, and Being* (Minneapolis: Fortress Press, 2010), 90. However, Carter's argument also complicates Copeland's claim that human personhood necessarily includes "racial" embodiment (ibid., 92).

[36]See Carter, *Race*, 383, n. 14 and 410, n. 113; and R. Kendall Soulen, *The God of Israel and Christian Theology* (Minneapolis: Fortress Press, 1996), esp. 47-48. Soulen could support a more modest version of Carter's claim that Irenaeus avoids supersessionism (*Race*, 13), inasmuch as the anti-Judaism of the Gnostics and Kantians goes beyond what one finds in Irenaeus (Soulen, *The God of Israel and Christian Theology*, 57ff.).

[37]Goldberg, *The Threat of Race*, 106-45, 163-69. See also Carter, *Race*, 399, n. 2, in which he mentions, but does not dwell upon, the grave problem that Zionism poses for Palestinians.

[38]Charles Taylor, *A Catholic Modernity: Charles Taylor's Marianist Award Lecture*, ed. James L. Heft (New York: Oxford University Press, 1999), 25ff.

[39]Derrida, "Hospitality," in *Acts of Religion*, 361-62.

[40]See "Faith and Knowledge: The Two Sources of 'Religion' at the Limits of Reason Alone," in Jacques Derrida, *Acts of Religion*, ed. Gil Anidjar (New York: Routledge, 2002), 59-60 and "khōra," in *On the Name*, 104-9.

A Response from a U.S. Hispanic Perspective

María Teresa Morgan

In his challenging, scholarly paper Andrew Prevot has contributed significant insights and scholarship on issues of race, ethnic identity, and the historical struggle of minorities and demonstrated the key role that deconstructing the categorizations language imposes on identity plays in elaborating a praxis of liberation. From the rich lode of ideas and complex interrelations he provides, I was drawn to comment on three areas: The first is the use of "indeterminate and determinate speech in discourses of race and identity" in his introduction. The second is that of hospitality, understood as "radical indeterminacy," in his commentary on Derrida's use of this term. The third offers a brief comment on the Pentecostal universality proposed by Maximus the Confessor and its influence on J. Kameron Carter. Though my approach does not focus on race but on ethnic and linguistic minorities, I believe that all oppressions and yearnings for liberation are shared by all dispossessed groups.[1]

My choice of these three areas arises from my contextuality, one shaped by identity, social location, and pastoral agency. By identity I am a U.S. Hispanic,[2] and by location I am borderline, though often uprooted. A third of my life has been spent in Miami, a city defined by a racial and ethnic diversity that has been a source of violence, friction, and, in the past fifteen years, concerted efforts at being with and learning from one another.[3] The last component of my contextuality is that of ministry; for the past twenty years I have been involved in faith formation with immigrants struggling with language and acculturation. These immigrants are almost exclusively Hispanics and Haitians. Their struggles include but are not limited to issues of culture, ethnic, and racial affiliations, language, and diffusion between nation of origin and nation of choice, along with intersections with other ethnicities.

Prevot's opening sentence forms the subject for my first correlation. "In discourses of race and identity indeterminate and determinate speech present themselves, in distinct ways, as simultaneously dangerous, necessary, and incompatible." I ask your permission to launch these words toward a metaphor of place. My purpose is to retrieve and relocate Prevot's terminology to the realm of habitat: meaning the determinacy for immigrants of being in one place, the United States, and the indeterminacy they experience of not really being here.

The U.S. Hispanics and Haitians who shape my ministry live in between location and dislocation. In his introductory section and throughout his paper, I identified several points of intersection between Prevot's work on the aporia of race[4] and identity and the work of some U.S. Hispanic theologians such as Virgilio Elizondo,[5] Roberto Goizueta,[6] Ada María Isasi-Díaz,[7] and Justo González,[8] among others, on the immigrant experience of U.S. Hispanics. These theologians speak of the self-identity of Hispanic (and I would add, Haitian) immigrants as one of indeterminacy, caught between the elusive contexts of their past and their present.

The immigrants with whom I work are, in the words of Roberto Goizueta, "in between."[9] They are defined by lives in between hyphens. In addition, given the current nativistic anti-immigrant climate in this country, ethnic categorizations ascribed to them by the dominant Anglophonic culture are often used against these cultural and linguistic minorities as a tool for marginalization, exclusion, and shame.

Prevot raises the problematic of naming. While identifying with a group serves as a source of solidarity, the structures of defining identity are used to create the very dichotomies that relegate minorities to the margins. He states, "Historical struggles for liberation tend to oscillate between advocating determinate identities, on the one hand, and striving to transcend them through a rhetoric of indeterminacy on the other." He affirms that "the goal of liberation demands that the concrete not be left behind. And yet, to the extent that the concrete becomes ossified into restrictive structures of identity, liberation in a postmodern age also requires that these structures be overcome." There are parallels between Prevot's affirmation, Goizueta's way of "both/and," and Alejandro García-Rivera's theological aesthetics.[10] All three proposals safeguard the affirmation of one's culture, race, and identity while affirming the necessity to move beyond them. Racial and/or ethnic identification is then seen not as creating a dichotomy where otherness means exclusion; rather it affirms the concreteness of identity while moving into a communion wherein, as Prevot states, "the determinate structures of humanity's historical existence are transcended in some respects but retained in others."[11]

The second area of my response centers on the Derridean problematic of hospitality. My reflection is anecdotal, based on the methodology of *mujerista* theology that ponders the quotidian of our experiences ("*lo cotidiano*") so as to discover therein the self revelation of God.[12]

Ten years ago I worked in a faith formation program at a Haitian Mission in South Florida. I participated in this weekly endeavor for three years. A group of Haitian teens regularly gathered outside the church, seemingly oblivious to my comings and goings. One evening, somewhere into my second year, they asked me if I was "a white Haitian." I was startled by their question and have long pondered its multiple dimensions and implications. These kids probably thought that only one of their own would visit their neighborhood. Whatever their reasons, they identified me as Haitian. I was no longer the foreigner invited to be with them for a few hours a week; the hospitality they offered me blurred the lines between welcoming a stranger and seeing me as one of their own. I, too, crossed the border of my own self-understanding and safety and became one of them. The "concrete universal" of a Christopraxis "that shapes both self and society in kenotic or ecstatic relation with the other" of which Prevot writes became real to me that night.

Finally, over time scholars of diversity have proposed four traditions on which to base a liberating praxis of racial, ethnic, and linguistic minorities in the Christian community. Prevot intertwines these traditions throughout his essay. The first, ecclesiological communion, views the church as the gathering of the *laos*,[13] a people of many races and nations.[14] The second is a Christopraxis that is based on the Incarnation, a model Prevot indicates is part of Carter's project.[15] In his conclusion Prevot states that in the inclusivity and concreteness of the Incarnation "God's love for a diversely beautiful and yet destructively bellicose humanity" is revealed. The third tradition is the Trinitarian paradigm proposed by Elizabeth Johnson[16] and Catherine Mowry LaCugna,[17] in which the unity and Trinity of God models the relationality of human beings. Diversity is thus seen not as oppositional but as relational.

The fourth tradition is the account of Pentecost, developed during the Patristic era[18] and in our time by Congar and Montague.[19] Pentecost has been a root source for my self-understanding and ministry.[20] In my personal and professional life, the language issue has been a "necessary aporia," which Prevot defines as "a predicament from which there is no way out." The most divisive issue at the social, political, and parish level of my encounters is that of the linguistic preference and needs of non-English-speaking first-generation immigrants. The Spirit's descent at Pentecost in "tongues as of fire" offers a paradigm where, as the Fathers of the church discerned, the racial, linguistic, and ethnic divisions of Babel are overcome in a true catholicity, proclaiming, as Prevot notes, the fulfillment of covenantal history. I close with a verse from Walt Whitman, whose poetry is being rediscovered as one of inclusion[21]:

> Not till the sun excludes you, do I
>   exclude you;
> Not till the waters refuse to glisten for
>   you, and the leaves to rustle for
> you,
>   do my words refuse to glisten and
>   rustle for you.[22]

Notes

[1] The theme that all oppressions are intertwined and all yearnings for liberation are shared by minorities is central to feminist, womanist, and *mujerista* theology. See, for example, *Feminist Ethics and the Catholic Moral Tradition*, ed. Charles E. Curran, Margaret A. Farley, and Richard A. McCormick, S.J. (Mahwah, NJ: Paulist Press, 1996). See also María Pilar Aquino, "Feminist Intercultural Theology: Toward a Shared Future of Justice," in *Feminist Intercultural Theology: Latina Explorations for a Just World*, ed. María Pilar Aquino and María José Rosado Nuñes (Maryknoll, NY: Orbis Books, 2007), 9-28.

[2] I chose the self-understanding of "U.S. Hispanic" instead of Latino/a because of my focus on linguistic minorities. "U.S. Hispanic" denotes the linguistic homogeneity forming the basis of our identity as Spanish speakers from the Caribbean and Central and South America living in the United States. "U.S. Hispanic" is used because, as Justo González proposes, Hispanics form a new ethnicity in the United States. Removed from our country of origin, most of us would feel like strangers in our own land. We are, to borrow the term, "naturalized" in the United States, our adopted country. At the same time, aspects of our consciousness remain embedded in our mother language and in the often painful and "dangerous" collective memory of our birth country (Justo González, *Mañana: Christian Theology from a Hispanic Perspective* (Nashville: Abingdon Press, 1990), 41; Roberto S. Goizueta, *Caminemos con Jesús: Toward a Hispanic/Latino Theology of Accompaniment* (Maryknoll, NY: Orbis Books, 1995), 6-17.

[3] See *The Miami Herald* series (May 15, 16, and 17, 2010) by Casey Frank and Bea L. Hines on thirty years after the McDuffy Riot. On December 1979, Arthur McDuffy, a black motorcyclist, ran a red light and failed to stop while pursued by police. When he crashed, the officers beat him to death. On May 1980 an all-white, all-male jury in Tampa acquitted the four policemen; Overtown and Liberty City erupted in riots and fifteen people were killed. In the thirty years since the riot, we have had three black Miami police chiefs and one black Miami-Dade chief. See also Kathleen McGrory's series in *The Miami Herald* on race and diversity in *American Senior High*, May 9, 12, and 23, 2010, detailing the challenges, efforts, and progress of interracial and interethnic perspectives in American Senior High, a microcosm of Miami. The last of this series reports on the positive integration of ethnic studies curriculum in the public schools of Miami-Dade and Broward counties.

[4] The term raciology, the theory of race, has evolved from its original colonial conceptualization during the Victorian era to a prophetically laden meaning in post-modern racial discourse. I refer the reader to the section on "Delineating the Aporia" in Prevot's article for further elucidation of the term.

[5] See Virgilio Elizondo's groundbreaking work, *The Future Is Mestizo: Life Where Cultures Meet* (Bloomington, IN: Meyer Stone, 1988). See also Elizondo, "Transformation of Borders: Border Separation or New Identity," in *Theology: Expanding the Borders*, The Annual Publication of the College Theology Society, 43, ed. María Pilar Aquino and Roberto S. Goizueta. (Mystic, CT: Twenty-Third Publications, 1998), 22-39.

[6] Goizueta, *Caminemos con Jesús*, 1-17, 173-211. See also Goizueta, *Christ Our Companion: Toward a Theological Aesthetics of Liberation* (Maryknoll, NY: Orbis Books, 2009), 126-56.

[7] Ada María Isasi-Díaz, *Mujerista Theology* (Maryknoll, NY: Orbis Books, 1996), 13-27, 59-82, 86-102.

[8] González, *Mañana*. See also González, *Santa Biblia: The Bible through Hispanic Eyes* (Nashville: Abingdon Press, 1996).

[9] Goizueta, *Caminemos con Jesús*, 2, 5, 6, 9.

[10] Ibid., 5, 16, 17.

[11]The limits of this paper prevent further elaboration on this crucial issue of identity, difference, and transcendence. I do, however, want to include a citation from Alejandro García-Rivera illuminating this theme: "Theological aesthetics asks the question of 'difference' rather than the question of 'identity.' For only the question of 'difference' asks about the nature of true love, a freedom making possible a sacrificial transcendence of identity" (Alejandro García-Rivera, *The Community of the Beautiful: A Theological Aesthetics* [Collegeville, MN: A Michael Glazier Book, Liturgical Press, 1999], 73).

[12]See Isasi-Díaz's elucidation on *lo cotidiano* as the epistemological source of theologizing in *Mujerista Theology*, 66-73.

[13]The Septuagint and the New Testament employ three words to designate a people. The first is *ethne*, referring to nations whose strife with one another arises from their differences. The second is *laos*, indicating the people of God, chosen from many races and nations. The third, *ochlos*, means the marginalized multitude for whom Jesus showed a preference (see Casiano Floristán, *La Iglesia: Comunidad de Creyentes* [Salamanca: Ediciones Sígueme, 1999], 169-70).

[14]*Gaudium et Spes*, 53-62; and Floristán, *La Iglesia*, 297-316, 616-17. See also Bradford Hinze's article, "Ethnic and Racial Diversity and the Catholicity of the Church," in *Theology: Expanding the Borders*, The Annual Publication of the College Theology Society, vol. 43, ed. María Pilar Aquino and Roberto S. Goizueta (Mystic, CT: Twenty-Third Publications, 1998), 162-99. I am indebted to Bradford Hinze for his excellent exploration of the four paradigms mentioned in my response.

[15]This paradigm is rooted in Paul's Letter to the Galatians, which proclaims the equality of all the baptized in Christ Jesus (Gal 3: 27-29). Prevot traces the influence of Irenaeus on Carter's adoption of this model. On this theme, Alejandro García-Rivera states, "Indeed, the incarnation suggests that all 'difference' is a gracious epiphany, a loving revelation" (García-Rivera, *The Community of the Beautiful*, 73).

[16]Elizabeth Johnson, *She Who Is: The Mystery of God in Feminist Theological Discourse* (New York: Crossroad, 1996), 224-45. See also Dennis M. Doyle, "Communion Ecclesiology on the Borders: Elizabeth Johnson and Roberto S. Goizueta," in *Theology: Expanding the Borders*, The Annual Publication of the College Theology Society, vol. 43, ed. María Pilar Aquino and Roberto S. Goizueta (Mystic, CT: Twenty-Third Publications, 1998), 200-17. I am grateful to Dennis Doyle's article for launching me on the path of possibilities for this response. On the Trinitarian paradigm, see also Isasi-Díaz, *Mujerista Theology*, 81.

[17]Catherine Mowry LaCugna, *God for Us: The Trinity & Christian Life* (San Francisco: Harper, 1992), 377-411.

[18]Origen, *In Genesim*, c 1 (PG 12, 112); St. Gregory Nazianzen, *Oratio* 41, 16 (PG 36, 449); St. John Chrysostom, *Hom in Pentec.*, 2 (PG 50, 467); St. Augustine, *Enn.* In *Ps 54*, 11 (PL 36, 636; CChr. 39, 664 ff.); *Sermon 271* (PL 38, 1245); St. Cyril of Alexandria, *Glaphyra in Genesim* II (PG 69, 79); St. Gregory the Great, *Hom in Evang.* Lib II, Hom. 30, 4 (PL 76, 1222); St. Bede *in Hexaem*, lib. III (PL 91, 125). See *Ad Gentes* 4.

[19]See Yves Congar, *I Believe in the Holy Spirit*, vol. 1, *The Holy Spirit in the "Economy": Revelation and Experience of the Spirit*, trans. David Smith (New York: Crossroad, 2003). See George Montague, *The Holy Spirit: Growth of a Biblical Tradition* (New York: Paulist Press, 1976).

[20]See my article " 'Tongues as of Fire': The Spirit as Paradigm for Ministry in a Multicultural Setting," *The Spirit in the Church and the World*, The Annual Publication of the College Theology Society, vol. 49, ed. Bradford E. Hinze (Maryknoll, NY: Orbis Books, 2003), 105-23.

[21]See Jeremy McCarter's review of C. K.Williams's book, " 'On Whitman': The Real American," *Newsweek*, May 17, 2010, 47-48.

[22]Walt Whitman, "To a Common Prostitute," *Leaves of Grass*, cited in McCarter, 48. Though McCarter does not mention the title of the poem, and thus makes the theme of mutuality all the more universal, I chose to identify it because Whitman plies the beauty of his words to include and honor the most historically marginalized and oppressed group.

Conflict and Solidarity Ethics

Difficult Conversations on Economics, Religion, and Culture

Rebecca Todd Peters

Barbara Padilla is a Roman Catholic laywoman who was marginally involved with her local parish in Tucson until 2002 when she joined a local immersion trip to Altar, Mexico. Barbara was not particularly moved by the formal presentation of the harsh realities of migrant life on the border and her response, "Oh, that's sad," indicates that the compassion that she felt did not particularly translate into anything more meaningful than pity—that is, until the group met with some migrants at a restaurant hideout. Barbara noticed a woman sitting by herself in the corner who was about her age and who looked very sad. Wanting to talk with her, she asked a member of her group to interpret. As they spoke, Barbara discovered that the woman had migrated north from Chiapas in search of a better life for her children. Despite the fact that what motivated her to migrate was her children, she had left all four of them behind under her sister's care because she was uncertain about what prospects she would find after reaching the United States. As they talked, the Mexican woman began to cry, and Barbara reached out to her, unable to stop her own tears from flowing. As Barbara described it,

> For me, that was the moment, the feeling of knowing that *this* is the reason why I came. To see this lady and know that someone would leave their kids like that to try to make something better. That's just not right. And where was I before? Why wasn't I paying attention? Until you see people

and meet people and hear the things that people go through, you just don't get it. At least I didn't.[1]

Like Barbara, most educated U.S. Americans are familiar with the desperate conditions of poverty that drive immigrants from Mexico to seek work in this country. We are also familiar with the problems of child labor, human trafficking and forced prostitution, sweatshops, climate change, and a litany of human-created social injustice in our world. We live in a world of both dizzying wealth and extreme poverty. In 2003, 7.7 million people were millionaires.[2] Their combined wealth was US$28.9 trillion, close to three times the U.S. GDP.[3] On the other end of the spectrum 3 billion people (nearly half of the world's population) live in poverty. This disparity, this conflict between wealth and poverty in our world is the starting point for my own work as a Christian social ethicist.

As a white woman, who stands in a position of relative wealth and privilege as an educated, first-world academic, I struggle with a multitude of difficult conversations about economics, religion, and culture as I strive to discern how my work as a Christian ethicist can contribute to building up the common good—a task that has become counter-cultural in a world bent on individualism and wealth accumulation. Perhaps the most significant moral challenge for many first-world Christians is that while we are often able to recognize the moral failings of the present system and even, to some extent, our complicity in perpetuating these systems, many people simply do not know what to do. The situation appears overwhelming—how can we possibly alter the direction of globalization? Too many people respond by simply shutting down and ignoring the problem; after all, this response functions to protect us from the guilt that can accompany recognition of complicity in a system that benefits us at the expense of others—a guilt that can be paralyzing.

Increasingly, my interest is in addressing the moral conundrum that first-world people face as we strive to live with integrity in the midst of a global economic order that has been structured to privilege individualism, wealth creation, efficiency, and the maximization of profits. While my work continues to be focused on addressing social injustice through the transformation of structures of society, my real insight in recent years has been to understand the question in new ways. While I still find myself asking the broader theoretical question, "how can I help transform social injustice," I have found that my entry point into this problem has shifted in response to the many people who continue to ask me what *they* should do in response to the conflicts of wealth and poverty that shape our world. Quite frankly, "Sell all that you have and give it to the poor" is not an adequate ethic—not simply because it is unrealistic, but, more importantly, because it does nothing to change the structures of our social order that are oppressive. For me, getting married, having children, earning tenure—all of these experiences in my own life have also contributed to a different way for me to think about both the problems that we face and realistic ways of trying to address them.

These days I find myself asking, "How is God calling me to live faithfully in the place where I find myself?" The remainder of my comments on the topic of conflict and solidarity ethics are shaped by my current research project that aims to develop an ethic of solidarity as a model for first-world Christians who are struggling to discern how to live faithfully in the midst of a globalizing world.

In a world on the precipice of epochal change and facing an environmental crisis of our own making, what we need is a new theology for a new age. A new theology that helps us make sense of the chaotic and unjust world in which we live. Just as our religious experiences are shaped by our social location, so too, are our theologies. The form of liberation theology in Latin America that arose out of a context of poverty and oppression does not make sense for privileged Christians in first-world countries. There is a dangerous tendency for first-world Christians to spiritualize our understanding of what we mean by "oppression" and to do very real violence to the radical insights of Latin American liberation theologians who work in the midst of severe material deprivation. When poor people in Latin America read the story of the Exodus, it makes sense for them to identify with the Hebrew slaves and to seek liberation from the bondages of poverty, illiteracy, political oppression, and violence that have marked the lives of many poor communities throughout the global South. But, as first-world Christians read the story of the Exodus, most of us are far more like the Egyptians than the Hebrew slaves. Like the Egyptians, we are the landowners, the task masters, the ones who benefit from the exploitation of the labor of the workers. As we read Exodus with these eyes, we must ask ourselves who God is calling us to be and how God is calling us to live.

A theology for people of privilege in the first world will, necessarily, be different from a theology that helps people in the developing world make sense of the world around them. This does not mean that the ultimate reality of the divine is different, just that our experiences of the world in which we live necessarily shape our theology in distinct and meaningful ways. A theology of solidarity is a meaningful response for first-world Christians to the injustice, economic disparity, and unjust globalization that plagues our world today. It requires a recognition of the disparity that exists between the dominant norms of economic globalization that are currently shaping economic discourse and practice in our society and an acknowledgment of the necessity to have deeper moral norms to guide our economic interactions.

For most people in first-world contexts, the ability to practice an ethic of solidarity requires an experience of metanoia, and by that I mean an authentic transformation that enables people to see the world with new eyes, to recognize the disparities that exist between the cultural myths of economic success and the reality of making a living. Only when we are able to see the world through new eyes are we able to increase the likelihood of true partnership and solidarity with our global neighbors.

Barbara Padilla is an example of how an authentic experience of metanoia can became a life-changing experience. After her encounter with the woman who was seeking a better life for her children, Barbara's worldview was transformed. She recognized that she had been reading about immigrants struggling and dying in the desert for years, but she did not know these people. Now, she knew one of them, and she decided that she was going to do whatever she could so that no mother had to endure what the woman she met was enduring.

Barbara became a leader on immigrant issues in her parish and in her community. She joined Samaritans, a group that patrols the desert offering food and water to people in distress, she organized the sale of Just Coffee in her church, using the opportunity to educate people about the complex problems that prompt immigrants to leave their home countries, and she began to lead parish visits to Altar that were modeled on her first trip.[4] Barbara's experience of metanoia turned her life upside down as she began to live out a relationship of solidarity with the immigrants that she had met.

While Barbara's experience offers a concrete snapshot of how an ethic of solidarity might shape an individual's life, let's turn now to the larger question of the theological basis for solidarity and how it might become a moral norm and foundation of a Christian ethic.

An Ethic of Solidarity

A theology of solidarity offers us a new foundation upon which to build an ethic that calls us into covenant relationship and partnership with our brothers and sisters from the two-thirds world. While primarily a description of human relations and behavior, a theology of solidarity grows out of and is modeled on God's love and delight with the created world and God's unbounded mercy and care for creation. It offers hope and the promise that sustainability is a more faithful and fulfilling life for Christians than consumption and convenience.

I am proposing that we first-world Christians consider solidarity as a way of defining our obligation to the other in a world where the forces of globalization privilege us at the expense of our brothers and sisters in the global South. In this context, solidarity can be defined as an active relationship of support between two people or groups of people who are different from one another, in which one party stands with, supports, advocates for, or otherwise generally acts as a partner to a person or group under duress. The starting point of a relationship of solidarity is mutuality.

From a position of mutuality, people act to help others; this stems from their understanding that the well-being of all creation is interdependent. In this new relationship of mutuality, there is a desire to know one another and to develop a relationship of partnership and respect that contributes to the ongoing well-being of both parties. Mutuality offers the possibility of a new way of responding to injustice that focuses on building relationships between people whose lives are marked by social and economic difference and on working together to address a problem.

A foundation of respect for other people's worldviews and life experiences allows for people from different backgrounds and social locations to engage one another in a dialogue that can help lead to the development of new solutions to age-old problems. People who work out of a position of mutuality understand that they can work together with others to solve social problems that impact all of them, but that they cannot solve other people's problems for them. Partnerships based on mutuality demonstrate a capacity for each party to use their strengths and assets to work together toward the common good.

If a theology of solidarity helps us understand how to think about living in the world, an ethic of solidarity gives us a blueprint for how to live by calling us to four tasks—metanoia, honoring difference, accountability, and action. Let's examine each of these tasks in turn to see how they might shape the practice of a solidarity ethics.

Metanoia

An ethic of solidarity begins with an experience of metanoia. While metanoia is often translated in the New Testament as repentance, it is more accurately understood as a total personal transformation that is reflected in both thought and behavior.[5] Metanoia is a radical transformation of heart, mind, and soul that literally makes us a new person. The concept of metanoia does not simply refer to a spiritual experience of transformation, but it suggests an accompanying transformation of behavior and lifestyle as well. The change that occurs is manifested in a change in how one both thinks and acts.[6] We have already seen how the experience of metanoia served as the foundation for Barbara Padilla to begin to develop her own ethic of solidarity with immigrants in her community.

Honoring Difference

Solidarity implies a respect for difference, a desire to work together with others toward a common goal, but it also reflects a desire to maintain our differences because they are uniquely important to our identity and to our common humanity. This

requires that we learn how to understand and respect the lives of
our global neighbors, a task that entails a good deal of listening
on our part. The lessons of post-modernism have taught us that
not only are differences real, they are also essential aspects of our
identity that shape our consciousness and our consciences in different ways. Identity politics do not dominate our social and political
discourse simply because they are "trendy"; they dominate our
discourse because people on the periphery of power who have
not historically had a recognized voice or political role in shaping
politics, culture, and economic systems have unique perspectives
to offer, perspectives that help us understand the world and its
problems in new and different ways. Democratizing our political,
economic, and civil society discourses is important because the
new voices that come to the table bring new perspectives that help
to shape public policy, economic systems, and corporate culture
and behavior in new ways that are responsive to a broader set of
constituencies in our world. Ultimately, the incorporation of new
voices and perspectives into the discourse leads to the development
of more practical, more realistic, and more egalitarian solutions
to our collective social problems.

Accountability

Twenty-five years ago, feminist social ethicist Beverly Harrison described solidarity as concrete answerability to oppressed
people, arguing that solidarity required genuine accountability
that included vulnerability and an openness to being changed by
our relationship and encounter with people who are oppressed.[7]
If we understand solidarity in Harrison's terms, it must move
beyond superficial expressions of support that require little effort
on our part and into a genuine partnership with others. Learning
how to live in solidarity with our neighbors is an expression of
our call to "love our neighbor as ourselves." Provincial attitudes
about who counts as our neighbor can engender a social ethic in
which we can continue to care for our local community, church,
and family and remain oblivious to the ways in which our lives
impact the larger world. In the Gospel of Luke, Jesus teaches us
in the parable of the Good Samaritan that he expects us to see
our neighbor even in those people we do not know and whom

we might not even like. In an era of globalization, we may never meet the neighbors we are called to love as ourselves; nevertheless, they remain our sisters and our brothers, loved and cherished by God and deserving of dignity and respect.

Action

One of the key distinguishing factors of solidarity is that it is a state of being that demands that people who are in a relationship of solidarity be willing to act on behalf of one another as a result of the bond that they share. What this means is that an ethic of solidarity is an ethic of action rather than simply an attitude toward others. Just as Jesus' solidarity with the poor and marginalized of his day and his commitment to transform his social world led him down a dangerous political path that ultimately led to his death, the actions that first-world Christians are called to take in solidarity with our sisters and brothers in the global South hold the possibility of sacrifice. As we denounce neoliberal globalization as sin and work toward changing the direction of globalization in our world, we must live in the world in new ways. Admittedly, this is not easy work.

Conclusion

Botswanan New Testament scholar Musa Dube points out that "those on the dominant side are not always adversely affected by international imperialism, unless they make a conscious effort to identify with the oppressed for ethical reasons."[8] One of the foundational questions that an ethic of solidarity asks is how is it possible for us to be right with God and to be right with each other and the earth—when there is so much unnecessary suffering and exploitation? It is time for Christians in the first world to take up Dube's challenge and to make a conscious effort to identify with the oppressed. This is particularly important for U.S. Christians who occupy positions of relative power and privilege vis à vis the poor and the marginalized peoples of the world. An ethic of solidarity thus requires that people actively engage in the building up of ties of mutuality and friendship with persons and/or communities of people who have been marginalized by our privilege.

A theology of solidarity offers us a vision of covenant relationships and partnership with our brothers and sisters from the two-thirds world. It requires that we listen to the voices of people from the global South, and it requires that we think more carefully about how our lives are bound to theirs through our economic transactions in the global economy. Economic justice is, at its heart, an issue of systemic transformation that requires that we look more carefully at how we have theorized and structured our economies; and an ethic of solidarity requires that we be engaged in working toward structural change in our societies.

As important as individual behavior is, we cannot solve the problems of poverty, environmental degradation, and inequality in our world simply by the individual lifestyle choices that we make. Individual behavioral transformation is a necessary, but insufficient condition for changing the direction of globalization. As long as children born in the United States require eight to nine times the world's resources as children born in India, Cambodia, and Zimbabwe and dozens of other countries around the world,[9] we must recognize that inequality is built into the structures of our society—including our economic structures. It is essential for us to recognize that the larger challenges that face us as a human community will require a concerted effort at systemic transformation.

A theology of solidarity is not an intellectual exercise for understanding life and our relationship with the sacred in the twenty-first century. While it may help us to do that, it is primarily an ethic that can help us understand how to *live* in ways that honor God and God's creation in the contemporary world. Embracing solidarity as a moral norm means embracing an ethic of accountability that requires us not only to evaluate our personal and collective actions in terms of how they impact our neighbors, but also to pursue concrete relationships with oppressed or marginalized communities that open us up to personal transformation and help us to live out our calling to transform the world.

Notes

[1]Jeffry Odell Korgen, *Solidarity Will Transform the World: Stories of Hope from Catholic Relief Services* (Maryknoll, NY: Orbis Books, 2007), 28.

[2]Alternative Globalization Addressing People and the Earth—AGAPE document (Geneva: World Council of Churches, 2006), 3.

[3]Ibid.

[4]Korgen, *Solidarity Will Transform the World*, 27-29.

[5]Johannes P. Louw and Eugene A. Nida, eds., *Greek-English Lexicon of the New Testament Based on Semantic Domains*, 2nd ed., vol. 1: Introduction and Domains, 41.52 (New York: United Bible Societies, 1989), 510.

[6]Ibid.

[7]Beverly Wildung Harrison, "Theological Reflection in the Struggle for Liberation," in her *Making the Connections: Essays in Feminist Social Ethics*, ed. Carol S. Robb (Boston: Beacon Press, 1985), 244.

[8]Musa Dube, "Postcoloniality, Feminist Spaces, and Religion," in *Postcolonialism, Feminism, and Religious Discourse*, ed. Laura Donaldson and Kwok Pui-lan (New York: Routledge, 2002), 102.

[9]Ecological Footprint of Nations 2004, http://www.rprogress.org/new-pubs/2004/footprintnations2004.pdf.

A Response to Rebecca Todd Peters

Traci C. West

My response to the essay of Rebecca Todd Peters would ordinarily include attention to the points of agreement in our perspectives on Christian ethics and economic life. There are many more points of convergence between us than disagreements on the topic of how one builds just global political economies through intercultural relationships informed by a radically liberationist Christianity. However, in our preparation for this dialogical presentation, we decided beforehand to try to practice respectful dialogue on areas of conflict. We believe addressing conflict is necessary in building intercultural global relationships. In keeping with this assignment, therefore, my brief response deliberately highlights possible divergences in our approaches.

The emotionally gripping interaction between Barbara, the Roman Catholic Arizona laywoman and "the Mexican woman" that Peters narrated immediately caught my attention. The scene resonates with some of the same challenges of personal, intercultural interactions with which I struggle in my own approach to crafting ethical strategies that contribute to economic justice across nation-state borders. Peters points out the emotions that were part of the exchange that took place in the discussion between the two women: "As they talked, the Mexican woman began to cry and Barbara reached out to her, unable to stop her own tears from flowing."

When I reflect on the economic relationship between the United States and Mexico, I find it difficult to understand how one can create an authentic, egalitarian friendship between wealthy U.S.-Americans and the poor in Mexico. Can such a friendship exist when people who are poor in Mexico are severely harmed by socio-economic political agreements and environmental impacts that, by design, yield privileges for the quality of life U.S.-Americans enjoy? Especially when such political dynamics are not directly confronted, is it ever possible to create personal, intercultural relationships where U.S.-American Christians can see people who are poor in Latin America as something other than another mission project to which they dedicate themselves?

U.S.-American Christians tend to have a one-way understanding of who has the problem to be solved, of who brings the problem to be worked on by them. Do these examples of friendship that Peters describes create a paradigm that is still too individualistic to disrupt that one-way understanding? An individualistic understanding that addresses economic problems by forging intercultural friendships with the poor can simply reinforce a growing trend of U.S.-American Christians who engage in a form of poverty tourism that is dubbed a "mission trip." When Barbara sees "the Mexican woman" cry, she has an intense, engrossing sense of the woman's suffering. How will this contribute to the needed work of systemic change? Or will it merely enrich Barbara's description for her friends of what she saw on her trip?

I maintain that to create solidarity that addresses global economic inequalities and the suffering of the poor in the two-thirds world, we U.S.-Americans have to be able to see what we do and how we live within the political framework of a common problem, and not simply by focusing on helping *them* (poor people in other countries) with their problem of poverty. There will be differing tasks for each of us committed to this work in our vastly differing cultural and political contexts, but the nature of our shared broken socio-economic system has to be the common focal point for us (U.S.-Americans). This is the only way we can even recognize the work that we must undertake.

The Cost of Violence and Finding
the Resources to Change

Traci C. West

I am on a quest, a methodological quest that concentrates on a single aspect of the interdependent, global political economies that currently exist. I seek a method of analysis that recognizes the elimination of gendered, intimate violence, specifically, the sexual and physical assault of women, as a central criterion for economic healthiness. Therefore, accompanying me on this quest, even briefly, will require a broader framework for understanding economic relations than that to which many of us may be accustomed.

In any estimation of what is necessary for global economies to genuinely thrive, we must include the criteria of women's safety from abuse in their intimate relationships with men, such as their fathers, uncles, or husbands, as well as their freedom from sexual assault and harassment regardless of whether the perpetrator is a stranger, co-worker, acquaintance, or intimate relation. The costs of tolerating this violence should not be measured merely in terms of lost economic productivity and innovation, as such violence can also diminish women's health, workplace performance, education and training, and even access to their own homes.

There is also a more systemic and profound loss: a steady attenuation of moral capital, a crucial foundation needed by all facets of civil society to fulfill their constructive potential. In order to address the problem, we must recognize a combination of resources needed for stable globalized political economies, including actions to eliminate intimate violence, a human dignity-honoring community ethos, and gender equality. My quest focuses on the process of identifying these resources, especially some of the racial dynamics involved.

Building on my prior research on violence against U.S.-American black women,[1] I utilize more recent interviews that I conducted with leaders in Ghana, South Africa, and Brazil. The interviewees were activists and scholar-activists committed to addressing gender violence through varied public and private sector approaches. Claiming the benefits of global interdependence, I want to learn from the ideas of these African and Afro-Brazilian leaders to help formulate a liberationist Christian ethics that challenges white supremacy and its capacity to foster violence against women. I believe that learning from these non-U.S. sources of knowledge and activism offers an opportunity to garner fresh ethical critiques. I believe that learning more about anti-violence methods from these African and Afro-Brazilian contexts might help recognize the role of racism in supporting or tolerating gender violence in our U.S.-American culture, with its resulting economic consequences. But what allows honest, intercultural learning to occur across such vast continental and cultural divides? This fundamental question about utilizing outsider perspectives as a resource needs a detailed response that, frankly, I am still working out.

Looking Back

A few of my basic assumptions about the contextualization of Christian ethics may provide conceptual rudders for this pursuit. First, partnerships between Christian mission and globalized capitalist greed that centrally involve violence against women certainly do not represent new historical phenomena. I find references to a supposedly recent trend called "globalization" in current academic conversations about contemporary political economies so distressing because historical memory is absent. The economic legacy of the trans-Atlantic slave trade, for instance, provides ample evidence of organized, globalized capitalist greed on a massive scale several centuries ago that also incorporated sexual violence against women. This trade in human beings helped to generate the wealth and economic advantages currently enjoyed by the United States and several other so-called first world nations in Europe. In the U.S.-American south, the success of the eighteenth- and early nineteenth-century chattel slavery economy relied upon the rape of black women who were used as "breeders."

This rape history can be observed even in the architectural design of Elmina Castle in Cape Coast, Ghana, the last holding place for enslaved Africans on their home continent before they were shipped to the Americas. The fort was originally built by Christian Portuguese traders in 1482 when they named the region the "Gold Coast." After the Dutch took over the fort, they developed the slave trade on a bigger scale than the Portuguese (at its height in 1630-1794). The fort's design reminds present-day visitors of the normalcy of sexual assault in that commercial enterprise. A visitor can learn this information as she walks up the narrow stairway at Elmina Castle reserved for female slaves who had been selected for rape by the European trader governing the fort. The steep, winding stairway leads up to his private bedroom. Also, the chapel of the European slave traders found in the center of the castle is still adorned with their Christian scriptures. That place of worship stands as a monument to the Christian blessing of the violence and commerce that took place there. Much more reflection is needed in Western Christian ethics on the interlinked history of anti-black, racist practices and intimate violence against women within globalized economic relations.[2] This historical context informs my project, but my questions about creating alternative, emancipatory economic practices are contemporary.

Looking at the Present

A second assumption about the contextualization of ethics that I bring to this quest creates a differing emphasis. I insist on the need for an ethical framework that includes a universalized recognition of gender violence as emblematic of globalized political economic unhealthiness, instability, and immorality. Yet I realize that authentic ethical analysis can occur only when this universalized recognition of harm is placed in dialogue with particular cultural realities. The commonly shared notion of justice I seek must operate with principles of fairness and compassion, as well as historical memory about the treatment of subjugated and marginalized peoples, while also guided by the cultural complexities and injustices experienced by women within particular sociohistorical groups and particular community contexts.

In my seminary teaching, for example, I asked masters of divinity students in one of my classes this past semester the following question: "Where do you look in your local communities in order to ethically evaluate economic life?" In response, the class jointly created a chart comprised of widely ranging economic indicators including the availability of recreational parks (publically accessible open space), the availability of affordable housing, the reliability of police and fire emergency services, and the extent of an illegal economy that could span prescription drugs sold in high schools by students to pornographic images of trafficked girls accessed via internet in the privacy of their homes. In addition, throughout the semester, each member of the class had to present a weekly ethical analysis of one news story that was reported in one of their hometown media outlets. I encouraged the students to identify what they considered to be truncated or biased views that were represented to the public as adequate mass media news coverage of the economic or financial affairs of their communities.

One student who grasped the breadth of economic life was from the Democratic Republic of the Congo. An example he presented from his hometown newspaper (accessed by internet) mentioned an ongoing problem of the ambush and rape of women on their way to the market in a local Congolese community.[3] The student offered his own view of this problem as an economic one created by war and explained his criticisms about the inadequacy of the news coverage he had found. But then he quickly added that he knew that these kinds of economic problems were not present in the U.S. because of our very fortunate, safe, stable community environments. Other students in the class nodded their heads in agreement with this characterization of the United States.

This observation is discouraging. Their certainty about the peacefulness of U.S. culture baffles me and represents a direct challenge to my prospects of successfully communicating with an educated U.S.-American Christian audience about a liberationist Christian ethical method that highlights the insights of my African sources. My future audience is likely to be well aware, for instance, of the kinds of statistics about violence against women in the United States found on the National Coalition against Domestic Violence website,[4] such as "one in every four women experience domestic violence . . . one in six women experience an attempted or completed rape . . . in seventy to eighty percent of heterosexual intimate partner murders the man physically abused the woman before the murder no matter which partner was killed."[5] But a kind of imperviousness to the impact of those realities prevails.

It does not even seem to matter how many reports are published about little girls sexually trafficked into our cities and suburbs[6] to be exploited by ordinary heterosexual suburban husbands, or studies that describe heterosexual fathers who have raped and molested their daughters.[7] Christian readers of my project are likely to remain unaffected, given their perception of the over-whelming safety and peace in U.S.-American communities. It is hard to break through the myth that "we" are the economically developed, superior, stable, leader-in-all-things nation in contrast to "them," the hoards of distressed brown and black faces featured in mass media news reports who are found in unstable places in need of Christian mission work.

Since my work focuses on gender violence, it may be particularly difficult to displace our society's commitment to the comforting falsehood of innate U.S.-American cultural superiority with regard to women's freedoms and socio-economic opportunities. This sense of superiority often produces an arrogant presumption that "we may have some problems here, but we definitely treat women better than they do in Africa."

In response, I despairingly wonder how I could hope to commu-nicate a method that contradicts these lies. The anti-black racism feeding this prevalent attitude of cultural superiority functions too productively to be defeated. That is, gender-based attitudes of cultural superiority help to produce a sense of moral entitle-ment that is so generative for maintaining white supremacy in our society. Moreover, these self-delusions are costly, particularly for U.S.-American victim-survivors of violence whose ongoing anguish is ignored. Some attention to the economic maintenance of cultural hierarchies that hide the reality of domestic and sexual violence may help to reveal the moral infrastructure of this cultural process. In particular, how does U.S. Christianity participate?

Some Christians, for example, in their recent public insistence that "the definition of marriage is a union between a man and a woman" have made substantial contributions to U.S.-American self-delusions about gendered morality. This view not only attempts to preserve the supremacy of rights and privileges accorded to heterosexuals in our society, but it also isolates heterosexual identity as the defining ingredient of marriage rather than mutual respect and love between a couple. This heterosexist formulation creates deception about what is moral in intimate couple relations. In short, this definition reinforces the morally bankrupt and Christian gospel-negating idea that the social label given to your sexual identity matters morally much more than how you treat one another.

Churches have spent, for example, hundreds of thousands of dollars on campaigns to protect the privileges of heterosexual marriage in Maine,[8] or tens of millions of dollars to protect marriage in California. They literally purchase a cultural lie about the nature of morality in intimate, covenantal relationships. When Christians identify heterosexuality as the defining ingredient that renders marriage moral, they deny the moral significance of the beating, abusing, raping, and sometimes femicide that too often occurs in heterosexual marriages in the United States. Christian church chicanery about protecting the morality of marriage, together with the use of Christian money to purchase the political power to legitimate its chicanery, exemplify an extreme commitment to maintaining hierarchies of superiority, ignoring the abused, heterosexual wives. In response to such lies and deceptions, an initial step in the Christian liberationist method that I seek must engage in truth-telling that radically shifts economic priorities, including those of the church, toward equality.

A process of recognition has to be cultivated in order to notice the staggering U.S.-American cultural impoverishment created by our cultural superiority complexes and social hierarchies. This self-critical step is necessary in order to authentically engage in relationships of solidarity across differing cultural, nation-state, and religious groups in support of socioeconomic justice. Fortunately, the necessity for U.S.-American self-criticism is not something that must be completed prior to engagement in such relationships; rather it is part of the beneficial learning that results from even deciding to try to learn, for example, from black African sources of knowledge about addressing male-perpetrated intimate violence.

Notes

[1]Traci C. West, *Wounds of the Spirit: Black Women, Violence, and Resistance Ethics* (New York: New York University Press, 1999).

[2]Although it does not focus on intimate violence, for an important contribution to this historical work, see Katie G. Cannon, "An Ethical Mapping of the Transatlantic Slave Trade," in *Religion and Poverty: Pan-African Perspectives*, ed. Peter J. Paris (Durham: Duke University Press, 2009), 19-38.

[3]Kalombo Ngoy Nelson, unpublished paper, April 15, 2010.

[4]http://www.ncadv.org/.

[5]http://www.ncadv.org/files/DomesticViolenceFactSheet%28National%29. pdf, accessed September 4, 2010.

[6]For example, see Adolescent Girls in Georgia's Sex Trade, Juvenile Justice Fund, 2008, http://www.uniteus.org/files/AFNAP_In-depth_Tracking_Study_Official_version.pdf.

[7]Lynn Sacco, *Unspeakable: Father-Daughter Incest in American History* (Baltimore: Johns Hopkins University Press, 2009); Judith Lewis Herman and Lisa Hirschman, *Father-Daughter Incest* (Cambridge: Harvard University Press, 1981).

[8]The Catholic Church reportedly gave over five hundred thousand dollars to help pass a ban on marriage equality in Maine (Chuck Colbert, "In Maine, Same-sex Marriage Is a Catholic Issue," *National Catholic Reporter*, October 29, 2009, http://ncronline.org/news/politics/maine-same-sex-marriage-catholic-issue, accessed September 10, 2010). Also see Associated Press, "Catholic Church Steps Up Anti-Gay Marriage Effort," *Boston Herald*, September 6, 2009.

Part II

EMBODIED CONFLICTS AND CONVERSATIONS

The Church as the Flesh of Christ Crucified

Toward an Incarnational Theology of the Church in the Age of Globalization[1]

Anselm K. Min

The globalizing world is not only a different but also a divided world demanding a concrete sense of the solidarity of all humanity and creation across all particular boundaries. I highlight certain aspects of the incarnation or hypostatic union as an especially relevant Christological basis for that global and cosmic solidarity. I argue that our task today is not to abandon the traditional Christology of the hypostatic union, as many are tempted to do, but to retrieve and deepen its universal existential significance as the "recapitulation of all things." I take the traditional theology of the church as the Body of Christ in his hypostatic union, concretize it into the church as the flesh of Christ crucified, and develop the classical essential attributes of the church—unity, holiness, catholicity, and apostolicity, with reference to the sufferings and hopes of the globalizing world.

The Hypostatic Union for the Age of Globalization

Jesus' proclamation of the reign of God and his praxis of that reign make it clear that his life provides an important example of compassion for the poor and those marginalized for reasons of social differences. It also provides an important model of identifying with the poor and excluded in their political struggles for liberation. Recent biblical studies and liberation theology have shown that the reign of God that Jesus proclaimed contained a preferential love for the poor and marginalized of society and for those excluded from the system of identity based on holiness and purity. This latter group included Gentiles, menstruating women, shepherds, tax collectors, prostitutes, lepers, eunuchs, and the maimed.

Jesus lived to preach the reign of God and to practice its demands, encouraging the poor and oppressed with hope in the approaching reign. He also challenged the powerful and wealthy to repentance, service, and solidarity with the marginalized, and subverted prevailing systems of identity based on religion, power, and wealth that dominate and exclude.

As he lived, so he died, not of disease, old age, or an accident, but by crucifixion as a political criminal for claiming to be "the king of the Jews" (INRI). His death took place outside the gates of Jerusalem at the hands of a mighty empire of the ancient world; it was the political price for his provocation in the name of God's reign. For the sake of the reign of God and for the solidarity of the oppressed and excluded Others, Jesus was murdered by those whose security and interest was threatened by his proclamation and praxis.[2] His was the death of a martyr for the cause of solidarity with those who were excluded for religious, political, and economic reasons. His acceptance of death as the ultimate Outsider was both a critique of the prevailing system of identity and a sign of solidarity in resistance.

What we know about the historical Jesus, then, is sufficient to warrant the argument that Jesus provides an inspiring example relevant to the challenges of the globalizing world. With appropriate interpretation and application, Jesus seems to provide the motivation to respond to the needs and crises of the globalizing world: special compassion for the victims of economic injustice and ecological disasters, identification with the oppressed in their struggles against political and military imperialisms, solidarity with those excluded for reasons of religious differences, effective resistance to the deceptions and illusions of shallow materialism, and the preferential option for the migrant worker. We may even go further and say that Jesus can also serve as an inspiring example of simplicity of life, without greed for power and wealth, someone who lives in harmony with nature, the "lilies of the field and the birds of the air," protecting the environment rather than harming it.

Generally, this is also where those who do not accept the incarnational Christology of the hypostatic union stop and go no further. At this level Jesus is a great prophet of God's preferential love for the poor and a moral exemplar of identification with the marginalized practiced to the point of martyrdom. This is to say a great deal about any human being.

The Nature of the Hypostatic Union

What, then, does the hypostatic union do to Jesus as a moral teacher, prophet, and martyr? Given all its historical relativity and particularity, the hypostatic union confers on Jesus' very humanity, without destroying it, a significance that is as divine as the eternal Son with whom it is hypostatically united. This gives Jesus a significance, therefore, that is as universal and as transcendent as the eternal Son and Word of God himself. Only the divine can overcome the temporal and spatial externality and distance characteristic of all finite creatures and become immanent in all things and at all times. Only the divine has the immediacy of presence and relation, identifying with them and participating in them while also empowering creatures to identify with and participate in the divine and, through the divine, also in one another. Only the divine can "represent" us in the totality and depth of our existence, both individual and social, in all aspects of life, in our interiority and exteriority, in our relations with all humanity and nature, and in our aspirations toward the divine.

God alone can do this because God is the creative source of our being (*esse*) in its totality and depth. The divine transcends all the irreducible differences and externalities of distinct essences and empowers us to share in the destiny of the Son. God can represent us in the most comprehensive ontological sense because we exist as the kind of beings that we are only because our whole being participates in its ontological source that creates us out of nothing.

As a symbol of renewed and reconciled humanity and creation, Christ means the relativization of all human distinctions, whether natural or artificial. He is the sacrament of the solidarity of humanity among all peoples, the solidarity of humanity and nature, and all of these in the prevenient ontological solidarity or

communion of all creation with the Father produced by the Holy
Spirit. Theologically, this solidarity of all humanity and creation
in Christ the Son is the most profound reality that relativizes all
the divisive human distinctions based on gender, nationality, class,
culture, and even religion. In Christ we can recover our solidarity
with one another because we can see Christ in one another and one
another in Christ as members of the same Body. The symbols of
the New Adam and the Body of Christ within the saving economy
of the triune God provide the theological basis for sublating all
the divisions and differences into a profound solidarity of Others,
for which the globalizing world is crying out.[3]

The Hypostatic Union as Transformative

The perspective of incarnational Christology, then, entirely
transforms the meaning of Jesus. Jesus is no longer just a moral
teacher exhorting us to give ourselves to the poor and marginalized of society; he is also the Son of God inspiring us to find him
in the poor and suffering and to identify ourselves with him and
with one another in him. Whatever we do to "the least of these
my brothers" we do to him, something no human being can say.
The hypostatic union thus inspires and motivates us to see Christ,
the incarnate Son, in every human being.

The poor themselves have all the theological motives and reasons for struggling for their own liberation because they know
that their struggle is not only theirs but also that of Christ. They
know that in *their* struggle *Christ* is also struggling with them,
and that they too can share in the hope of Christ himself, his
resurrection.

The citizens of powerful nations should also know that when
their own governments dominate small nations politically, economically, and culturally, they are themselves implicated in that
domination and theologically responsible for the suffering and
dehumanization their governments are wreaking on the citizens
of small nations. These people are, theologically, members of the
same Body of Christ and thus their own sisters and brothers in
Christ. Political solidarity with those who suffer in other nations
will be the necessary concrete expression of their theological solidarity with them in the Body of Christ. The struggles to help the

poor and suffering, the struggles of the poor for their own liberation and dignity, and the struggles of the non-poor to enter into
political solidarity with the poor across the boundaries of nation,
culture, and religion are not just politics but also theology. The
connection between politics and theology is precisely the ontology
of participation provided by the hypostatic union.[4]

The Church as the Flesh of Christ Crucified

Avery Dulles has popularized the "models" approach to
ecclesiology, describing the five distinctive models of institution,
communion, sacrament, herald, and servant, and advocating the
community of disciples' model as his own.[5] All of these models
and images have something to contribute, and it is important to
retrieve the profound insights contained in each.

Not all images or models, however, are equally important.
Some models are more significant because they are more central
to the heart of the Christian faith, more illuminative of the rest
of Christian existence, and more unifying of the entire Christian
vision. For the theological reasons elaborated in the preceding
section I prefer the model of the Body of Christ because it refers
to the becoming-flesh of the Word, the primary analogate to which
all meanings of the Body of Christ must be traced and in which
they participate.

Most contemporary ecclesiologies deal with the theme of the
Body of Christ, which is inevitable, given the Christological basis
of all ecclesiology. The church as the people of God or the temple
of the Spirit or the communion model all presuppose something
of the organic communion of all in the Body of Christ. They all
emphasize the fact that the church is the Body of Christ, providing appropriate biblical and traditional-theological reasons, but
there are also three conspicuous absences.

First, they do not show why something like a church is an essential necessity in the first place; they fail to develop the relevance
of the church for the social structure of human existence, especially
for the contemporary world in the very throes of globalizing
that structure with all its tensions and problems. They tend to
be positivistic, and convey a picture of a self-sufficient and self-
satisfied community completely isolated from the world. Second,

they do not adequately develop the full meaning of the hypostatic union of Christ whose Body the church is. In his hypostatic union Christ unites, reconciles, and recapitulates all things, creator and creature, humanity and nature, and humanity with one another, serving as the divine source of the global and cosmic solidarity of all creation.

Further, when they do develop the global and cosmic meaning of Christ, they do not concretize and contextualize that meaning by connecting it with the cries and screams for solidarity and reconciliation in the contemporary world. Most ecclesiologies tend to be narrowly ecclesiological, dealing with intra-ecclesial issues (such as models of the church, biblical and theological foundations, institutional structures of the church, marks of the church, and ecumenical issues) and not sufficiently contextual or sufficiently Christological, which would position the nature and mission of the church in the concretizing context of the global and cosmic solidarity of all creation in God. I propose to restore these missing dimensions.

Theology as theology is not in a position to provide specific policies and solutions to all the problems of the globalizing world. However, theology can and should inspire certain general sensibilities that can serve as the horizon for discerning problems and motivating the will to pursue relevant solutions. This is particularly true for Christian communities, which is the primary audience of theology. While theology cannot substitute for empirical expertise in providing solutions, it can and should provide the basic perspectives and the inspiring motivation for recognizing problems and pursuing responses. Problems can appear as problems only to certain horizons and perspectives, and the solution of problems requires motivation and commitment. The Pentagon and Wall Street view the world and its problems in one way. Theology may view them in quite a different manner.

The Body of Christ primarily and literally refers to the flesh that the divine Word became, but it is also the saving recapitulation of all things, the solidarity of God and creatures and of all humanity and creation with God and with one another in God. All creatures, whether human or non-human, are created to become members of this Body and share in the transcendent solidarity with God and with one another. As the most visible manifestation of the recapitulation of all things, the Body of Christ contains the whole of theology from the triune God, of which the Word is the second person, to the destiny of all humanity and all creation to the economy of that destiny.[6]

The church is not literally the body of Christ and is not hypostatically united with Christ, but it is also the Body of Christ in more than a purely metaphorical sense. It is the community of those who ontologically share in the life and grace of Christ, its head, and share that life and grace with one another in the Holy Spirit. This sharing is even more intimate than the manner in which the members of a living body share in the same life of the body. However, the Body of Christ is a great metaphor because it has the capacity to point to the ontological unity of community members with Christ and through him with all of history and creation. In itself, the Body of Christ as a metaphor contains all the classic marks of what the true church should be: unity (with the head and among one another), holiness (as sharing in the new life communicated from Christ in the Holy Spirit), catholicity (as recapitulation of all things in Christ the head), and apostolicity (of its origin from Christ the incarnate Word, the source of unity, holiness, and catholicity and thus also of its eschatological destiny).

The Use of "Flesh" versus "Body" as Metaphor

I propose to substitute "flesh" for the "body" of Christ as an analogy for the church for three related reasons. First, while "body" sounds very neutral, "flesh" refers not only to the basic materiality, sexuality, sociality, and historicity of human existence, but also to all of these in their fragility, vulnerability, mortality, and sinfulness. It captures the resistance of unredeemed human nature and creation to the reconciling work of the Holy Spirit by dominating, exploiting, dividing, and destroying. It stands for fallen humanity and fallen creation and their need for redemption and reconciliation.

In addition, understanding the church as the "Flesh of Christ" reminds the church of the self-emptying of the Son in becoming flesh and sharing most intimately in the frailties of the human condition. Jesus' self-emptying redeemed that condition from within. It also reminds the church of the theological imperative to more explicitly imitate the redemptive kenosis of the model in which it participates and of which it is meant to be a sign.

The church should not forget that it is the "Flesh of Christ" precisely in the sense that the Word "became flesh" so as to empower and invite the church to likewise become flesh in the human condition. As the Flesh of Christ the church is invited and inspired to participate in the redemptive self-emptying of the Word into the depth of the human condition in all its sinfulness and suffering, in its divisions and conflicts, in its exposure to hunger, lust, and mortality.

A third reason to take on the metaphor of "flesh" is that while Christ fully participated in the humility of the human condition without sinning, the church as the Flesh of Christ is not necessarily protected from sinning; it participates not only in the humility of the human condition but also in its outright "carnal," sinful existence. The church is immersed not only in the redemptive self-emptying of the Word who became flesh, but also in the contamination of "all flesh," "the lust of the flesh and the lust of the eyes and the pride of life" (1 Jn 2:15).

The church can proclaim the word of redemption only as a human group itself in need of redemption. To refer to the church as the "Flesh of Christ" is to be reminded not only of the primordial model in which it participates and which it is called upon to proclaim and imitate, but also of the distance between Christ and the Flesh. Christ and the church are not hypostatically united, and the church is always under the temptation to become flesh in the sense of sinful, carnal existence. To call the church the "Flesh of Christ" is to remind the church of its carnal character in the biblical sense and to warn it against the constant temptation to divinization, triumphalism, spiritualism, idealism, and intellectualism.

Considering the Crucifixion

I further propose to understand the church as the "Flesh of Christ Crucified." This accentuates the incarnation at its most dramatic, most concrete, and most intense. By the same token, it is most revelatory of God's solidarity with all humanity and all creation and it highlights the role of the church in its witness to the "logic of the cross" (1 Cor 1:18) in the contemporary world.

The incarnation is not something that took place at the moment of conception but was a continuing event throughout the life and death of the incarnate Son. It means more than becoming a human being in the abstract because it involves participating in the depth of the agonies and struggles of human existence in its materiality and sociality, with all its divisions and conflicts. The crucifixion constitutes the most dramatic moment of the particular historical dialectic into which the divine Son emptied himself to bear witness to the reign of God. It meant bearing witness to the reign to the point of accepting death, perhaps the most decisive act of self-emptying love possible. Death came in the form of crucifixion by the mighty empire of the ancient world.

No symbol captures the profound agonies and yearnings of the globalizing world more appropriately, more theologically, and more compellingly than the Christ Crucified who continues to bear his cross in his suffering members all over the world today. It is not yet the time to indulge in the joys of the resurrection, although a good theology must insist on the unity of the death and resurrection in Christ. It is a question of emphasis, and the emphasis that we need today is a theology or logos of the cross, not that of glory, even if it is also true that our participation in the logic of the cross needs the sustaining hope of the resurrection.[7]

To call the church the "Flesh of Christ Crucified" is to call on the church to participate precisely in this most dramatic and decisive event of the incarnation and to bear witness to the inherent logic of the cross, which still remains a scandal and a folly to all humanity, including the church itself. In this age of globalization when all humanity is internally divided and alienated from one another and from nature as a whole, it is critical to pay special attention to the demand of the logic of the cross, the praxis of universal solidarity in God. The immensity of human suffering we cause one another today calls for us to remember the suffering that we are so anxious to conceal. The global and cosmic stretching of human sympathies and the yearning for forgiveness and reconciliation such suffering demands need to be nurtured and encouraged by the universalizing union of the human and the divine in the Suffering Servant.

As the Flesh of Christ Crucified, then, the basic mission of the church is to continue to concretize, exemplify, and memorialize the incarnational dynamic primordially unleashed by Christ in his crucifixion in the flesh. This is a dynamic of global and cosmic solidarity and reconciliation in the triune God. The incarnation of Christ calls for the continuing incarnation of his original dynamic by the members of his Flesh in the concrete circumstances and dialectics of their different times and places. It is the imperative to concretely actualize solidarity and reconciliation in a divided and conflictual world on a global and cosmic scale.

The Flesh of Christ Crucified and the Marks of the Church

The traditional marks of the church—unity, holiness, catholicity, and apostolicity—provide the context for discussing certain essential characteristics of the church.[8] What would these marks mean in light of the incarnational dynamic of global/cosmic solidarity in sin and grace unleashed by the Word in this hypostatic union?

Globalization and the Unity of the Church

From the perspective of the church as the Flesh of Christ Crucified, the conventional discussion of the unity of the church seems very intra-ecclesial and abstract; it is too detached from the concrete struggles and destinies of all humanity. We tend to define the church in terms internal to itself, faith, scripture, liturgy, sacrament, clergy and laity, church history, and so on, and forget its original and essential involvement in the struggles and destiny of all humanity and creation by virtue of its being the Flesh of Christ. The age of globalization that heightens our consciousness of the mutual dependence of all humanity with itself and with all creation should remind us of the global and cosmic solidarity of all things in Christ the Word. It should also help us rediscover this most profound dimension of the Christian faith—the unity of the church—without which the church would become a self-enclosed group in complete isolation from the world.[9]

The age of globalization demands that we appreciate this global and cosmic solidarity in all its concreteness, with its internal differentiation, its divisions and sufferings, and its concealed yearning for a new order of human relations. This is not to import an external social problem into the church. Rather, we must think dialectically.

Large-scale external trends, such as globalization, do not remain merely external to the church but invade and penetrate its interior and pose an internal problem. The cultural, political, and economic differences and conflicts among the nations and cultures of the world certainly complicate the relation among the "particular" churches within the universal church as well as the role of regional and national conferences of bishops. The political economy of globalization further complicates the "internal" issues of the church by bringing together Christians of many different nations, cultures, and even religious backgrounds, raising sociological questions about group dynamics and the theological problem of what unity concretely means in a multicultural church and parish.

Globalization thus interrupts our traditional idea of the unity of the church by challenging us to think of the entire globe and all creation theologically as part of the recapitulation of the hypostatic union. Globalization is not just a historical or social phenomenon but also a theological phenomenon. We are reminded of our ultimate theological destiny as human beings, and the unity of the church is meaningful only as a sign and sacrament of this global and cosmic unity of all things in Christ.

The church must become a sign of this human unity concretely by establishing solidarity through the reconciliation of differences and divisions so rampant today. It must learn to recontextualize the traditional question of love of neighbor without which we cannot love God. What is the most effective way of showing love in a globalizing world that suffers from mutual alienations and hostilities among nations and cultures? To be a sign of unity in a divided world necessarily demands the praxis of love. The unity of the church must be reconceived in terms of the theological unity of all humanity and creation in Christ and concretized in the praxis of multicultural love. All institutions of the church must incarnate this sense of human solidarity in their concrete differences and divisions. The whole relationship between church and world must be reconceptualized.

Globalization and the Holiness of the Church

The holiness of the church has usually been discussed in terms of the sanctifying presence of the Holy Spirit, the sacraments that make grace present, and the saints who exemplify the transforming union with God. Holiness refers to our relation to God who alone is holy, and expresses a yearning for union, intimacy, and connection with God who transcends us all. The church is holy because it is specially chosen by the triune God to exemplify to the world the sanctifying presence of God. It is God who inspires and empowers us to participate in the divine by participating in the hypostatic union of the divine and human in the Son.

This makes the status of the church more than a little delicate. The church is neither identical with God nor hypostatically united with the divine in the way that the body of Christ is. It is not, therefore, to be worshiped or idolized. This does not, however, make it a human community pure and simple, to be understood and measured by empirical sociological or historical criteria alone, although it does have these dimensions. It is a human community gifted with the special presence of the triune God that inspires and empowers it to be a paradigm of the call to humanity and all creation to participate in the divine. The church is holy because its ultimate subject, its ultimate goal, and its ultimate content are divine.

The holiness of the church is also interrupted by the challenge of globalization in a twofold way. The church is a relationship with God whose presence alone makes it holy. But who is the God who dwells in the church and to which the church bears witness? Globalization brings many different religions and many different conceptions of the divine together for mutual competition and dialogue. The church cannot ignore the challenge of these religions and their different conceptions of God and salvation if it truly believes that God is indeed the "God of all creation," as it professes at every Eucharistic celebration. God also provides ways for all humanity, in their different situations and through their different religions, to find ultimate liberation from the fragility of the human condition. The church must love them in their differences as God does.

The struggle of the church to love involves a delicate negotiation between two equally indispensable poles of our Christian relationship to God—to God's transcendent incomprehensibility, and to God's incarnational closeness in which the always transcendent God nevertheless has become one of us. Both poles are necessary.

Without transcendence, God ceases to be God, while without incarnation, God ceases to be the Christian God. Globalization interrupts the holiness of the church as it challenges the church to constantly negotiate the space between the transcendent and the incarnational poles. This must be done in the context of the different concepts of the divine embodied in other religions.

Globalization poses another challenge to the holiness of the church. The church, which is meant to be an effective sign of grace, the presence of God in the world, necessarily faces the questions of whether the church is a sign at all and of what kind of a sign it is. In its sinfulness the church can be a countersign, as the clergy sexual abuse seems to indicate, while in its saintly examples, like Mother Teresa, it is a credible sign. How can the church be an effective sign of the incarnational dynamic unleashed by the global and cosmic solidarity of all creation in the triune God?

The compelling multifarious needs of the globalizing world call special attention to the hungry, thirsty, foreign, naked, sick, and imprisoned of Matthew 25, found today mostly in the poor, divided, and exploited nations of the world. Any assistance to them will be an act of saving identification and solidarity with the Son who identifies with them. The hypostatic union makes Christ present in them, still bearing his cross, and crying out, "My God, my God, why have you abandoned me?" This is perhaps the real test of the holiness of the church, its relation to the Flesh of Christ Crucified. It cannot bear witness to the holiness of the Lord it serves without serving the most humble needs of the neediest members of his Flesh. The holiness of the church will shine all the more brightly in and through the praxis of its members as members of the Flesh of Christ are still crucified in more than two thirds of humanity.[10]

Globalization and the Catholicity of the Church

Historically, catholicity has been understood in terms of the vocation and movement of the church beyond the local and particular to the universality of the whole world to which the gospel is meant to be proclaimed. The concept has been further developed to include the universality of saving doctrines in relation to all essential aspects of human life, universal humanity that must be addressed regardless of differences in condition and status, and the universality of sins and virtues of which human beings are capable. That is to say, the church is called upon to embody the "wholeness" or "integrity" of life beyond particularism, exclusivism, partiality, and one-sidedness. This is part of the incarnational dynamic that reconciles all things and that increasingly universalizes the self-consciousness of the church so as to make it more open and more receptive to all that is true, good, and beautiful.

Globalization also interrupts and challenges the catholicity of the church in many ways. The church is called upon to expand its self-consciousness to the entire globe and indeed to the entire universe, to appropriate the insights and treasures of different religions and cultures. It is called upon to integrate into a wholeness the various dimensions of life—economic, political, and cultural—and shed light on its transcendent meaning. It is called upon to sanctify all aspects of human existence and reconcile all human groups in their often divisive differences. There is literally no area or aspect or group outside or beyond the concern of the church as the Flesh of Christ. The call to catholicity in the globalizing world is a call to global catholicity in the sense of an all-comprehensive and radically ontological call to appreciate all things that are insofar as they participate in the being of the triune God. It is a call to be as open as God is open, to be as merciful, perfect, and receptive to all things as is our heavenly Father (Mt 5:48; Lk 6:36).

Globalization and the Apostolicity of the Church

Concern with the apostolicity of the church focuses on its origin as mediated by the apostles through their knowing of Jesus Christ. It also focuses on the fidelity of the church to that origin, and the church's collective memory. Its collective memory is also the church's collective hope because it remembers the Christ Crucified who is also risen and who empowers all to anticipate the hope of sharing in his resurrection.[11] Apostolicity, therefore, is not an antiquarian concern; it remains a constant challenge to the identity, fidelity, and renewal of the church as a community of shared memory and shared hope. Apostolicity means not only originating from Jesus through the apostles but also being "sent" precisely to live that subversive memory and empowering hope in the midst of history, both past and present.

Globalization is a special challenge to the apostolicity of the church. It demands that the church, with its origin in the Word become flesh, respond to its ontological call to the solidarity in Christ of all humanity and creation in both sin and grace. Humankind has always had some sense of its common humanity, but that sense has remained rather abstract. Different cultures and religions have remained in relative isolation from one another, and their sense of humanity has likewise been colored by their particularity and narrowness. The age of globalization has transformed isolation, particularity, and narrowness by bringing national, religious, and cultural differences together in the most concrete fashion. The resulting divisions and conflicts compel all of humanity to find a mode of living together as human beings with all their differences and beyond all their differences. Added to the stress of differences is the ecological crisis, which forces a consciousness of our common destiny with nature: human beings are part of nature, and when they harm nature, they harm themselves.

Conclusion

Globalization thus challenges the church to return to a sense of global and cosmic solidarity, and to the source of its most ancient identity in the Word incarnate whose hypostatic union recapitulates all things and calls for the church to participate in that work of recapitulation.

It should also be clear that the church's unity, holiness, catholicity, and apostolicity do not refer to different areas of reality but only to the different dimensions of one and the same reality of the church. The unity of the church refers to the dimension of interdependence and the need for harmony and communion among its members. Holiness also refers to the transcendent aspirations toward God immanent in our struggles for this harmony with one another. Catholicity relates to the totality of the created world to be reconciled and recapitulated in Christ in those struggles, while apostolicity stands for the origin of the very incarnational dynamic that inspires these struggles for unity, holiness, and catholicity.

Notes

[1]I would like to thank Professors Laurie Cassidy of Marywood University and Maureen O'Connell of Fordham University for inviting me to present a plenary address at the fifty-sixth annual convention of the College Theology Society held on June 3-6, 2010, at the University of Portland, Portland, Oregon. It was a great honor and a great pleasure to share some of my thoughts in progress with colleagues. This article is a revised version of that address.

[2]John Dominic Crossan, *Who Killed Jesus?* (San Francisco: Harper, 1995).

[3]I provide a detailed discussion of the Trinity as the ontological source of this solidarity of Others in *The Solidarity of Others in a Divided World: A Postmodern Theology after Postmodernism* (New York: T & T Clark, 2004), 91-155.

[4]It is critical to remember that the theological ontology of representation, participation, and recapitulation made possible by the hypostatic union of the human and divine in the Word incarnate was precisely what was at stake in the Nestorian controversy. See St. Cyril of Alexandria, *On the Unity of Christ*, trans. John Anthony McGuckin (Crestwood, NY: St. Vladimir's Seminary Press, 1995). It is also a prominent theme in Maximus the Confessor; see Lars Thunberg, *Man and the Cosmos: The Vision of Maximus the Confessor* (Crestwood, NY: St. Vladimir's Seminary Press, 1985), 80-91; and Hans Urs von Balthasar, *Cosmic Liturgy: The Universe According to Maximus the Confessor* (San Francisco: Ignatius Press, 2003), 273-74. For a masterful twentieth-century reconstruction of that ontology, see Emile Mersch, *The Theology of the Mystical Body* (St. Louis: B. Herder, 1951), 197-246; also Henri de Lubac, *Catholicism: A Study of the Corporate Destiny of Mankind* (New York: Sheed & Ward, 1950; Mentor-Omega Book, 1964), 17-32.

[5]Avery Dulles, *Models of the Church: Expanded Edition* (New York: Doubleday, 1987).

[6]See Mersch, *The Theology of the Mystical Body*, 51-54.

[7]I present a fuller discussion of a theology of the Body of Christ in the age of globalization in my *Solidarity of Others in a Divided World*, 134-55.

[8]For standard theological and biblical discussions of the four marks of the church, see Hans Küng, *The Church* (New York: Sheed & Ward, 1967), 263-362; Johann Auer and Joseph Ratzinger, *Dogmatic Theology 8: The Church: The Universal Sacrament of Salvation* (Washington, DC: Catholic University of America Press, 1993), 345-469; George Tavard, *The Church, Community of Salvation: An Ecumenical Ecclesiology* (Collegeville, MN: Liturgical Press, 1992), 99-111; Jürgen Moltmann, *The Church in the Power of the Spirit: A Contribution to Messianic Ecclesiology* (San Francisco: HarperSanFrancisco, 1977), 337-61; Wolfhart Pannenberg, *Systematic Theology*, vol. 3 (Grand Rapids: William B. Eerdmans Publishing Co., 1998), 405-30.

[9]J.-M. R. Tillard, *Church of Churches: The Ecclesiology of Communion* (Collegeville, MN: Liturgical Press, 1992), is perhaps the best recent ecclesiology of communion, but it is also a good example of a discussion of communion

without any significant reference to the divisions and conflicts, often bloody, so rampant in the world to which the church is meant to be a sign of unity and communion. It is a very abstract discussion of the church in complete isolation from the world, its transcendental and historical context.

[10]It is no coincidence that Emmanuel Levinas sees an authentic relationship to God only when it is interrupted and mediated by a loving relationship to a human Other in the undesirability of his or her hunger and need; see Anselm K. Min, "Naming the Unnamable God: Levinas, Derrida, and Marion," *International Journal for Philosophy of Religion* 60 (2006): 100-103.

[11]For a recent discussion of the apostolicity of the church, see John J. Burkhard, *Apostolicity Then and Now: An Ecumenical Church in a Postmodern World* (Collegeville, MN: Liturgical Press, 2004), which takes apostolicity as the apostolicity of the origin, doctrine, and life of the church as such.

The Body Globalized

Problems for a Sacramental Imagination in an Age of Global Commodity Chains

Vincent Miller

Globalization is a concept with myriad definitions. This is certainly fitting for so large and complex a reality. Too often, however, our imagination of globalization remains on the macro scale. We consider globalization a matter of things "out there"—other cultures, global economic activity, environmental change. While its scale is, by definition, global, the changes it brings about take place on the local, even the personal and intimate level.

In his survey of debates on the cultural effects of globalization, John Tomlinson offers the helpful description of globalization as "complex connectivity."[1] Rather than seeing globalization as a new form of something we already understand (for example, a "global village" or "space-time compression"), complex connectivity alerts us to attend to the particular sorts of influences, impacts, and relationships that take place in everyday life in a global world. Most people spend much less time in the front sections of jets and in business hotels than *New York Times* columnist and globalization guru Thomas Friedman. Yet even people of modest means in advanced capitalist societies eat food from around the world, worry about diseases that arrive from far away, feel that their jobs and their retirement account balances depend upon decisions and dynamics over which they have little control, and watch distant events—revolutions, natural disasters, political upheavals—on their television or computer screen in the comfort of their private space.

Each of these common experiences emerges from very specific sorts of connections. Consider two examples. Almost any purchasing decision involves acting on a global scale. My choice of coffee, socks, shampoo, or a computer all have effects around the world that I never see. It's as if we have long hands that can reach around the world to obtain anything we desire. But some moral *corpus callosum* has been severed. We cannot see what our hands are doing. At the same time, we have a separated global sense of sight. We watch the victims of disaster—natural and human—around the world, in real time. Hundreds of thousands of years of human moral instinct and wisdom cry out within us to act on their behalf. Yet we have no hands to accompany this sight. We see the orphan in the village wrecked by a tsunami, the family left homeless by an earthquake, but can make no direct response. We have become global actors, but the nature of our agency is profoundly different from the sorts of moral situations we have dealt with traditionally.

These are but two examples of the "complex" nature of the connections in which we are entangled in our global age. In order for the church and theology to respond adequately to the epochal challenges posed by globalization, we must attend to the particularities of these connections.

This essay focuses on one of these myriad global connections: the impact of globally sourced consumption upon the imagination that emerges from our lived experience of embodiment. This essay grows out of two interrelated concerns: one a memory of a conversation that has long left me uneasy, and the other an assumption that I made within *Consuming Religion* that requires revisiting. The first was an informal conversation I participated in years ago about the liturgical use of digital media such as video clips and PowerPoint. There was a shared and forceful dismissal of such things as an encroachment of virtual reality upon the liturgy, resulting in the loss of its embodied, sacramental character. I'm not at all a promoter of PowerPoint. I'm profoundly hesitant to use it in the classroom, let alone the liturgy. Nevertheless, something about this conversation never sat right with me. In the years since, I've looked back repeatedly, coming to various answers about what was wrong. One has stabilized recently. It has to do with the body as the ground of the sacramental imagination. In a world of global commodity food chains, where we have no idea where the food that nourishes and constitutes our bodies comes from, the body might not be the bedrock we desire. Virtuality might haunt us even in sacred rituals from which video screens are banned. Our experience of our own bodies is often as disconnected as the digitally mediated realities that so rightly cause us concern.

In *Consuming Religion* I argued that the Catholic sacramental imagination can provide a resource to counter the abstraction of commodification.[2] A robust belief in creation and incarnation push us to respect things in their materiality. These doctrines help us not only to see things as valuable in themselves, but also to resist the workings of commodification that reduce the tree, the wool, the ore, and the human labor that transforms them, into mere disposable carriers of the ephemeral style. I still believe this is true. Grounded in bedrock dogmatic convictions of Christianity, these will remain intellectual resources. Whether they continue to inform a shared ecclesial imagination is a different question; one that rests on matters of liturgical practice, cultural, and religious formation. The latter, I have argued, is deeply implicated in the basic material difficulty we face in consumer culture: commodification. The sacramental imagination, so important a resource for countering commodification, may indeed be undermined by our imaginative formation in commodity consumption.

In this essay, I consider how commodity abstraction impacts the sacramental imagination via its construction of our bodies. If, as we will see below, many theologians have argued that a proper understanding of embodiment is essential for an adequate sacramental theology, what happens to our sacramental sensibilities when commodification hides the very connection to the world, the contingency, the locatedness, the relatedness, that theological treatments of corporeality have sought to build upon?

Embodiment and Sacramentality

In Susan Ross's words "post-Vatican II sacramental theology has focused on the inherent goodness of physical reality" and corporeality. Yet, she observes, it "fails to address embodiment in any but the most general sense."[3] Ross's work emphasizes the inevitably gendered component of embodiment that is too often ignored in theological treatments of corporeality. She also argues, however that abstract essentialism haunts more gendered accounts of embodiment as well. These often "fail to put . . . bodies in real socio-economic contexts."[4] The latter lacuna is the location of my concerns about the formative influence of commodification.

I will consider its consequences by engaging two major works in general sacramental theology that address embodiment, those of Edward Schillebeeckx and Louis-Marie Chauvet. Both accounts suffer from the gender abstraction that concerns Ross. However, out of the broad literature on sacraments and the body, they offer the most sustained and direct theological reflections on the relationship between embodiment and sacramental theology. While others may engage particulars better, these two theologians focus on the link that connects embodiment and sacramentality.

Sixty years after its publication, Schillebeeckx's *Christ, the Sacrament of the Encounter with God* remains one of the most direct accounts of the relationship between sacramentality and embodiment. In it, Schillebeeckx developed Aquinas's anthropology and sacramental theology using phenomenological resources: "Mutual human availability is possible only in and through man's bodiliness." The incarnation is continued in the sacramental work of the church. Christ takes up "earthly, non-glorified realities into his glorified saving activity."[5] The sacraments are "the divine act of redemption itself, manifest in the sacred environment of the living Church, making a concrete appeal to man and taking hold of him in a living way, as really as does the embrace of a mother for her child." Just as the child needs more than knowledge of the mother's love, so the sacraments are the "actual embrace" necessary to "perfect the experience of love."[6]

Schillebeeckx's argument is more than an exposition of Aquinas's dictum "*quidquid recipitur per modum recipientis recipitur*" in terms of embodiment. In addition to his epistemology of embodied encounter, Schillebeeckx offers a comprehensive anthropology of corporeality that encompasses agency as well: "In human activity a person's own bodiliness is an aspect of the active subject. The bodily expression is not merely a manifestation of a free spiritual act after it has already been achieved in pure interiority; the spiritual act can only be achieved in incarnation." Schillebeeckx distinguishes between the "central acts of life" and more mundane everyday acts that do not engage the fullness of our personhood, arguing that sacraments are best understood as belonging to the former.[7]

Three decades later, Louis-Marie Chauvet (whose work Schillebeeckx was engaging in his final unfinished manuscript on sacraments) continued to engage the relationship between embodiment and sacramentality. Where Schillebeeckx grounded his sacramental theology on the incarnation, Chauvet focuses instead upon the paschal mystery: God's ongoing work in history to bring about salvation. Corporeality in this account is linked to mediation in a different sense, our unavoidable location within language, culture, and history. Chauvet speaks of a triple body of culture, tradition, and nature.[8] The order is quite intentional; there is no access to our relationship to nature save through the mediation of language, culture, and tradition. "[N]o word escapes the necessary and laborious inscription in a body, a history, a language, a system of signs, a discursive network. Such is the law. The law of mediation. The law of the body." In this regard, Chauvet cites Dominique Dubarle's description of the body as the "arch-symbol" of the human symbolic order.[9] We are spoken long before we ever speak. As humans we receive our subjectivity from our culture. We do not make ourselves. This anthropological fact is also the basis for understanding God's gift of salvation in the church. God's act precedes us. Christian identity is a gift.

At times Chauvet sounds as if he's making a sociological or anthropological point. His engagement of anthropological studies of traditional initiation rites can be read as anthropological nostalgia for a degree of cultural formation and immersion that modern societies lack.[10] He is, however, making a fundamentally Christian theological argument. The sacraments, even more than the scriptures, convey the scandalous entrance of God into human history. Our entering into them within the church conveys our embodiment in a tradition founded on God's gracious self-gift. This logic lies within the sacraments themselves. "Baptismal immersion, the first *sacramentum* of the Christian, is a good example: the body is completely plunged into the symbolic order proper to the church, an order metaphorized by water in baptism."[11]

Our embodied engagement of the sacraments draws us into the paschal mystery:

The very fact that we receive a sacrament does involve us . . . we either make the gesture or not. When everything seems to fail for believers, when the ground of their firmest convictions gives way beneath their feet, when anguish grabs them by their throats as the idea runs through them that perhaps there is no God, what remains for them, so that they are still able, in spite of everything and if it is possible, to communicate with "God," if not their bodies? What else remains for them but their bodies taking in hand what the Church takes up—a little bread and wine—and saying what the Church says—"my body given for you"—taking and saying these the gestures and words of him whom the Church confesses as its Lord? But when faith has lost every illusion about its good "reasons," when it no longer has anything but the body, then is it not eminently "faith"?[12]

Both Schillebeeckx and Chauvet locate the body at the center of their sacramental theologies. Corporeality holds important truths that theology ignores at its peril. In addition to offering an account of embodiment, each also assumes these correspond in some way to experience. Schillebeeckx, despite the supplement of the phenomenological notion of encounter, continues to offer a rather abstract account of the embodiment. His distinction between the "decisive, central acts of life" and "everyday acts of a lesser kind" illustrates this abstraction. As many have since shown, the mundane practices and structures of everyday life form, construct, and discipline us.[13] Our subjectivity is achieved not only in our reflexive engagements with others in the world, but also in the more mundane formation in everyday life.

Chauvet offers a compelling account of embodiment as locatedness, mediation, and formation within a tradition that precedes oneself. This account is offered as a strategic challenge to the extrinsicism of ontotheological views of God and humankind, and to business models of exchange that cannot see the gratuitousness of God and other persons that exceeds all calculation.[14] But the problem we face is not merely one of competing conceptions of exchange. The everyday structure of commodification inclines us to ignore bodily mediation and its consequences in a particular way. This leaves us particularly ignorant of the many complex relationships that sustain us, rendering the wisdom of embodiment mute.

Commodity Distancing and the Body

There are many sites of concern regarding the body and commodification: labor, sexuality, pornography, plastic surgery, the commercialization of human tissue and genetic material, and so forth. Here I will focus on a less explicit, but far more pervasive one: food and the literal global sourcing of our bodies.

In *Consuming Religion* I presented commodification as an overlooked formation of the imagination. Commodities come to us without information about their origins in land, labor, and life. Our daily commerce with them teaches us to engage the world in this way: expecting that things are readily intelligible outside of their originating contexts. Thomas Princen speaks of "distancing" to describe how global commodity chains systematically deprive us of feedback regarding the conditions and consequences of the production of the things we consume. He describes various ways in which feedback is severed in global commodity chains.

The simplest is geographical distance: producers act differently when consumers could, in principle, see their production. I'd be unlikely to eat a fast food burger if behind the parking lot there were one hundred thousand cattle crammed into a feed lot, standing knee deep in their own excrement. But since that lot is actually in Kansas or Brazil, I smell only the cooking meat.[15]

More complex is what Princen terms "cultural distance." This involves a lack of detailed knowledge of the predicament of producers, such as, for example, the effects of export agriculture on subsistence farming societies, the bargaining power that farmers have with export firms, or how economic pressures influence their choices about land use and the safe application of fertilizer and pesticides.[16]

At each moment of exchange in commodity chains that now span the globe, only information that encourages a sale is passed along, namely design, and price, and perhaps, quality. With each exchange, the purchaser becomes more distant from the origins of the commodity and less likely than ever to find out how it was produced, and it becomes more likely that many of the full costs of the product will be externalized. The consequence of this is that for the consumer, all production seems to arrive from an infinite frontier: a place where resources are infinite, waste can be disposed of without consequence, and labor costs can be infinitely reduced.

Although the objects we consume come to us from around the world, the feedback we receive about our consumption is decidedly local: the credit card bill, domestic clutter, and our waistlines. It's as if we have extremely long hands that reach into every corner of the world. Reaching into my refrigerator to pour a glass of orange juice, I touch three continents: the can tells me it contains concentrate from the United States, Mexico, Brazil, or China. But these long arms are coupled with extreme near-sightedness. My reach may stretch thousands of miles. My gaze goes about as far as the light from the refrigerator.

Our current economic system does not provide any ready means for us to think about our relationships with others. Other socio-economic systems provide this information quite directly. Even the exploitative system of the slave plantation made clear the owner's reliance upon the labor of the slaves. A subsistence-oriented family farm, of the sort that a large percentage of humankind lived on just a few generations ago, provided feedback concerning consumption. The fall harvest had to last until crops became available again in late spring. Thus a desire for bourbon, for example, had clear limits. If you feed too much of your corn to the still, your family would go hungry and you might not have any seed corn. Our present economic system provides us no ready feedback. We don't know what too much is. We never really know when we're taking more than our share from the commonwealth or when we are eating our (or our children's) seed corn.

In teaching and lecturing, I've long sought to stress the intimate nature of these relationships. Underwear was my example of choice: something very intimate, the first thing we put on in the day, a complex item that is generally quite cheap. Probably none of us has ever made a pair. To illustrate the global reach of our consumption, occasionally I would consider the strange brew in my compost pile: local fruits and vegetables from farmers' markets, regional produce, but also orange peels from California, avocado skins from Mexico, bananas from Costa Rica, and mangoes from India. This is a strange humus indeed, but not unusual. My compost pile, like every other one in the first world, hosts unprecedented blends of nutrients and microbes; a strange geography, myriad bioregions tossed together in one small bin.

It took me a surprisingly long while to notice the rather obvious fact that my compost pile is, well, me. My bones, muscles, organs, viscera, brain, skin are the same strange blend. I eat the things whose rinds end up in my compost, plus feedlot cattle from Kansas and Brazil, salmon—some that swam wild in the North Pacific and others that were confined in pens in Chile, plagued by unnatural swarms of sea-lice, dropping a toxic sludge of excrement and antibiotics that endangers the ocean ecosystem in the area.

My body is constituted in global relationships. Even the nerve cells that host my thoughts, the neurotransmitters that surge and fade in their synapses, are drawn from plants, animals, and the labor of others around the globe. My corporeality has just the kind of finitude and relatedness that Chauvet evokes. Yet I see none of it. Implicated, imbricated, insinuated in myriad relationships, all this remains beyond imagining. I can summon these connections, but I am not confronted by them. Relationality describes me, but it does not mark the default of my imagination.

While the hidden truth of our global consumption conforms to our more complex accounts of corporeality, the formation of our imaginations on this side of the veil of the commodity makes us appear autonomous, unrelated to anything. We are not implicated in the world, but rather are individual, sovereign subjects who choose from a range of objects at our disposal.

Zygmunt Bauman speaks of the "subjectivity fetish" to describe this formation of the self. The subjectivity fetish is the flip side of the commodity fetish. Commodities "stick to the role of Cartesian 'object'—fully docile, obedient stuff for the omnipotent subject to handle, give shape to, put to good use. By their sheer docility they elevate the buyer to the noble, flattering, ego-boosting rank of the sovereign subject, uncontested and uncompromised."[17] This relationship, more than any legacy of Descartes or neo-scholasticism, confirms us daily as abstract subjects unencumbered by the physical entanglements of embodiment. Even as we obsessively monitor diet and nutrition, the connections of our bodies remain hidden beyond our sovereign choice from the grocery aisle or menu. Or more precisely, this is a mode of embodiment that is profoundly unconnected. Furthermore, it is one that has great difficulty understanding the self as a gift. Constructing ourselves by choosing among and acting upon passive objects, we are particularly ill suited to understand ourselves as gift.

The commodity sourcing of our bodies is an obstacle to learning of our mutual dependence and interconnection from our embodiment. This, as much as any digital mediation, threatens to reduce our bodies to virtual realities. Indeed, it is striking how virtual our attempts to understand our connections must become. This is precisely what the environmental practice of "footprinting" aims to do: artificially reconstruct the context of our consumption. Since we lack any direct feedback regarding the scale of our consumption in relationship to the finite biotic area of the Earth, this process aims to construct that feedback virtually. These calculations require that one model and morally inflect one's conception of the whole, and catalogue and evaluate one's total impact on that whole.[18]

The terminology is striking. Our "footprint" far exceeds the ground seen or felt beneath our physical feet. We are forced to imagine it through an abstract reconstruction: a numerical figure of the acres of bioproductive land we require, the number of "Earths" that would be required for everyone to live as we do. An abstract proportion of an unimaginably large space stands in for the more direct knowledge of location and connection upon which humans have long based their actions. In the advanced capitalist nations, we no longer stand in the fields or see the herds from which we eat. Knowing the difference between the "enough" our bodies require, and the "too much" of our hyper-stimulated desires now requires this exercise in abstraction as much as attention to embodiment.

And so the long-delayed answer back to that conversation about liturgical PowerPoint: There is no safe refuge to be found in more embodied forms of liturgy. We bring global and abstract bodies to ancient liturgies conducted with oil, bread, and wine from God knows where (we certainly don't!).

Responding

There is a real danger here of falling into the "winner loses" paradox of critique.[19] By successfully portraying the protean power of the forces of false consciousness and domination, one runs the risk of rendering resistance impossible. At their best, however, such analyses have truly critical value in that they clarify the specific nature of the challenges we are facing. Rather than showing how commodification will always win in the end, the goal is to show precisely how commodification works, so we can best direct our efforts at resisting it. This often troubles some of our most ready-to-hand responses, showing them to be more implicated in the problem than we think. Thus, authenticity, spirituality, and as I have argued here, embodiment, are more tangled in consumer abstraction than we would like.

That does not mean, however, that they are compromised beyond usefulness. Rather it alerts us to the fact that the struggle is much closer to hand than we first imagined. Embodiment remains a valuable turn in sacramental theology. It is rooted in central doctrines and in the lived practice of the eucharistic liturgy and the other sacraments. This turn to corporeality has only become more important with the rise of new virtual spaces and the reinforcement of disembodied subjectivity by our formation in commodity consumption. The body, traditional liturgies, and sacraments are not, however, a land outside these erosions; a foothold amidst the flood. Indeed, they never were.[20] We should instead view them as pointers toward a fullness that we must work toward through the transformation of our imaginations and the structures and practices in which our imaginations are formed.

Seeing how the virtual haunts even our flesh can push us to develop a more fine-grained analysis of the problem. Here we return to Tomlinson's notion of "complex connectivity." We must attend to the particular sorts of connections in which we are insinuated, and attend to the specific ways in which they discipline us and the particular liberative possibilities they provide. Thus, rather than romanticizing flesh (even in suffering) as a bedrock contrast to the evanescence of the virtual, we need to develop criteria for an adequate Christian theology of embodiment. Such criteria would include finitude, vulnerability, interdependence, the ability to recognize grace/gift, openness to transcendence, and sanctification.

Such criteria can, in turn, help refine our engagements with globalization and the technologies that we lump together as the "virtual." What sorts of connections and relationships do they make possible, prefer, and prohibit? How do these mediations build upon, reinforce, replace, or undermine our relationships in shared space, face to face, and in more intimate forms of relationship?

I conclude with the central example in this essay: there is no shortage of awareness of our bodies. We are fascinated with our diets, but this does not necessarily convey to us our interdependence with the rest of the world. Likewise, we are often quite aware of, indeed haunted by, our finite fragility and vulnerability. However, absent a sense of our interconnectedness, these anxieties do not blossom into solidarity with others who, like us, are also vulnerable. Thus, our response to the challenge of global consumption must focus on cultivating awareness of these interconnections.

The church perennially struggles to accept the full consequences of the doctrines of creation, incarnation, and resurrection: that creatures in their finite particularity really matter. It struggled to accept this in a Greco-Roman philosophical horizon. It struggled in a different way in the hierarchical societies of the medieval world and the mass societies of modernity. The present moment presents yet the latest challenge to the central truths of the Christian faith. The response demanded of us is practical and ecclesial, not just intellectual. Our intellectual theological work can contribute by attending to the challenges of the particular relations in which globalization implicates us.

Notes

[1] John Tomlinson, *Globalization and Culture* (Chicago: University of Chicago Press, 1999), 5ff.

[2] Vincent J. Miller, *Consuming Religion: Christian Faith and Practice in a Consumer Culture* (New York: Continuum, 2004), 188-92.

[3] Susan Ross, *Extravagant Affections: A Feminist Sacramental Theology* (New York: Continuum, 1998), 98.

[4] Ibid., 227.

[5]Edward Schillebeeckx, *Christ, the Sacrament of the Encounter with God* (New York: Sheed and Ward, 1963), 42.

[6]Ibid., 199.

[7]Ibid., 198.

[8]Louis-Marie Chauvet, *Symbol and Sacrament: A Sacramental Reinterpretation of Christian Existence* (Collegeville, MN: Liturgical Press, 1995), 149-51.

[9]Ibid., 151.

[10]Ibid., 359-63.

[11]Ibid., 375.

[12]Ibid., 375-76.

[13]For two very different accounts of such mundane formation see the work of Michel Foucault, for example his *Discipline and Punish: The Birth of the Prison* (New York: Vintage, 1977), and Michel de Certeau, *The Practice of Everyday Life*, vol. 1 (Berkeley: University of California Press, 1984).

[14]Chauvet, *Symbol and Sacrament*, 106ff. For a use of the whole of Chauvet's sacramental theology to address the problems of consumerism and liturgy see Timothy Brunk, "Consumer Culture and the Body: Chauvet's Perspective," *Worship* 82 (July 2008): 290-310. See as well Timothy Gabrielli's essay in this volume "Chauvet in Space: Louis-Marie Chauvet's Sacramental Account of Christian Identity and the Challenges of a Global Consumer Culture."

[15]Thomas Princen, "Distancing: Consumption and the Severing of Feedback," in *Confronting Consumption*, ed. Thomas Princen, Michael Maniates, and Ken Conca (Cambridge: MIT Press, 2002), 116-17.

[16]Ibid., 117-18.

[17]Zygmunt Bauman, *Consuming Life* (Malden, MA: Polity Press, 2007), 16ff.

[18]Many simple footprint calculators are available on the Internet. For a more comprehensive example see Jim Merkel, *Radical Simplicity: Small Footprints on a Finite Earth* (Gabriola Island, BC: New Society Publishers, 2003).

[19]Fredric Jameson, *Postmodernism, or, The Cultural Logic of Later Capitalism* (Durham: Duke University Press, 1991), 5.

[20]It is important to avoid romantic nostalgia here. Our current global economic order is not simply the unrighteous usurper of a previous order of justice and transparency, but rather the latest successor in epochs of more or less exploitative social orders. The bread and wine of the eucharistic liturgy in Jesus' time, and more often than not since then, have been the products of profoundly unjust systems of production.

Formation(s) of the Mystical-Political in the Age of Globalization

Suffering as Agentive Choice in Dorothee Soelle and Talal Asad

Johann M. Vento

Dorothee Soelle begins her book *The Silent Cry: Mysticism and Resistance* with this quote from Jalal Al-Din Rumi: "Why, when God's world is so big, did you fall asleep in a prison, of all places?" and she returns to this image frequently throughout the book.[1] She uses it as shorthand for the human being, shut off from community, from joy, from beauty, from pain, from God. Near the end of the book, this image becomes her name for the current crisis in a chapter subheading, "The Prison We Have Fallen Asleep In: Globalization and Individualization."[2] *The Silent Cry* came out in 1997 in German, and undoubtedly much about globalization has changed in the ensuing thirteen years. This essay will not attempt an analysis of globalization; instead I assume as the context of this discussion the economic relations that structure our current global reality and the dominant position of privileged North Americans within these global relations. What I do consider is the possibility for comfortable, privileged Christians in the Northern Hemisphere to engage suffering, both their own and that of others, as a mystical-political practice of social relationship within our globalized context. I suggest that the "formations" (following Asad)[3] of suffering available to us are characterized by the avoidance of pain and the cultivation of numbness to suffering. The ability to wake up in this prison requires a process of formation based on the cultivation of openness to pain.

Political theology has long pointed to the ways in which avoidance of our own (private) suffering and our moral blindness to (public, political) suffering form and feed upon one another. We do indeed find ourselves, in our current age of global capitalism, poorly outfitted with privatized forms of Christian faith and anesthetized against suffering in ways that deny our fundamental (global) inter-subjectivity and the foundations of both our personal and communal well-being. Rumi's metaphor is indeed an apt one for our anesthetization. I will not be asking, with Rumi, why we fell asleep in this prison, but rather trying to describe what happens when we wake up in it.

Soelle describes the ever more efficient global market as an engine that

> runs on, driven by the coercion to produce more and confirmed by technological success of unimaginable proportions. And this engine is programmed for ever more speed, productivity, consumption, and profit, for about twenty percent of humankind. . . . Within this super-engine, human beings are not only "alienated" as Karl Marx observed, but they are also addicted and dependent as never before.[4]

If we are addicted and dependent (and anaesthetized) as never before—if we are formed to avoid suffering, our own and others, we might ask, what set of practices can form us differently—what can allow us to engage suffering? Political theology speaks of the mysticism of suffering, the lament to God in the face of unjust suffering. This essay seeks to be a meditation on that lament—to open up that moment, as it were—to reflect on it as in itself a formative practice of remaining present to suffering, of waking up in this prison in which we have fallen asleep.

I will discuss suffering and agency by reading together one of the founders of the new political theology, Dorothee Soelle, and the contemporary anthropologist of western secularism, Talal Asad. Drawing primarily on Asad's *Formations of the Secular* and Soelle's *The Silent Cry: Mysticism and Resistance* I will describe their ideas on suffering as agentive choice, suffering as formative of social relationships, and suffering and the formation of *habitus*. Reading Soelle with Asad illumines these aspects of Soelle's work related to suffering and agency and provides the basis for a conclusion on the implications of this discussion for the mysticism of suffering.

Suffering as Agentive Choice

In the second chapter of *Formations of the Secular*, entitled "Thinking about Agency and Pain," Talal Asad calls into question widespread related assumptions about agency and resistance in the field of anthropology and within secularism more broadly. He argues that: "A crucial point about pain . . . is that it enables the secular idea that 'history-making' and 'self-empowerment' can progressively replace pain by pleasure—or at any rate, by the search for what pleases one."[5] He questions the belief that pain is always "external to and repressive of the agent."[6] Asad maintains that there are a variety of ways in which agents engage suffering beyond resistance to it and, in particular, he is interested in "whether pain is not simply a *cause* of action, but can also itself be a *kind* of action."[7]

As an example of suffering as chosen, Asad cites religious ritual drama such as the stations of the cross or the Shiite Muharam processions marking the martyrdom of Hussain where "[p]artici-pants . . . enact, identify with, undergo the predetermined agony of figures in the Christian and Islamic narratives. In subjecting themselves to suffering (in some cases self-inflicted wounds) they seek in part to extend themselves as subjects."[8] Offering another religious example, he alludes to Methodist piety in eighteenth-century England in which agency is understood as self-surrender to the power of Christ's atonement as lived out in active tension with agency understood as self-mastery.[9] We will see below other examples that Asad offers of agentive pain in relationship.

Thus although Asad finds evidence for multiple conceptualiza-tions of agency, especially with regard to religion, he argues that in cultural theory, agency becomes reduced to "the metaphysical ideal of a conscious agent-subject having both the capacity and the desire to move in a singular historical direction: that of increasing self-empowerment and decreasing pain."[10] The common assump-tion that follows from this regarding pain is that one is either an agent or a victim. Asad argues that we tend to think of suffering as merely a passive state, as something that happens to us. It may become the cause of action to seek the end of suffering, but we do not think of pain as an action itself. On the contrary, Asad wants to argue that we can think of pain "not merely as a passive state (although it can be just that) but as itself agentive."[11]

Asad's ideas about suffering and agency find resonance in the work of Soelle. In her book *The Silent Cry*, Soelle wants to challenge the assumption that suffering is always only a passive and alienating experience: "Does not suffering always mean that I am exactly *not* what I do when other powers are doing something to or against me?"[12] As Soelle builds her argument about suffering as agentive choice, her critique is not only of secular modernity, as is Asad's, but also with other Christian conceptions of the choice to suffer. She therefore draws a sharp distinction between *compassio* and dolorousness, which she associates with the Christian tradition's "extreme, often pathological obsession with suffering . . . ," in order to distance her own position in the strongest terms from any suggestion of advocating a cult of suffering.[13]

Compassio and dolorousness each have their roots, she argues, in devotion to the crucified Christ that emerged in the High Middle Ages. For Soelle these two "mystical trends" form "a polarity of different, often overlapping ways of living one's life. . . ."[14] To illustrate dolorousness, Soelle recalls medieval ascetics who imposed on themselves practices such as lying on shattered glass, sleep deprivation, exposure to cold, extreme fasting, and self-flagellation. She calls the pursuit of ever greater suffering through extraordinary ascetical practices an addiction and sees it as entirely valueless:

> Such craving for suffering no longer distinguishes between fruitless, avoidable, and self-inflicted suffering and that which Paul accepted "for the body of Christ's sake," that is, for the sake of the community that suffered persecution in the Roman Empire. *Compassio* in this sense is not suffering that people bring upon themselves through unparalleled demands of asceticism. It arises with those who have to bear it. Dolorousness draped in mystical yearnings has nothing to be glossed over. It patently bears the marks of masochistic substitutionary satisfaction.[15]

The "mystical trend" that Soelle wants to extol is *compassio*, the choice to bear with innocent suffering or the choice not to flee from or become numb to the suffering of the other in solidarity. Throughout her treatment of suffering in *The Silent Cry*, to suffer in this way as choice, as practice, is put forward as an essential and formative aspect of mysticism. For Soelle, the choice to suffer in this way is related to the ability to love, to love God, and to love others through pain—to forgo numbness and to feel the pain that comes, to be present to it, and to love actively through it. For Soelle the suffering of God makes taking suffering on as an action within the life of discipleship possible:

> then suffering is not simply something bad to which one can surrender or stand up in resistance. It becomes instead a reality that has something to do with the far-near God and that fits into God's incomprehensible love. The way of suffering that is not just tolerated but freely accepted, the way of the passion, becomes therefore part of the disciples' way of life.[16]

Rather than a passive acceptance of fate, such acceptance of suffering becomes a way of encountering God as Love, "and thus the accepting person becomes a participating subject instead of remaining a mere object of the power of fate. Acceptance deprives icy meaninglessness of its power because it clings to God's warmth also in suffering."[17] Soelle emphasizes here that she does not impute to suffering itself any salvific significance, but rather that she sees the acceptance of *compassio* as an action, as a choice: acceptance of suffering "expresses the participation of humans who do not acquiesce but who, in mystical defiance, insist through their suffering that nothing become lost."[18]

Suffering as Formative of Social Relationships

Talal Asad argues against theorists who define pain as essentially a private experience that pain is also a "public relationship."[19] In this regard, he references Wittgenstein's work on "pain behavior" and Veena Das's work on Wittgenstein in her powerful writing on mass violence against women during the partition of India and Pakistan. Recalling Wittgenstein, Das notes that we should understand the sentence, "I am in pain," not as a propositional statement, giving us information, but rather, as a relational one, as one asking "for acknowledgement and recognition; denial of the other's pain is not about the failings of the intellect but the failings of the spirit."[20] For Asad, then, addressing the pain of the other is "not merely a matter of judging referential statements. It is about how a particular kind of relationship can be inhabited and enacted."[21]

Countering those who maintain that pain is essentially incommunicable and that there must always remain doubt about the pain of another, Asad argues that knowing and sharing the pain of the other is often possible in lived relationships. He uses here examples such as a mother who suffers because her child is wounded and a rape survivor whose healing process depends in part on others' hearing, understanding, and feeling outraged with her about her violation: "The person who suffers because of another's pain doesn't first assess the evidence presented to her and then decide on whether and how to react. She lives a relationship."[22] Pain in these cases is not private and is not experienced only as something to be escaped for the sake of pleasure, rather, it is "an active, practical relationship inhabiting time."[23]

Another example that Asad uses to drive home this point is the pain a woman experiences during childbirth. In particular, he is discussing a study of a group of religious women in North America who prefer un-medicated home birthing and for whom the pain of childbirth takes on an empowering function. Here again, pain establishes relationship, and while it may be escaped, and while the woman is every bit a mother to the child if her pain is medicated during delivery, the point Asad makes in bringing up this example is that in particular situations when pain is a natural part of the birthing process "it is not simply the negative experience of a patient, as biomedicine tends to regard it, but an aspect of a distinctive social act. . . ."[24]

Asad emphasizes that he is not trying to argue that pain in and of itself is "a valuable thing" or that people should not seek to change conditions that cause pain, but rather that the ways persons engage pain are "modes of living a relationship" and that "[t]he ability to live such relationships over time transforms pain from a passive experience into an active one, and thus defines one of the ways of living sanely in the world."[25] Noting that ideas about sanity differ through time, he argues that the progressivist, secular way of understanding pain as merely passively experienced and agency as always seeking to escape pain prevents us from seeing other modes of living out pain as relationship.

Moreover, Asad argues that pain can be felt between and among people: "The secular emphasis on the integral human body as the locus of moral sovereignty makes it difficult to grasp the ideas of pain as an imagined relationship in which such 'internal' states as memory and hope mediate sociality."[26] Asad wants to emphasize that while pain is certainly felt differently by the person primarily injured than by the person who suffers because of the pain of the other, sufferers are social persons and that "their suffering is partly constituted by the way they inhabit, or are constrained to inhabit, their relationships with others."[27] The pain itself, in a very practical, concrete way, is a vital part of what establishes and/or maintains relationship.

Soelle, the theologian, speaks of suffering as arising out of relationship with God and with suffering others. Describing the pain one feels because of the suffering of others as an experience of the absence of God, she writes, "Mystical love for God makes us open to God's absence: the senseless, spiritless suffering that separates humans from all that makes for life. The privation and eclipse of God ought at least to be felt and suffered. The nausea caused by this world of injustice and violence ought at least to be perceptible. . . ."[28]

Soelle notes that for John of the Cross "the suffering for the neighbor grows the more as the soul unites itself through love with God."[29] Maintaining that this kind of suffering is not imposed from without or chosen for the sake of attaining a certain mystical state, she emphasizes that it "arises from a relationship to the world that is not immersed in the I alone."[30] This aspect of agentive choice bears echoes of pain as an action within a relationship, as Asad describes it, and it is clear that this pain is an integral part of lived relationship: "in its anguish about unliberated life, it is drawn into suffering . . . the voluntary element here [is] the risk contained in every partiality for the victims of history and every commitment to the cause of the losers."[31]

Soelle unpacks the poet Reinhold Schneider's statement that the choice before everyone who encounters suffering is either agony or numbness or, in her words, either *compassio* or apathy. She sees this as a conflict

> between the avoidance of suffering, not-having-seen and not-wanting-to-see anything, and seeking to protect oneself with the diverse and increasingly improving means of numbing, on the one hand; and the preferential option for victims wherein people voluntarily enter into the pain of others, and, in the extreme case, choose the pain of death, on the other.[32]

Clearly for Soelle, *compassio* is a mystical act, and first and foremost it enacts and deepens a relationship with God. But what the foreground set by the reading of Asad helps to make clear is that *compassio* as Soelle conceives it is at the same time constitutive of social relationship. As a lived response to the suffering of the other, even when it is only a lament, even when it is, as Asad says, part of an "imagined relationship" consisting of "memory and hope," sociality is mediated. This helps us to begin to see the mysticism of suffering not only as an action, but one that forms and maintains relationship across space and time.

Suffering and *Habitus*

I will turn now to Asad's discussion of *habitus* in order to explore the idea of agentive suffering over time as formative of a disposition and to propose that a reading of Asad and Soelle together on this point suggests that we can think of the mysticism of suffering as an ongoing practice of formation.

In his various discussions of pain and agency in both *Genealogies of Religion* and *Formations of the Secular*, Asad draws on the concept of *habitus*,[33] primarily as it is formulated by French sociologist and anthropologist Marcel Mauss, as "an embodied capacity that is more than physical ability in that it also includes cultivated sensibilities and passions, an orchestration of the senses."[34] Asad is interested in how persons may intentionally cultivate certain dispositions through a program of discipline of the body and emotions.

He enlists his argument about pain as agentive choice in his discussion of the ability of the body to be trained as part of a program of formation:

Although the living body is the object of sensations (and in that sense passive) its ability to suffer, to respond perceptually and emotionally to external and internal causes, to use its own pain in unique ways in particular social relationships, makes it active. Many traditions therefore attribute to the living human body the potential to be shaped (the power to shape itself) for good or ill.[35]

Asad argues that through his use of the concept of *habitus*, Mauss was developing "an anthropology of practical reason—not in the Kantian sense of universalizable ethical rules, but in that of historically constituted practical knowledge, which articulates an individual's learned capacities."[36] Mauss saw the human body not as incidental to culture or its passive recipient, but rather "as the developable means for achieving a range of human objectives, from styles of physical movement (e.g., walking), through modes of emotional being (e.g., composure), to kinds of spiritual experiences (e.g., mystical states)."[37]

Asad is particularly interested in Mauss's references to mysticism at the end of an essay where, referring to Taoist body techniques, Mauss suggests that body techniques are at the basis of all mystical states and that "there are necessarily biological means for entering into 'communion with God.' "[38] For Asad, Mauss's work on the role of body training in the formation of various forms of practical knowledge, especially mystical experience, suggests that "embodied practices (including language in use) form a precondition for varieties of religious experience. The inability to enter into communion with God becomes a function of untaught bodies."[39]

Soelle does not use the term *habitus*; however, I find significant echoes of the way that Asad uses the term in her work. In the way that Soelle describes living out the mysticism of suffering, I read intimations of what Asad understands as *habitus*, in particular in its embodied and formative aspects.

In a paradoxical way, Soelle speaks of unjust suffering as the experience of the absence of God, but, at the same time, the acceptance of that suffering as a locus of the encounter in mystical union with the God who suffers with us.[40] She defines *compassio* first and foremost as "suffering with the crucified Christ" and all those who continue to suffer unjustly.[41] For Soelle this is not a series of isolated events but a way of suffering, "a way of the passion [that] becomes therefore part of the disciple's way of life."[42]

Soelle describes various practices that embody *compassio*, such as protest, intercessory prayer, and boycotting. She offers these examples not as ethical choices in response to suffering so much as the choice to "do" suffering in a particular way. Quoting a South African anti-apartheid activist on prayer, Soelle offers this: "I suddenly realized that praying was important for me, that I needed it. Not as a retreat from (dreadful) reality but much more as a time of holding still to face that reality in its horror and beauty, face it as a part of it, but also experience at the same time that it is not the last word."[43] The acceptance of suffering, suffering with Christ, and suffering with the victims of injustice are the ongoing embodied practices of the Christian life as Soelle conceives of it that form the *habitus* of the mysticism of suffering.

The Mysticism of Suffering as Spiritual Formation in the Age of Globalization

A mystical-political practice of suffering defies the etiquette of social relationships established through global capitalism whereby some pain is anesthetized and some pain is imposed, ignored, or justified, by turn. What are the forms that this embodied practice demonstrates? Perhaps they are not so different from the practices common to relationships, to the spiritual life, and the life of activism: crying, hugging, keening, and other forms of mourning and lament, prayer, meditation, song, dance, marches, sit-ins—but all understood as ways of "doing" pain, of refusing to be anaesthetized.

Reading Asad and Soelle together amplifies the fact that the mysticism of suffering forms and maintains social relationships. It is not a hopeless feeling sorry for oneself, nor an addiction to suffering for its own sake, nor an acceptance of injustice. As an openness to the pain caused by injustice and, in particular, to the pain caused by our own position within global economic relations, it is the outcome of relationship. Connection is made, whether imaginatively in prayer or physically in weeping or marching alongside others. I am not conflating the mysticism of suffering with activism necessarily. Although the mysticism of suffering may manifest itself in activism at times, it may manifest itself in a multitude of other ways as well. It might be a cry to God, an aching heart, a silent presence with a victim or a poem of outrage. Soelle's treatment, informed by a reading of Asad, suggests that such actions constitute relationship in their own way. For Soelle, they form ever deeper connection with the suffering God and with others at the same time. It is this mystical move, for her, that is the act of resistance. The encounter with the suffering God of those who suffer with others enfolds all—victims and co-sufferers—with God in a relationship that denies the final word to injustice.

The work of Asad and Soelle suggests that the mysticism of suffering is a process of formation, part of the formation of one's *habitus*, one's way of being in the world. As Soelle describes it, it is a "way of suffering," not isolated cries but an ongoing mystical practice of openness to pain and acceptance of suffering in a life of resistance to injustice. In the prison in which we sleep, the global market gets to decide who suffers and who gets to remain anaesthetized.

The wisdom of political theology suggests we, North American Christians in positions of privilege, are addicted to numbness—to isolating ourselves from the pain of the other in our global economic relations. Surely in our current age of globalization, we have ever new ways of doing so. Indeed, it is in the interest of those who want us to keep consuming in such proportions that we continue to do so.

Waking up is a choice to be present to pain. Knowing about the pain of the other is not enough for most of us to wake up in this prison. Global capitalism is too crafty a warden and our stupor is too powerful. Soelle refers to the impotence of knowledge to fuel change among the comfortable and insists that only a "long-term praxis that is learned" by acts of resistance themselves can change us.[44] We wake up in this prison, and are kept awake, by a sustained openness to relationship with the other that is also open to living pain and remaining present to it. This is more than a cognitive exercise. It is more than choosing from among a set of actions in any one given moment. It is a mysticism of suffering as *habitus*, a way of living, formed over time by embodied practice, out of which our own pain and the pain of the other are taken on as actions of love, discipleship, and resistance.

Notes

[1]Dorothee Soelle, *The Silent Cry: Mysticism and Resistance* (Minneapolis: Fortress Press, 2001), 1.

[2]Ibid., 191.

[3]Talal Asad, *Formations of the Secular: Christianity, Islam, Modernity* (Stanford: Stanford University Press, 2003).

[4]Ibid.

[5]Ibid., 68. Asad argues that attributing an essential agency to the human person and defining that agency as the "responsibility to power" was related to emerging property law in early capitalism and to defining persons as objects of social discipline in the modern nation state (74).

[6]Ibid., 71.

[7]Ibid., 69.

[8]Ibid., 78.

[9]Ibid.

[10]Ibid., 79.

[11]Ibid.

[12]Soelle, *The Silent Cry*, 137.

[13]Ibid., 138.

[14]Ibid., 139.

[15]A comparison with Asad here is interesting, because in an earlier work, *Genealogies of Religion: Discipline and Reasons of Power in Christianity and Islam* (Baltimore and London: The Johns Hopkins University Press, 1993), Asad discusses certain practices of mortification among medieval Christian monks, including physical mortification, as part of a program of forming in themselves certain desired dispositions, most importantly the will to obey what is considered to be the truth (see Asad, *Genealogies of Religion*, 133). He neither condemns nor praises these practices nor tries to distinguish between less and more extreme forms of them in terms of their value or saneness, as does Soelle. For the purposes of his argument, such practices fit into a larger program, logically consistent with medieval monastic Christian thought about the power and pervasiveness of sin and the possibility and nature of virtue formation within believers. For him, that the practitioners themselves understood these practices as part of a program that would form in themselves indispensable Christian virtues is enough to make his point: in that context, given the prevailing understandings of sin and virtue formation, the character of social life, and the structuring of self-understandings, these practices of humiliation were the acts of agents. Since relations among religious authority, ritual, and self-understanding are different in different times and

places, he argues that how and why they change continue to be the subject of anthropological study (see Asad, *Genealogies of Religion*, 167).

[16]Ibid.

[17]Ibid., 149.

[18]Ibid.

[19]Asad, *Formations of the Secular*, 81. Asad references Ludwig Wittgenstein, *Philosophical Investigations* (Oxford: Blackwell, 1953), 100.

[20]Ibid., 82, n. 31, quoting Veena Das, "Language and Body: Transactions in the Construction of Pain," in *Social Suffering*, ed. Arthur Kleinman, Veena Das, and Margaret Lock (Berkeley: University of California Press, 1997), 88.

[21]Ibid.

[22]Ibid., 82.

[23]Ibid., 83.

[24]Ibid., 88.

[25]Ibid., 84.

[26]Ibid.

[27]Ibid., 85.

[28]Soelle, *The Silent Cry*, 140.

[29]Ibid.

[30]Ibid.

[31]Ibid.

[32]Ibid., 150.

[33]Asad notes the Aristotelian and medieval Christian heritage of this term. See Asad, *Formations of the Secular*, 251. He alludes to Pierre Bourdieu's later work on *habitus*, faulting him for not acknowledging Mauss's use of the term. See Asad, *Genealogies of Religion*, 75, n.20. Asad's understanding of *habitus* remains much closer to that of Mauss, defined here as the intentional formation of certain dispositions, rather than Bourdieu's development of the concept of *habitus* as inculcated in the person by social forces outside of one's control. See Pierre Bourdieu, *Outline of a Theory of Practice* (Cambridge: Cambridge University Press, 1993), 76-78.

[34]Asad, *Formations of the Secular*, 95.

[35]Ibid., 89.

[36]Asad, *Genealogies of Religion*, 76.

[37]Ibid.

[38]Ibid. Asad is referring to Marcel Mauss, "Body Techniques," in Marcel Mauss, *Sociology and Psychology: Essays*, ed. and trans. B. Brewster (London: Routledge and Kegan Paul, 1979).

[39]Ibid., 76-77.

[40]Soelle, *The Silent Cry*, 138.

[41]Ibid., 141.

[42]Ibid., 138.

[43]Ibid., 206.

[44]Ibid., 204.

Chauvet in Space

Louis-Marie Chauvet's Sacramental Account of Christian Identity and the Challenges of a Global Consumer Culture[1]

Timothy R. Gabrielli

Contemporary studies of globalization argue that its dynamics encourage the projection of identities devoid of the depth of tradition necessary to maintain a complex identity.[2] The literature illustrates that in addition to homogenization, in which particular cultures are replaced by a global one, globalizing forces also cause heterogenization and deterritorialization; that is, they facilitate difference, while detaching community and culture from geographical space.[3] If these studies are correct, the plethora of questions about what makes Christians Christian is part of the scramble initiated by these global dynamics, which encourage a narrowly defined, niche identity. Disconnected from geography, identity becomes something sought after and constructed piecemeal, rather than inherited and assumed.

Further, these spatial structures, as Vincent Miller has argued, make the maintenance of narrow identity an overriding religious concern. The identities constructed therein lack both the depth of engagement with an extended tradition and the room for legitimate disagreement characteristic of a complex identity. Practices of dialogue and reasoned argument are not necessary when communities become mere "enclaves of the like-minded," fronts for the cultivation of a narrow identity.[4] Miller has succinctly stated the problem for Christian theology: "The church must engage a situation that demands clear identities without allowing itself to be reduced to a mere identity front."[5] That is, the church must find a way to conceptualize, embody, and nurture Christian identity in a more substantive way than that demanded by contemporary spatial configurations.

The far-reaching work of sacramental theologian Louis-Marie Chauvet offers a wealth of resources for conceptualizing Christian identity in a complex way. Chauvet has received much scholarly attention since the publication of *Symbole et sacrement*, his 1987 effort at a *"sacramental reinterpretation . . . of what it means to lead a Christian life."*[6] Initially, much of the acclaim was centered in his native Europe.[7] Chauvet is a parish priest in the diocese of Pantoise and a professor emeritus of theology at the Institut Catholique of Paris. More recently, especially after the 2001 translation of *The Sacraments*, his work has received greater consideration on this side of the Atlantic. Since, as Chauvet claims, sacramental theology is a dimension that runs through the entire theological enterprise, rather than a specific subdivision of it, the implications of his work have been explored across theological disciplines.[8]

At the beginning of the earlier work, Chauvet mentions that a certain clamoring for the "marks" (or principal pillars) of Christian identity in France was one of the promptings for undertaking that project. He identifies scripture, sacrament, and ethics as the three "marks" proper to Christian identity and explores the relationship among them throughout the rest of the book. Of course, concerns about Catholic identity are not limited to France. In the United States, universities and hospitals have been particular loci of the concretization of the identity question.[9] And, if studies of globalization are correct, the pressing question of identity is embedded in global spatial constructions themselves.

While Chauvet would readily admit that the church does not function in a vacuum, the contours of his project do not lead him to engage specifically with globalization. In what follows, I will attempt to "place" Chauvet's account of Christian identity in today's globalized space. First, I will explicate some of the elements of Chauvet's project that make his account of identity rich and complex, including his symbolic turn and his emphasis on corporeality and gift. Second, I will identify some of the challenges posed to Chauvet's account by analyses of our globalized context. Third, I will point to some of the resources in Chauvet's own work with potential to respond to the challenges of living a complex identity in globalized space.

Chauvet's Turn to the Symbolic

In order to explicate Chauvet's account of identity from within his sacramental theology we must first consider two important aspects of his work that reveal his emphasis on Christian identity as corporeal and as gift: his critique of scholastic sacramental theology and resulting turn to the symbolic, and his notion of symbolic exchange.

Part of the difficulty with scholastic approaches to the sacraments, argues Chauvet, is their productionist discourse about grace, which renders it a "thing," an "object" to be produced, gotten, and augmented.[10] In this mode, humans can only stand externally to God, as takers of some object from God. Relationships among people and between people and God can only be conceived in the "technical model of cause and effect."[11] Therefore, he posited that the nature of grace requires another approach, a *"discourse from which the believing subject is inseparable,"*[12] a symbolic one where body is primordial and language is central.

Chauvet finds the symbolic order more fruitful because it can more aptly discuss grace as constitutive of a *relationship* involving subjects situated in life. By the symbolic order, Chauvet understands

> the system of connections between the different elements and levels of a culture (economic, social, political, ideological—ethics, philosophy, religion . . .), a system forming a coherent whole that allows the social group and individuals to orient themselves in space, find their place in time, and in general situate themselves in the world in a significant way—in short, to find their identity in a world that makes "sense."[13]

The theologian who takes the symbolic order as a point of departure moves to answer the question "Who is God?" from the concrete life of the Christian community, beginning with the New Testament witnesses.

If theology begins with the New Testament, then, according to Chauvet, the specific starting point is the cross.[14] The folly of the cross is that we always-already stand in a relationship of mediation. Jesus of Nazareth, the "body of God" in humanity, was situated in a time and place. Those who "pledge allegiance" to him owe him a human body in this time and place. Therefore, the "body of God" in humanity also has a reality in the church, Christ's primary mediator. The sacraments are "the most distinctive representations" of the church and continually and constantly "force us to confront *mediation* . . . by way of the senses." The link between the body and the soul runs so deep that it cannot be any other way for us in this life. "And so we find ourselves in the end sent back to the *body* as the point where God writes God's self in us."[15]

The symbolic order is characterized by symbolic exchange, which is a second building block of Chauvet's thought, rather than the market exchange characteristic of the order of production. Symbolic exchange involves the exchange, not of things, but of subjects themselves; as such, it is the process by which subjects come to be subjects in the symbolic order.[16]

Chauvet draws upon sociologist Marcel Mauss (1872-1950) to elaborate the contrast between symbolic exchange and market exchange.[17] Mauss studies "archaic societies" (such as Samoa and Melanesia) and ancient Rome, finding operative there a form of gift economy. Chauvet explains that in the cultures that Mauss studies symbolic exchange is a "total social fact" in that it is operative across social strata and in all manner of exchange from smiles to wives to goods.[18] One cannot turn down hospitality, food, jewels, and so on, and upon reception of the gift, one is obliged to offer a return-gift, not to the giver, but to a third party. This manner of exchange, given the oxymoronic name "obligatory generosity," is not the *quid pro quo* of the market because the primary "interest" in the gifting cycle is not object-driven, but relational: "*to be recognized as a subject*, not to lose face, not to fall from one's social rank, and consequently to compete for prestige."[19] From the order of production, in which "equivalence" reigns (lend/borrow, buy/sell, give/take), the extravagant gift exchange appears silly.[20] Impoverished people gift others with kingly extravagance because the symbolic order demands it of them in order to be recognized as subjects.

The insight of Mauss is not simply an historical one, but also an anthropological one: it tells us something about how human beings work, how they become subjects, and how they live within the symbolic order. The structure of symbolic exchange is ternary (gift-reception-return gift), whereas market exchange is binary (product-value). Gift-giving includes a moment of "reception" in which the gift is received *as gift* and not as anything else. This moment is irrelevant in market exchange because it involves merely the exchange of things. In symbolic exchange, subjects exchange each other through the object. The gift works as symbol.[21]

Thinking about grace primarily in the mode of symbolic exchange situates it as "non-thing" from the start.[22] As non-value, grace is both gratuitous and gracious. Grace is gratuitous, not merited, earned, or deserved in any fashion. It is gracious, that is, it does not work in the mode of production, but is given "free of charge."[23] Nevertheless, symbolic exchange necessitates a response, for without a response the subject is turned merely into an object, devoid of any recognition as "other." If God's grace has been received *as* grace and not as anything else, the receiver will respond to it with love, not by evaluation or measurement.[24] Since, in the Chauvet-Mauss model, gifts make us persons and relate subjects to other subjects, in the gift exchange of grace Christians become Christians via their relationship to God.[25] Christians do not precede God's grace, but rather proceed from it in the gradual coming to be "of their identities as children-for-God and as brothers-and-sisters-for-others in Christ."[26] As such our selves are received from a gift that pre-exists us.[27]

Exegeting the resurrection appearances in the gospels, Chauvet draws attention to the tripartite structure of each: an appearance of Christ (a gift of grace), the recognition of the glorified Christ as the same person as the one who was crucified, and a missionary component. The last two components together teach us that the reception of the gift of good news cannot occur without the return gift of Christian witness.[28] Affirming grace as gift necessitates our reception of ourselves and our response in *caritas*.[29] Chauvet's turn to the symbolic and his attendant emphasis on mediation and gift result in an account of identity that undercuts a simple production and projection of identities.

Identity in Chauvet's Schema

Identity, for Chauvet, only makes sense in the wider complex reality of a symbolic order. Therefore, identity is always mediated and caught up in the gift exchange that characterizes the symbolic order. One cannot call Jesus "Lord," an indispensable confession for Christian identity, Chauvet maintains, without necessarily being taken up into the symbolic order of the church. Thus, "Christian identity is not self-administered." One must receive baptism.[30] This does not mean that identity does not have a personal dimension, but it must, in some measure, follow a common ecclesial pattern. In other words, identity is corporate. The sacraments are the agents of identity because ritual gesture and word are the acts of the ecclesial body constitutive of the symbolic order of the church.

In the church, subjects are unendingly transformed into believing subjects. Thus, Christian identity is never complete. It, too, is mediated. Because there is a measure of absence in one's possession of Christian identity, there is never a point where a Christian can say, "I have it. I am now fully a Christian and understand all of the implications of that identifier."

In the sacramental rites, Christian identity is continually inscribed on bodies. We recall here Chauvet's demand that the "folly of the cross" be central to the symbolic turn. Expressed in the sacraments symbolically, the cross represents the corporeality of Christian faith. Performed ritually, these inscriptions make Christians "a people set apart." Chauvet writes, "By inscribing symbolically the marks of the Church's identity on the body of each person, rituals testify to the Christian difference."[31]

Corporeality, in the context of Chauvet's work, works directly in opposition to the temptation to construe the ontological difference between God and creation as negative, as obstructing a supposed more direct relationship.[32] Chauvet's symbolic turn aims at rendering it more positive. This symbolic approach also includes a positive reading of absence. Since all encounters with God, at least in this life, are mediated, there can be no such thing as a raw encounter with presence, so any encounter with God is also an encounter with God's absence. This is not bad news, but rather the good news of the incarnation. The Eucharist, as mediation par excellence, makes this most clear. Chauvet writes:

> As a symbol, the Eucharist *radicalizes the absence* of the Risen One: why would I celebrate it if I were able to be in immediate possession of him? To celebrate the Eucharist is precisely—contrary to all illuminisms of the Gnostic sort—to consent to this absence; or, rather, to learn little by little to consent to this absence. . . . Putting to death in us the mortal dream of an immediate presence of Christ—mortal, for such a presence can only be suffocating—the eucharistic symbol opens up an emptiness, a *space where God can come to be* in the very heart of our corporeity, *without destroying us* or diminishing our autonomy and our responsibility as humans. . . .[33]

Just as there is no pure, primitive Christianity to which one can appeal because of the necessity of mediation, so too there is no "core" Christian identity. To take on a Christian identity is a complex and difficult task fraught with paradox. On the one hand, to be Christian is to be part of the church and thus to enter into a defined group. The temptation is to recoil into that particularity, to become insular. On the other hand, to make a confession of Christ as Lord is also to open oneself to the universal, the entire kingdom of God. The temptation here is that the church so bursts open that it can no longer serve as sacrament of the kingdom. The paradox is that the church is never more itself, never more faithful to its particular marks, than when it opens to the universal, to the kingdom which grows in the world, through the particular.[34] Therefore, Christian identity betrays itself if it is not, in some sense, open-ended. Attempts to narrow that identity to a mere sign or to a "thing" that is self-selected and easily achieved, as global spatial structures seem to demand, are rendered wrongheaded by Chauvet's account.

Chauvet also understands identity as gift. In his structure, where sacrament works as a bridge between scripture and ethics, sacraments symbolically connect the letter to the body. The "mark" of "Scripture" in Chauvet's model "encompasses everything that concerns the *understanding of the faith*" from catechesis to theology because all of these comment on scripture.[35] The sacraments in their rituality "tell us that to become a believer is to learn to consent, without resentment, to the corporality of the faith."[36] Therefore, the move in the sacraments is from knowledge of the faith to its recognition, to its being seen *as faith*, as gift shot through with absence. Christian identity, then, is not asserted but rather constantly received as gift from God, mediated by the church. While individuals have religious feelings, theological ideas, and so on, these are not what motivate action in liturgical ritual. "Here the self is put at the disposal of the Other whom it can let act in the Church's mediation. The self lets the Other act by performing a gesture which is not from itself, by saying words which are not its own, by receiving elements which it has not chosen."[37]

Chauvet finds this corporeality at the center of the Eucharist. Because one is not participating in one's own actions or expressing one's own religious feelings in the church's ritual, even if one's deepest convictions seem to be floating away and the very idea that perhaps there is no God runs through one's body, the Eucharist remains. Indeed, "what else remains for them but their bodies taking in hand what the Church takes up—a little bread and wine—and saying what the Church says—'my body given for you'—taking and saying these as the gestures and words of him whom the Church confesses as its Lord?"[38] The bodily, and deeply symbolic, act of chewing on the Body of Christ, this rumination on the supreme folly of the cross, counteracts our temptation to make faith merely human wisdom.[39]

The specificity of the Eucharistic sacrifice—it is Jesus Christ, Word made flesh, on which we chew—precludes any generalized, vacuous ethic. Christians favor ethical action, not because that is the essence of all religion, but rather because in Christian action Christ is once again made known to his people.[40] In the Eucharistic celebration the paschal mystery is anamnesized. We are placed in touch, if only through a dark glass, with the eschaton. God wants to be alive, to assume flesh in the world. The Eucharist impels Christians toward concrete ethical action, that is, being Christ, loving as Christ loved, for the sake of the world.

To be a Christian, then, is to be caught up in this gift exchange that demands one's whole life as response, that makes Christians into Christ in the world. In our globalized world, we are encouraged to construct our own identities, oftentimes piecemeal. Chauvet emphasizes that identities are not merely asserted by individuals, but also received in the gift exchange of the symbolic order.

Chauvet in Space: Challenges to Chauvet's Account of Identity

With the structure of Christian identity constituted by the marks of scripture, sacrament, and ethics, Chauvet has articulated something greater than a shallow cultural practice of projecting a niche identity. By placing this structure of identity within the framework of gift exchange and situating it firmly within the corporeality that marks our human existence, Chauvet has both further enlightened and complexified the picture. Nevertheless, bringing Chauvet's sacramental account of identity consciously to bear on the question of forming identities among U.S. Catholics in our contemporary globalized world presents some problems.

Chauvet's articulation of identity implies that becoming Christian is not simply overlaid on becoming human; it is rather a coextensive and continuous process that makes Christians particular *kinds* of human beings: those who receive Christ in word and sacrament and go to be *alter Christi* in the world. There is a continuing dialectic between identity as a Christian and identity as a human being.[41] To take Chauvet seriously, then, one must attend to the wider context in which human beings become human and Christians become Christian. Christians are made into Christians not only in the imperfect symbolic order of the church (the relevant symbolic order for Christian identity),[42] but in the messy stuff of late modern global capitalism.[43]

Danièle Hervieu-Léger, in her sociological study of religion in this messiness, explains that the rapid change of modern life crumbles any collective sense of memory, thereby undermining the structures of religious institutions and creating new forms of religious belief that are often more individualized.[44] It is not surprising that in a commodified context, where our habits are shaped in abstraction by constantly engaging end products apart from their complex coming-to-be, we have difficulty entering into the deep memory of tradition.[45]

These individualized forms of religious identity are self-constructed in concert with multiple other political, economic, cultural, and social factors. When appropriated by an individual to her own end, religious traditions "function as [a] stock of symbols, capable of being mobilized especially when the secular projections of historical fulfilment [sic] (modernist ideologies of progress, in their several variants) are called into question."[46] The coherence of a religious tradition is brought into a space where individuals "construct meaning" on their own, looking only for a type of social confirmation from a group.[47] When this happens, the whole enterprise of deep identity is defeated because modernity creates a desire for tradition *on our own terms*, rendering participation in a thick non-voluntarist tradition impossible.

Witness, as an example, the linguistic slide in the word "confirm" in the Catholic sacrament of confirmation. In the early church, the agent of this "confirm" was Christ and later the bishop or the sacrament itself, who or which "confirmed" baptism.[48] Beginning about thirty years ago, the subject of "confirm" became the confirmandi themselves, who confirm their own baptism or faith.[49] Such a change in usage reflects, among other things, an emphasis on the individual's own construction of identity, verified by the church.

Moreover, the context described by Hervieu-Léger complicates the primacy of the church as the symbolic order in which Christian identity is formed and points to the perils and challenges of forming Christians in the contemporary context. Rather than obtaining across the strata of a relatively circumscribed society, the exchange of subjectivities is a challenging enterprise in globalized culture. This is made even clearer when we consider the factors of commodification and deterritorialization. While a globalized culture does not challenge the validity of Chauvet's theology of grace, it nevertheless requires some pause in its application to understanding Christian identity.

Chauvet's account of identity is dependent upon his account of symbolic exchange, best understood in the cycle of gift-reception-return gift, as articulated by Marcel Mauss. For Mauss, symbolic exchange is a "total social fact": material exchange constitutes sociality, which trumps any objective value of the goods themselves.[50] However, it might be said that in our contemporary context, commodification, rather than symbolic exchange, is the "total social fact." Commodity exchange impinges upon how we conceive of relationships, even beyond the marketplace. Steeped in commodification, we evaluate relationships in terms of an economic calculation. Families become mini corporations.[51] Friendships are conceived in terms of assets and liabilities.[52] Religious forms, symbols, and practices are constantly torn from their traditional context and laid in the marketplace for consumption.[53]

Ulrich Beck notes that "Cosmopolitanism has itself become a commodity; the glitter of cultural difference sells well."[54] Consumers are numbed to actual, concrete encounters with "the other" by an endless parade of false images, such as the aged Latina posted on the walls of Starbucks stirring *dulce de leche* in a pot on her stove. The problem is not simply that the average Starbucks patron does not know this woman, or that she has not actually made what they are drinking, but that the image itself romanticizes a quickly eroding reality. As Starbucks stores grow exponentially, more and more people come to taste *dulce de leche* only in Starbucks cups. And, of course, it is not actual *dulce*. As anyone who has watched a young barista serve up one of these lattes knows, the flavor comes not from thick, reduced sweetened milk, but from a pumped syrup. The depth of culture that one encounters in drinking *dulce de leche*-flavored beverages comes with the cosmopolitan mélange of both "frappuccino" blenders and Grammy-winning music of *The Chieftains*—the Irish folk musicians known for producing albums without borders—roaring in the background. Like in Chauvet's analysis of market exchange, the moment of receiving identity as *gift* and not as anything else is undercut. Indeed what is received in global consumer culture is rather like a "Lego set" of commodity-images with the potential of building one's own "patchwork" identity.[55]

We cannot maintain, in light of the pervasiveness of commodification, that the anthropological insights of Mauss hold *tout court*. Rather, it seems that we must work hard to re-imagine and practice relationships in terms of an exchange of subjectivities.[56] Gift exchange occurs, if it all, in pockets of direct resistance to the assumptions of the dominant culture of commodification.[57]

But Beck's sense that cultural difference "sells well" highlights a further complication. In our consumer culture, social groups appropriate commodities as markers of what Pierre Bourdieu called "distinction."[58] That is, certain cultural practices, such as knowing not to clap between movements of a symphony, identify those of one social group over another. This is somewhat reminiscent of Chauvet's account of gift exchange: though stratified, social groups allow for the coming-to-be of subjects in that social group by a gift-cycle centered on these practices.

Further, though, culture is constituted by the interplay of these social groups undercutting and maintaining distinction by employing particular identity markers. In the context of a highly attuned economic marketing apparatus, these identities are attractive for exploitation in the marketplace. They fit right into the ongoing need for new niche markets and the critical subcultures struggle to keep up. People's desire for deep agency is manifest here, though consumer culture only provides a carefully marketed set of building blocks.

Finally, the analogy to grace that Chauvet works hard to establish does not in fact come easily to those shaped and formed in consumer culture. It is, for the most part, a foreign mode of exchange. Further complicating the landscape is the voluntarism undergirding symbolic exchange in the contemporary context, in contrast to the "obligatory generosity" operative in the cultures studied by Mauss. While there are multiple philosophical and political factors contributing to voluntarism, "deterritorialization" contributes in a profound way as it dissolves the natural relation between geography and culture, rendering cultures voluntary from within.[59]

Cuisine is one of the most illustrative examples. The geography of Britain, for example, was largely determinative of "British cuisine"—pot roast, fish and chips, and so on.[60] In the machinery of global capitalism, British cuisine becomes a distinct entity from the geographical space in which it developed; it can be exported and eaten around the world. The same disjuncture and exportation, of course, happens to other cuisines. Therefore, deterritorialized eating is thoroughly voluntaristic. The seasons are no longer providers of specific foods. If one wants strawberries, one can choose to buy them from a warmer climate year-round. Fish is flown to landlocked locales before the sun sets on the day it was caught. National cuisines become more kitsch than necessity. On can still eat "British" in Britain by choosing fish and chips or roast beef, but it can be nothing other than a choice, for *bucatini all'amatriciana*, a *hamachi* roll, or a Big Mac are all available within a few miles' drive.

When culture is separated from territory, persons form their own particular networks of relationships from around the world, prescinding from numerous previously mandated geographical relationships in which the practices of argument and dialogue with others are cultivated.[61] In cultures where a gift economy is a "total social fact," persons are forced to develop relationships with those in geographical proximity in order to obtain certain services and goods. This is not the case after global capitalism. The flow of transnational communication enables one to find a particular identity free from locale and then undercut the placed structures that would necessitate getting along with others.[62] Cultivating identities becomes a dominant cultural practice and identities themselves become dwellings of the like-minded who choose, justify, and project them. Christians in the context of globalization struggle to comprehend and live the gift exchange of Christian identity precisely because it runs counter to dominant cultural practices. Indeed, the flows of globalization encourage people to choose a religious identity as an add-on rather than a way of life.

Mauss analyzes territorialized cultures. Therefore, these cultures do not demand that identities be chosen, constructed, and projected. Participation in the gift economy of those cultures was assumed and inculcated from birth. Like Tomlinson's example of British cuisine, the inherence of a gift economy in Mauss's examples seems to rely, at least in part, on the spatial dynamics of the cultures that are studied.

Relegating the practice of gift exchange to the sphere of voluntarism in the contemporary context challenges the anthropological insight that Chauvet derives from Mauss. Like cuisine, when one can only choose to participate in symbolic exchange, it is all too easy for Christian identity, formed via the practice of symbolic exchange, to be usurped and appropriated as merely a marker of identity instead of a way of life.

Chauvet in Space: Possibilities

While the challenges of commodification, deterritorialization, and shallow identity projection are serious, there are at least two ways in which Chauvet's account of identity offers possibilities for a theological response. First, it is complex and rooted in the liturgy, especially its anamnesis, and, second, being intentionally formed in the symbolic exchange of the liturgy, the moment of an ethical return gift involves responding to the logic of the liturgy in action that does not conform to the cultural default.

Contrary to the spatial structures and global dynamics that impel us to nail it down, to be very clear about the identity we are projecting, Chauvet is helpful in turning Christian attempts to do this on their head. His emphasis on "holding ourselves always in a mature proximity to absence" necessitates not only that we are continually coming to be as Christian subjects, but also that there is not a pure and simple identity to project. [63] As God cannot be reduced to idol, so too our very identity is not reducible to a projection, even though, as Chauvet warns, the transition is tempting and easy to fall prey to.[64]

Chauvet maintains a certain level of comfort with the open-ended, artistic aspect of ritual, which reminds us that there is no pure encounter with God, nor a pure Christian identity in this life. Rather than presenting a "simple theological discourse about its identity," in the liturgy "the Church lives its identity by manifesting it."[65] Likewise, our attempts to maintain and project a pure identity are sure to fail.[66] If they can be adequately lived, complex identities are the ones that resist both closing themselves off and marketing exploitation.

Christian identities are necessarily formed within the ecclesial "we." This "we" is continually made present during the anamnesis: *we* do this in memory of Christ. As such the gift of salvation is brought into the present from the past, but this only happens as "we." Anamnesis is necessarily a corporeal act. It drives us into Christ's saving action, placing us closer to that event than we were a few hours before. We receive the task, again and again, of rebuilding a deep sense of memory, even one that, in sacrament, brings the past to the present. Identity as "brothers-and-sisters-for-others in Christ" cannot grow in isolation, but is *necessarily* bound up with the body of believers, indeed, one extended through time.

Here, Chauvet offers us conceptual resources for the church to resist being made into a mere identity front. We would do well to emphasize the variegated nature of this body at every opportunity and to create situations in which that body, made at the Eucharist, can gather in its diversity. The second epiclesis, which calls upon God the Father to send the Spirit to make the ecclesial "we" into the Christ that we have received is a practice that orients us in this direction, especially in the second part of that supplication that asks for union with the whole church throughout history and in heaven.[67] Christian identity is both historical and eschatological.

In the voluntary spatial structures we inhabit, we must acknowledge that participation in the practices of the liturgy is necessarily more intentional than it was, for example, in the immigrant Catholic subcultures in the early twentieth-century United States. Therefore, in such a spatial dynamic, Chauvet offers an intentional kind of "secondary" formation in the sacramental life of the church. Formed in deterritorialized, commodified, pluralistic, and especially voluntary space in a primary way, Christian identity must be nurtured in more intentional ways.

While the geographical parish is a victim of these same changing spatial structures, parishes need to work to create, intentionally, an environment that was naturally created by geographical parishes. Kneeling next to and sharing a sign of peace with Christians of different socio-economic backgrounds can be a powerful liturgical symbol. As the Eucharist makes us into church, it can be much clearer that we are made one with those whom we perceive as different, whom we would not encounter at work or in a Facebook group.

As an anecdotal example, the beginnings of partnership between two Lutheran churches in disparate economic areas of Dayton, Ohio, holds great potential in this regard. While the outcome is uncertain, and there are many intricate issues to address, shared worship, shared pastors, and even shared finances have been discussed. Such a partnership aims to undercut the spatial structures we inhabit by making use of the church's spatial structures. Concerns regarding Chauvet's appropriation of Mauss on an anthropological level are relativized by thinking about how symbolic exchange operates as a matter of secondary formation in the church.

Chauvet's contention that we become brothers and sisters,

not simply of Christ, but for others in Christ, leads to the second point. Chauvet's construal of Christian action as the "return-gift" in the cycle of grace begun by God gives an important place for Christian agency in identity. In sacrament, Christians receive God's grace, *as grace*. Christian ethical action is owed, with symbolic weight, to both God and others. Identity is received as gift, but the completion of that gift exchange involves further agency on the part of the Christian in *caritas*.

On the level of primary formation, the practices of global consumer culture give rise to an excess of desire that tends toward desire for its own sake. Consumers exercise agency in generally rather banal and pre-programmed ways, though also in surprisingly profound ways. Along with ways to instill the depth of tradition and formation, we need to find ways to harness the desires that our context elicits in us to construct identities and to baptize them. Redirecting these wayward desires finds conceptual support in Chauvet's elevation of the human—that what is most divine is at the mercy of the most human. He writes: "the sacramental rites, as places in the wholly human—the too human—where grace is bestowed on the significant materiality of gestures, postures, objects, and words which make them up, while not the *only* representation, are still *the most eminent representation of this pro-cession of the divine God within God's re-cession at the heart of what is most human.*"[68] With the sacraments as paradigms, it must be that our excess of desire in globalized consumer culture can, somehow, be caught up in the gift of Christian identity.[69] Our broken, fragmented bodies are necessarily the very place that God takes on flesh in the world, bringing them into an uncomfortable and unsettling whole.

An example of channeling this desire arises from a particular strain of vibrant young Catholics, called "evangelical Catholics" by William L. Portier.[70] They have never known the U.S. immigrant Catholic subculture, nor the rancor over *Humanae Vitae*. Born into pluralistic, deterritorialized, heterogenized space, they have chosen Catholicism as their identity. This choice, doubtless, is conditioned, in some way, by the narrow identity politics of the space they inhabit. Having a strong desire to make an assertive choice, one that is sometimes narrow in its construal of the tradition, is part and parcel of their formation. Taking Chauvet's emphasis on our humanness seriously, we need to embrace this vibrancy and channel it into avenues in the tradition that will encourage a deeper, more complex identity.

Conclusion

In Chauvet's structure, the ethical return-gift, the third moment of the structure of gift exchange, is a particular place for desire to be re-appropriated in a way that makes the body of Christ present in the world. The gift of grace is received as a charge to a lived Christian response. The important point here is that this, too, makes Christians Christian. Re-directing Christian agency is not simply the output of Christian identity, but is, rather, caught up in the very exchange of subjectivity. It is, however, formally and logically after our absorption in the Christian tradition. Not only does this agency follow upon God's gift of grace mediated by the church, but it is also necessarily an intentional response to the logic of grace in the liturgy. Chauvet says that the proper character of Christian ethical practice "comes not from its degree of generosity but from its nature of *response* to the prevenient gift and commitment of God."[71] There are, of course, myriad ways that Christians make Christ present in the world by living lives that do not simply respond to the cultural default.

I offer here just one example. In the face of a government bill at the end of 2005 that required all non-profit organizations to inquire about the immigrant status of every person they served, then archbishop of Los Angeles Roger Cardinal Mahony authored a public letter to then President George W. Bush in which he appealed to the Gospel of Matthew, stating that, "Our golden rule has always been to serve people in need—not to verify beforehand their immigration status."[72] He found absurd the prospect of inspecting documentation before offering Catholics the Eucharist.

Mahony did not simply write a letter to President Bush and consider his responsibility complete. He vowed to disobey the law if passed, standing instead shoulder to shoulder with his Mexican brothers and sisters in Christ. Such a witness of solidarity, placing one's body next to those who may stand in harm's way, makes the body of Christ, formed in the sacraments, present in the world. Mahony then inaugurated an archdiocesan reflection on immigrant issues on May 1, the feast of St. Joseph the Worker. He recently introduced a new website, www.facesofimmigrants.org, that features personal conversations the cardinal has had with immigrants in southern California. About the site, he has said

> Instead of being side-tracked by heated rhetoric and political posturing, all of us should take the time to open our minds and hearts to hear the actual stories of the immigrants themselves. Who are they? Why are they here? How is our current immigration system failing them? How do their experiences impact our local communities and our nation?[73]

The immigration question, as Mahony sees, is not a problem only for the immigrants who have not received legal status, but a problem for the entire body of Christ, particularly the body of Christ in the United States, which has a profound immigrant history.

In terms of return-gift, in light of the current context, perhaps an unconventional set of specific ethical actions become deeply important and ought to be encouraged: those that intentionally bolster our memories—accounting for the deep histories of the various places we inhabit, immersing ourselves into cultural and family histories, identifying ourselves as much as possible with the sources of food and other goods—not simply for pleasure but as a discipline, sometimes painful, that forms in us a deeper openness to receive the gift of Christian identity.

Notes

[1] My thanks to Timothy Brunk, who offered some helpful comments during and after this paper's presentation, and especially to Vincent Miller who read several drafts of this paper, offering his insights. Thanks are also due to two unknown reviewers and Maureen O'Connell, one of this volume's editors, who made many helpful suggestions.

[2] See Danièle Hervieu-Léger, *Religion as a Chain of Memory*, trans. Simon Lee (New Brunswick, NJ: Rutgers University Press, 2000), esp. 127ff; Arjun Appadurai, *Modernity at Large: Cultural Dimensions of Globalization* (Minneapolis: University of Minnesota Press, 1996), esp. 39-42; John Tomlinson, *Globalization and Culture* (Chicago: University of Chicago Press, 1999). For a theological engagement with these sources see Vincent J. Miller, "Where Is the Church? Globalization and Catholicity," *Theological Studies* 69, no. 2 (June 2008): 412-32. From another angle, Philip Gleason, in "What Made

Catholic Identity a Problem?" in *Faith and the Intellectual Life* (Notre Dame: University of Notre Dame Press, 1996), 87-100, argues that the heightened interest in Catholic identity in the United States is historically located in the emergence of Catholics, around the time of the Second Vatican Council, from their diligently created immigrant subculture. Catholic identity was assumed in the subculture, but must be asserted in the context of pluralism. Both of these diagnoses betray a common concern for the spatial structures in which identity is articulated, formed, and lived. Identity is something different when shaped by an elaborate network of hospitals, schools, businesses, and neighborhoods in the U.S. Catholic immigrant subculture than when shaped by the demands of American pluralism.

[3]It is important to understand that these results come from the same technological and economic forces. Therefore, they occur simultaneously on different levels of our cultural experience. Many texts on globalization emphasize only homogenization; see, for example, George Ritzer, *The Mc-Donaldization of Society* (Thousand Oaks, CA: Pine Forge, 2004, orig. 1993), and David Howes, ed., *Cross-cultural Consumption: Global Markets, Local Realities* (London: Routledge, 1996). For alternative views, see the sources in the previous note. The difference arises primarily in methodology: cultural theorists read culture as not as strictly defined by ubiquitous economic brands as economic theorists tend to do. For example, many more people now have access to Coke, but many more people now also have a variety of ways to seek out, and only cultivate relationships with, the like-minded all over the world. See also *Theological Studies* 69, no. 2 (June 2008). The entire issue is dedicated to an array of theological perspectives on these and other aspects of globalization.

[4]Miller, "Where Is the Church?" 421.

[5]Ibid., 423.

[6]Louis-Marie Chauvet, *Symbol and Sacrament: A Sacramental Reinterpretation of Christian Existence*, trans. Patrick Madigan, S.J. and Madeleine Beaumont (Collegeville, MN: Liturgical Press, 1995), 1. The French original is *Symbole et sacrement: Une relecture sacramentelle de l'existence chrétienne* (Paris: Cerf, 1987). Chauvet's briefer book, *The Sacraments: The Word of God at the Mercy of the Body*, trans. Madeleine Beaumont (Collegeville, MN: Liturgical Press, 2001), distills the same argument for wider accessibility. All italics are Chauvet's unless otherwise noted.

[7]See, for example, Lieven Boeve and Lambert Leijssen, eds., *Contemporary Sacramental Contours of a God Incarnate*, Studies in Liturgy 16, Proceedings of the International Leuven Encounters in Systematic Theology Conference (Leuven: Peeters, 2001).

[8]See, for example, Philippe Bordeyne and Bruce T. Morrill, eds., *Sacraments: Revelation of the Humanity of God—Engaging the Fundamental Theology of Louis-Marie Chauvet* (Collegeville, MN: Liturgical Press, 2008). See also Todd Townshend, *The Sacramentality of Preaching: Homiletical Uses of Louis-Marie Chauvet's Theology of Sacramentality*, American University Studies, Series VII: Theology and Religion 286 (New York: Peter Lang, 2009),

and Joseph A. Bracken, "Toward a New Philosophical Theology Based on Intersubjectivity," *Theological Studies* 59, no. 4 (December 1998): 703-19.

[9]See, for example, the issue of *Christian Bioethics* (7, no. 1 [April 2001]) dedicated to the topic of Catholic identity in Catholic hospitals. See also Charles E. Curran, "The Catholic Identity of Catholic Institutions," *Theological Studies* 58, no. 1 (March 1997): 90-108. See also such book-length studies as: Daniel Donovan, *Distinctly Catholic: An Exploration of Catholic Identity* (Mahwah, NJ: Paulist Press, 1997); Michele Dillon, *Catholic Identity: Balancing Reason, Faith, and Power* (New York: Cambridge University Press, 1999).

[10]For a classic example, see Reginald Garrigou-Lagrange, *Reality: A Synthesis of Thomistic Thought* (St. Louis: Herder, 1950), esp. chap. 38, 39, and 49. Lagrange uses such phrases to describe Thomas's thinking as "grace . . . being poured into his heart" (298) and "grace . . . in the mode of production" (300).

[11]Garrigou-Lagrange, *Reality: A Synthesis of Thomistic Thought*, 22-24. Chauvet illustrates this onto-theological position with Plato's discussion of shipbuilding. Plato says that becoming is always in view of being in building a ship—in front of the builder is always the bringing to be of the ship. Plato says that the same goes for love. Chauvet disputes the second move, pointing out that the productionist scheme allows for no other way to talk about relationships.

[12]Ibid., 43.

[13]Ibid., 84. Chauvet is dependent upon Jacques Lacan for his understanding of "symbolic order."

[14]Ibid., 74. See also 453-89, where Chauvet contrasts his starting point for Trinitarian theology—the paschal mystery—with that of the Scholastics, in other words, the hypostatic union.

[15]Ibid., 82-83.

[16]Ibid., 100; Chauvet, *The Sacraments*, 119.

[17]Mauss's achievements are many, but his "Essai sur le don," in *Sociologie et anthropologie* (Paris: Presses Universitaires France, 1950), 143-279, elaborates his study of "gift" important for Chauvet's work. He also draws upon historian Georges Duby, particularly upon Duby's *Guerriers et paysans, vii-xiie siècle. Premier essor de l'économie européenne* (Paris: Gallimard, 1973).

[18]Chauvet, *The Sacraments*, 117-18.

[19]Chauvet, *Symbol and Sacrament*, 101-2. Both Mauss and Chauvet point to the inadequacy of our language to name this gift that obligates in turn and that cannot be refused; hence, the oxymoron.

[20]Ibid., 102-3.

[21]Chauvet, *Symbol and Sacrament*, 107. Chauvet is clear to point out, though, that "gift" as we often use it does not communicate the same reality as described by Mauss. Nevertheless, "presents" work in the symbolic order, even though they can be co-opted by the logic of the market—game shows and wedding registries are two examples of gift exchange in the order of production (see Chauvet, *The Sacraments,* 120).

[22]Chauvet, *Symbol and Sacrament*, 108. Chauvet finds the gift of manna in the Exodus narrative as concurrently the paradigmatic example of a "nonthing" and the paradigmatic example of grace (see ibid., 45).

[23]Chauvet, *The Sacraments*, 125.

[24]Ibid. The human response should not be construed as in competition with grace. Theologies beholden to productionist explanations of grace often find that the more grace works in competition with the free response of the subject, the more it is "grace." This cannot be if we consider the graciousness of the gift of grace as we consider its gratuitousness (see Chauvet, *Symbol and Sacrament*, 109).

[25]See Chauvet, *Symbol and Sacrament*, 110.

[26]Ibid., 537.

[27]Ibid., 108

[28]Ibid., 164-65.

[29]Ibid., 537.

[30]Chauvet, *The Sacraments*, 20.

[31]Chauvet, *Symbol and Sacrament*, 352.

[32]See Glenn P. Ambrose, "Eucharist as a Means for 'Overcoming' Onto-Theology? The Sacramental Theology of Louis-Marie Chauvet," Ph.D. Diss. (Graduate Theological Union, 2001), 161-63. See also Chauvet, *Symbol and Sacrament*, 92-95.

[33]Louis-Marie Chauvet, "L'Église fait l'eucharistie; l'eucharistie fait l'Église," *Revue Catéchèse* 71 (1978): 182. Quoted in Timothy M. Brunk, *Liturgy and Life: The Unity of Sacrament and Ethics in the Theology of Louis-Marie Chauvet*, American University Studies (New York: Peter Lang, 2007), 73. The translation is Brunk's.

[34]See Chauvet, *Symbol and Sacrament*, 181.

[35]Ibid., 178.

[36]Ibid., 153.

[37]Ibid., 375.

[38]Ibid., 375-76.

[39]Ibid. Chauvet recalls the seemingly bizarre scriptural accounts of Ezekiel and the visionary of Revelation literally "chewing the Book," which, after chewing, is "as sweet as honey." In the Eucharist, Christians symbolically translate scripture to ethics by chewing the Body of Christ. This chewing likewise aids reception of God's Word: "Precisely because it counteracts such a weakening of faith, the symbolic experience of the chewing, the rumination, and the ingestion of the Eucharistic bread as the body of the Lord is irreplaceable for us" (225-26).

[40]Ibid., 264.

[41]See Louis-Marie Chauvet, "Rituality and Theology," in *Primary Sources of Liturgical Theology: A Reader*, ed. Dwight W. Vogel (Collegeville, MN: Liturgical Press, 2000), 198-99. The selection that appears in this reader is excerpted and translated by Susan Wood from Louis-Marie Chauvet, "Ritualité et Théologie," *Recherche de Science Religieuse* 78, no. 4 (1990): 535-64.

[42]Chauvet, *Symbol and Sacrament*, 155.

[43]In his earlier work *Du symbolique au symbole: Essai sur les sacrements*

(Paris: Cerf, 1979), Chauvet spends the last chapter engaging to some extent with consumer culture, but not with the dynamics of globalization.

[44]Hervieu-Léger, *Religion as a Chain of Memory*, esp. 123-62.

[45]On commodification as abstraction and the habits it forms, see Vincent J. Miller, *Consuming Religion: Christian Faith and Practice in a Consumer Culture* (New York: Continuum, 2003), esp. 38.

[46]Hervieu-Léger, *Religion as a Chain of Memory*, 3.

[47]See ibid., 94.

[48]For an example of the first, see Ambrose of Milan, "On the Mysteries," chap. 7, sec. 42. Accessed online at: http://oll.libertyfund.org/Home3/EBook.php?recordID=0565 (February 1999). For an example of the second two, see Paul Turner, *Ages of Initiation: The First Two Christian Millennia with CD-ROM* (Collegeville, MN: Liturgical Press, 2000), CD: chap. 4, sec. 9.

[49]See Bernard Cooke, *Sacraments and Sacramentality*, rev. ed. (Mystic, CT: Twenty-Third Publications, 1994), 147-48; Dan Grippo, "Confirmation: No One Under 18 Need Apply," *U.S. Catholic* 47, no. 8 (August 1982), 31; Joseph Moore, *Choice: A Two-Year Confirmation Process for Emerging Young Adults* (New York: Paulist Press, 1986), 1; Lenore L. Danesco, "What Happens After Confirmation?" *Religion Teacher's Journal* 29, no. 8 (February 1996): 12. For an extended argument on this score see Timothy R. Gabrielli, "Confirmation and Being Catholic in the United States: The Development of the Sacrament of Confirmation in the Twentieth Century" (M.A. thesis, University of Dayton, 2010).

[50]Chauvet also relies upon historian Georges Duby, who describes a prevailing "mental attitude" in seventh- to twelfth-century Europe in which the collective exchange of goods was really about cementing relationships and social status (see Georges Duby, *The Early Growth of the European Economy: Warriors and Peasants from the Seventh to the Twelfth Century*, trans. Howard B. Clark [Ithaca, NY: Cornell University Press, 1974], 48-72).

[51]See, for example, Mary Claire Allvine and Christine Larson, *The Family CFO: The Couple's Business Plan for Love and Money* (New York: Rodale, 2004), which begins with the supposition that households should function like corporations complete with CFOs, a business plan, and job descriptions.

[52]See Miller, *Consuming Religion*, 36-39, for an analysis of the commodification of love. Miller provides a thoroughgoing investigation of the impact of commodification (and consumer culture as a whole) on Christianity.

[53]Ibid., 6.

[54]Ulrich Beck, *The Cosmopolitan Vision* (Cambridge: Polity Press, 2006), 41.

[55]See ibid., 5.

[56]Clearly, Mauss himself is engaging in this type of imagination to undercut utilitarian political notions. The anthropological study of Mauss relativized capitalism by providing an account of social cohesion that was not indebted to the operations of the market. In *The Gift* Mauss writes, "A considerable part of our morality and our lives themselves are still permeated with this same atmosphere of the gift, where obligation and liberty intermingle" (65). However, the examples that he offers occur more rarely than our consumer

practices: the birth of a baby in the village, a wedding feast. Even the more structural examples he cites are undercut in favor of consumer practices, for example, social insurance. The hefty tax cuts of the past thirty years in the United States make this clear (see Miller, *Consuming Religion*, 152-53).

[57]Hacker culture is perhaps one such example, where participants gift creativity and time writing code in exchange for prestige in the hacker community. While it would be interesting to explore hacker culture as a resource for understanding the workings of grace and, in turn, of Christian identity, such an example is nevertheless notably an exception to the mainstream and indeed legal practice of exchange practiced far more often in the daily lives of Christians (see Eric S. Raymond, "Homesteading the Noosphere," *First Monday,* 1998), http://www.firstmonday.dk/issues/issue3_10/raymond/ (accessed 16 May 2008).

[58]For Bourdieu's insights and their application to consumer culture, I am dependent upon Miller, *Consuming Religion*, 150-53.

[59]John Tomlinson, *Globalization and Culture* (Chicago: University of Chicago Press, 1999), 107, 128.

[60]Ibid., 124-25.

[61]See Miller, "Where Is the Church?" 419.

[62]See Appadurai, *Modernity at Large*, esp. 1-11 and 32-44.

[63]See Chauvet, *Symbol and Sacrament*, 74-75.

[64]See ibid., 403.

[65]Ibid., 274.

[66]The pure gift, too, is impossible—it cannot be solely and purely gratuitous or solely and purely gracious unless, of course, it comes from God. Only Christ on the cross is pure self-gift (see Chauvet, *The Sacraments*, 86-87).

[67]See Chauvet, *Symbol and Sacrament*, 271.

[68]Ibid., 373.

[69]On consumer desire see Miller, *Consuming Religion*, 107-45.

[70]William L. Portier, "Here Come the Evangelical Catholics," *Communio* 31 (Spring 2004): 35-66.

[71]Chauvet, *The Sacraments*, 138.

[72]Roger M. Mahony to George W. Bush, Los Angeles, 30 December 2005, http://www.archdiocese.la/news/pdf/news_704_President Bush Letter.pdf (accessed 10 September 2010). Mahony has since, of course, been involved with serious questions concerning sex abuse cases in his archdiocese. By offering his actions in this instance as exemplary, I do not intend to comment in any way on the other controversy.

[73]"Cardinal Mahony Launches 'Faces of Immigrants'" (29 April 2010), http://www.archdiocese.la/news/story.php?newsid=1174 (accessed 10 September 2010).

Desiring Place

Artists, HGTV/Travel Channel Cultures, and Eucharistic Topogenesis

Ryan Stander

Since getting married nearly five years ago, my wife and I have lived in student housing at various educational institutions. Our distant hopes for home ownership and travel are often buoyed and consoled with the vicarious experiences provided by cable programming designed to inspire creative design ideas and do-it-yourself solutions, while providing general entertainment. We distantly celebrate the young couples on *Property Virgins*. We critique design decisions. We imagine sampling worldwide street fare with Anthony Bourdain or hitting America's byways with Guy Fieri in search of *Diners, Drive-ins and Dives*.

But as we immersed ourselves in these seemingly innocuous corporately sponsored dreams we often became disillusioned with our own realities—our drafty windows, three different kinds of wood paneling, noise from our neighbors, and a general lack of space—and began to wonder about the effects that these beautiful homes and exotic destinations might be having upon our perspectives of place. We found ourselves within an alternate liturgy. This dynamic and polished program was replete with its own sacred times and rhythms (*Holmes on Homes* at 9:00 a.m. Saturday), spaces (Lowes, Home Depot, and the all-inclusive resort), objects (stainless-steel appliances and crown molding), texts (catalogs from Pottery Barn and Restoration Hardware), and even indications of liturgical reform following the housing market crash.

The problem, as Vincent Miller has argued, is not simply the "love of God versus the love of things."[1] Rather it is the strikingly similar formation structure utilized by both ecclesial and consumer liturgies that threatens to derail Christian desire. Like ecclesial liturgies, this alternative consumer-culture liturgy carefully crafts the most fundamental desires and orients the practices of its participants. This distorted sense of desire turns things, place, and people into consumable commodities, lifestyle accessories, and entertainment venues. By recasting the HGTV- and Travel Channel-type cultures within a consumer liturgy, we can look more specifically at this liturgy's cultivation of desire and its relationship to place.

This essay then considers human desire for place in the home and the world at large. It begins by examining the work of two visual artists—Martin Parr, a British photographer, and Jennifer Nelson, a North Dakota artist—to problematize the commodification of place. Through Parr's imaging of incongruous detail and Nelson's isolating white planes, both artists wrestle with their own distinct set of questions. Matters of homogenization, indulgence, frivolity, and kitsch applied broadly upon cultures and landscapes are pre-eminent for Parr. Nelson's focus, on the other hand, is on the shaping of cultural expectations, with particular regard to the American Dream as characterized by independence, equality, upward mobility, and home ownership. Both artists indirectly address the cultural construction and con-sumption of place with wary eyes upon appearances and sub-stances of reality.

Their questions and critiques form a visual landscape in which I explore two reconstructions of place in order to counter the consumer liturgy. First, the human geographer Robert Sack argues that humanity understands itself and its actions through the concepts and realities of place and space. Because consumerism fabricates disorienting and misleading contexts, Sack's proposal encourages humanity to see place and space as absolutely vital to any discussion about morality and ethics. Second, building on Philip Sheldrake's sacramental proposal for sacred space with what I've termed "Eucharistic topogenesis," I contend that the Eucharist creates a unique form of place that both subverts the consumerist world and offers an alternative space of formation. Eucharistic topogenesis implies the sacramental prolongation of the Body of Christ into the world, transforming and re-creating places from, in this instance, commodity consumption to places where humanity may flourish without economic obligations. When paired with Vincent Miller's analysis of commodification, the trajectories of the work of Sack and Sheldrake offer significant contributions to unmasking consumerism's disorienting tactics and, ultimately, the re-making of place.

Place in the Work of Martin Parr

The work of contemporary photographer Martin Parr functions as a mirror to global culture. The direct nature of Parr's documentary work often seems to image a new globalized form of normal or ordinary that delicately teeters between critique and lament, delight and disappointment. Parr has an uncanny ability to capture, often in very unflattering ways, the particular idiosyncrasies of Western culture through our food, our fashions, leisure activities, the things we buy, and the places we go. His remarkable ability to penetrate both American and British cultures often provokes angered responses, perhaps because we recognize many of our own patterns and practices unflatteringly reflected and publicly documented as works of art.

Parr's casual compositions and juxtapositions, garish colors, and strange lighting combine to create a peculiarly surreal quality. Through a unique combination of a ring flash, macro lenses, and overly saturated amateur slide film, Parr's images become bright parodies of our cultural excess. But important issues are at stake within the wit and gloss. Since the mid-1980s, Parr's work has turned a continual eye toward the middle-class, globalization, consumption, and tourism. Parr's book *Small World* looks specifically at global tourism and its effects upon the host culture.[2]

Geoff Dyer's artful introduction to *Small World* notes that Parr's work continues a long line of travel photography, imaging the exotic for those at home. Historically, as travel became easier, cheaper, and quicker, these images helped incite human desire to discover the exotic world beyond their own doorstep and culture. Adventurous souls explored beyond the common paths only to find that their trailblazing had quickly become the preferred path. Thus our search for some nugget of authentic culture ends in the sad realization that we are not the first, nor the last to enter these places.

Parr's work reminds viewers that landscapes are not simply

commodified backdrops to human endeavors and entertainment. Rather, they are reciprocally formative for those who inhabit them. While the backpacker's motto to "leave no trace" may generally work for the hiking trail, it does not translate as well with cultural forms as tourists might naively hope. Dyer suggests "that in order to escape the tentacles of this homogenizing 'civilisation,' it is necessary to travel further and further afield. And by so doing, you drag those tentacles after you. We are all responsible for the ruination we lament."[3] Parr has a particularly keen eye, especially for the tentacles of American imperium often seen as wearable Americana: a New York Yankees hat at the Notre Dame Cathedral, a Hollywood t-shirt at Karnak, a stars and stripes Speedo at the beach.

Martin Parr, *The Leaning Tower of Pisa*, Pisa, Italy 1990. Courtesy of Magnum Photos.

Another collection of Parr's images is of tourists recording their travels or themselves being recorded with an important cultural landmark. Whether striking a pose at the Pyramids, or straining to hold up the leaning tower of Pisa, these images function as "meta-photographs" to document the documentation of their presence. These images are the "proof of purchase" or the recorded assurance that they have indeed been at this site.

In much of Parr's work we are confronted with the landscape itself as a commodity for consumption. While tourism may offer opportunities to enjoy the world, it can simultaneously degrade the local environment while creating a homogenizing effect on the host place and culture.

Martin Parr, *Colosseum*, Rome, Italy 1993. Courtesy of Magnum Photos.

In turn, this raises problematic questions about authenticity. Is Parr documenting a replica of staged simulation?[4] Or, in our desire to consume the world through travel, has "the tourist Venice . . . or tourist Rome succumb[ed] to the tourist industry to become the real Rome?"[5] Whether it's the ubiquitous Visa logo, stacks of American cigarettes, or the onslaught of cheap knick-knacks, we feel cheated by the commerce that our desire for exotic experiences has created. Place and heritage have become industry and product.[6]

Place in the Art of Jennifer Nelson

Balancing Parr's garish parodies on both topic and style, North Dakota artist Jennifer Nelson's recent work pushes at ideas of desire and the cultural expectations of the American dream.[7] Nelson's remarkably simple line drawings of single family homes are situated within an uncluttered white surface that allows viewers to contend cleanly with concept without being bogged down with design. Where Parr looks at the effects of global tourism, Nelson considers marketing and the cultivation of desire for the home.

She states, "The idea of home . . . isn't just shelter, it's a place of one's own, often a single-family home with a yard."[8] As a recent homebuyer, her own anxiety over the process seems to have clarified her artistic vision. Through this process, she became intimately aware of the disparity between what she and her husband wanted (namely a garden and studio spaces), and "what everyone told [them they] needed and wanted."[9] Nelson suspects that both nostalgia and media influence were likely the subtle roots of her desire for a certain type of home. She contends that our ideas and desires for the idyllic home are often shaped by something unnatural, and perhaps even unreal.

Despite Nelson's critique, she acknowledges that the American dream remains firmly intact as a reality, though recent history reminds us that reality can be fragile. In two different series, Nelson has focused upon foreclosed homes in her hometown of Grand Forks, North Dakota.

Jennifer A. Nelson, *In the Red 158590*, 2008   Jennifer A. Nelson, *May 30, 2007*, 2008

One series of homes is illustrated in red, and the other is a series of glitter prints, in what she calls, "Barbie Dream House colors."[10] The *In the Red* series offers an oblique reference to the Red River Valley where Grand Forks is situated and an obvious reference to the financial toll and risks of the American dream, while the glitter suggests seduction and the unreality, or more precisely, the unsustainability of the dream.

Nelson also draws from popular media to explore its role in the cultivation of expectation and desire. By using images embedded in our collective memory such as the iconic homes of *Leave It to Beaver* and *The Waltons,* the houses become more than simple settings. Rather they become potent characters because "we know and embrace the images . . . they show us how the world should appear."[11]

Jennifer A. Nelson, *Hey Beaver!* 2008

In several works utilizing these houses from our collective memory, Nelson employs a particularly witty move where foreclosed homes dream about their ideal. Here, the real aspires to become the unreal as nostalgically imaged in the fictional homes of the Waltons and Cleavers.

Both Parr and Nelson help to articulate, in visual terms, observations regarding the cultural construction of place, particularly related to and perhaps exacerbated by mass media and cable programming. One piece of Nelson's work proves especially provocative in this direction.

In her work *There's No Place Like Home*, Nelson borrows Dorothy's iconic red slippers from *The Wizard of Oz.* In the film,

Dorothy uses the slippers as a means to achieve her dream of returning home. Nelson couples this sense with the intimacy of the traditional language regarding the woman's role as "homemaker," to suggest the birth process in the conjuring of home. While the birth process may be read into the image, it also emits a sexually charged scene of spread legs and fetishistic red glittering shoes. In this way, it provocatively images our culture's yearning for a home by sexualizing it, reminiscent of Vincent Miller's discussion of seduction and misdirection.[12]

Miller suggests that seduction concerns our *desire* for objects rather than the objects themselves. Commodity seduction drives consumption by "prolonging desire and channeling its inevitable disappointments into further desires."[13] Misdirection associates "commodities with needs, desires and values not directly related to the given product . . . encourag[ing] consumers to fulfill more profound needs and desires through consumption."[14] The glittering lust for a home is not simply to fulfill our need for shelter, but to extend the pleasure with renovating, using granite counters, crown molding, and perpetual redecoration. While the home itself is one giant identity-forming commodity, it also becomes the "primary repository of commodities used to define ourselves and isolate our private world from the public world."[15]

Miller's concern is that Christian desire is at risk of being distorted and exploited by consumer culture because it provides a powerful alternative that closely resembles the Christian structure of formation.[16] His insights are deeply rooted in a core Augustinian anthropology where the human heart is restless until it rests in God; consequently the ultimate goal of the spiritual quest is our union with God. Under the weight of consumerism, however, the human desire and the mystical search for God are sidetracked, subverted, and ultimately disseminated horizontally across an endless range of consumer options.

Following Miller's contention that the consumerist desire for desire itself is stronger than one's desire for the actual object, the work of Nelson and Parr extends that premise to include place. Whether seen as a never-ending series of redecorations or a whirlwind trip across Europe, place is intimately connected and cultivated through consumer desire. Programming as found on the Travel Channel, HGTV, the Food Network, and TLC, among others, presents place in easily digestible, achievable, entertaining segments punctuated (and ultimately funded by) a bevy of vendors ready to help you achieve your newly found dreams of travel and/ or home remodeling with their products and services.

Nelson questions the appearance of these realities by what is and isn't portrayed. She states, "In 30 minutes, kitchen remodels are completed and travels to remote areas of the planet can be accomplished. There is usually a mishap but there is always a happy ending." What viewers see is a highly edited and polished performance by show hosts and their crews. Viewers do not hear the later complaints about shoddy workmanship or the financial tolls, and even foreclosures that have accompanied receiving ABC's Extreme Makeover Home Edition or winning HGTV's Dream Home Giveaway. Nor are viewers privy to the ecological and social effects of travelers upon tourist destinations and host communities. Such effects do not fit the detailed marketing plans of paid advertisements. These deliberate editing omissions further obfuscate the connections between place and consumerism's cultivation of desire.

A Conceptual Examination of Place

Both Parr and Nelson have issued their concerns and critiques that parallel my initial misgivings about the effects of cable programming upon human perception and the use of place. Such concerns have spread across the disciplines, which have critiqued consumerism from a variety of positions and methodologies. Turning now from the arts, I offer a brief conceptual examination of place that will serve as a backdrop for human geographer David Sack and theologian Philip Sheldrake.

In many ways, place seems to speak for itself in our day-to-day spatial vocabularies. Common usage and conceptions of place are often interchangeable with space, territory, landscape, or location, depending upon a perceived specificity or abstraction. And yet, when place is pressed, its simplicity slides away into a complexity of historical and philosophical terrains of ontology and epistemology.

Similarities in our common usage of place can be readily seen historically in the divergent approaches toward place by Aristotle's preference for *topos* and Plato's emphasis on *chora*.[17] Aristotle's *topos* suggests an objective point on a map that exerts no actual influence upon those who enter. Topographical maps and global positioning systems are reminiscent forms of Aristotle's sense of *topos*. In contrast, Plato's preference for *chora*, the etymological root of "choreography," suggests the reciprocal dance between humanity and environment. Thus place is both object and a particular experience of being in the world.

It is this latter characterization of "being in the world" that has driven the fairly recent resurgence of place. Within modernity, concepts of *space* prevailed while *place* endured a slow and painful dismissal and subsequent suppression from both academic conversations and cultural practices.[18] Ultimately, both place and space were subjected to the hegemony of time. However, in the early 1970s, place re-emerged as a prominent philosophical inquiry in the work of Yi-Fu Tuan, Edward Relph, and Henri Lefebvre by turning from spatial studies of regional and cultural geography toward continental philosophy, phenomenology, and sociology.[19]

In particular, many have turned to Martin Heidegger's *Dasein*, which roughly suggests "being there" or "dwelling within" and carries connotations of care and cultivation.[20] For Heidegger, to be authentically human is to be rooted in place. Existence necessitates a physical and embodied reality. Heidegger's sense of place then is a much deeper concept than location or the GPS coordinates implied by Aristotle's *topos*. Place, as dwelling, engenders spiritual and political realities, communal and aesthetic aspects, and finds intimate connection to memory and narrative.

Robert Sack on Place

When place transcends topographical maps to include the fullness of human existence, other disciplines must take notice. Robert Sack's *Place, Modernity and the Consumer's World* considers the connection between place and morality with a critical eye on spaces of consumption. The crux of Sack's argument is that "moral agents . . . must be responsible . . . and must know the consequences of their actions."[21] Sack argues that actions travel through place and space; consequently geography emerges as an indispensable means for understanding our effects and responsibilities. As responsible moral agents, we must have the opportunity to analyze the effects of our actions and believe we can change our course of actions. The "good life," suggests Sack, is a "moral life" that necessarily involves examining the consequences of our actions upon time and space.[22] Consequently, any place that prevents us from understanding our actions is not moral.[23]

Sack further contends that consumption obscures these consequences by creating new places, processes, and effects that simultaneously sever connections by presenting themselves as a world apart—a consumer's cosmos, a showcase of goods, services, tours, and vistas.[24] In these spaces, individuals are trained to be the consuming center of the world, rather than a link in a global chain. In these contexts, place is one more product to be consumed.

Sack's model intends to cultivate a common ground for dialogue among the plurality of forces, fragmented theories, and competing practices. By uniting these voices, consumers may become more aware of the geographical conditions of production, distribution, and consumption. He states:

> This awareness automatically embraces the connections among the entire range of forces and perspectives. It requires that we imagine ourselves in a place that allows us to see the force of free agency and to see the connections of this place to other places. In this way, we build a picture of the webs of relations that our actions entail, and our awareness of these connections adds restraint.[25]

While Sack's framework is provocative, it lacks any means of tangible implementation.[26] Not only does his framework rarely touch the ground of actual consumers, it also idealistically assumes that awareness of spatial transgressions alone will naturally lead to restraint and a change of behavior that leads to a moral life. Furthermore, even though Sack acknowledges there is no universally held system of morality, his reliance upon ideas of "responsibility" and "generally accepted virtues" still assumes culturally embedded ideas and norms about human participation in the world. In the end, do these radically suspended, self-defined individuals who have been incessantly trained by consumerism possess the necessary desire and tools to unmask consumerism's disorientation? And subsequently, do they have the resources to reorient themselves in a "moral" non-consumer-based direction?

While I am not satisfied with the abstract and overly optimistic nature of Sack's program, it does offer a common space for discussion that the church must enter. From among the realms of meaning, its voice must be heard.

Philip Sheldrake on Place

By extending the meaning of place beyond location to reside at the heart of human existence itself, theological considerations have something significant to contribute. In *Spaces for the Sacred*,[27] Philip Sheldrake offers a robust inroad to this discussion by building upon Heidegger's *Dasein* and Ricoeur's sense of narrative to define the essence of place as "space that has the capacity to be remembered and evoke what is most precious."[28] Rooted in the liturgy and Eucharist, Sheldrake's Eucharistic catholicity[29] flows through his ecclesiology and into a sacramental sensibility where God's presence as action identifies with the radical particularities of place in the world, and yet is not defined by or bounded by it.[30]

For Sheldrake, sacramentalism implies more than simply a "graced world" because it requires a human response or action.[31] Likewise, Eucharistic ethics also imply more than simple behaviors or pious practices. Rather, they are the embodiment of the unique character and identity of the Christian community. The Eucharist is both the means and method of reconciliation that unites and reconfigures humanity's ambiguous stories and memories into the narrative of God in Christ. In the space of the liturgy and meal, the body of Christ is trained to enact this alternatively oriented place that welcomes the periphery, engages suppressed narratives, and resists homogenization.[32] As both means and method, the church is imagined as an embodied prolongation of God's transforming action and the real presence of Christ to faithfully engage the radical disorientation and dislocation of place caused by consumerism.[33]

Connecting Humanity and Place through the Eucharist

Both Sack and Sheldrake push for a clearer connection between humanity and place. While Sack's preliminary structure is abstract,

Sheldrake's proposal is more substantial and praxis-oriented. Through its reliance upon the sacramental structure of the liturgy and the Eucharist, his proposal offers an external structure of counter-formation and orientation that is lacking in Sack's proposal. From this perspective, the church offers a unique voice to begin a conversation about ethics and place from among the fragments of meaning and suggests five points of contact.

First, the proposals of Sack and Sheldrake rely upon the imagination. For Sack, the imagination allows humanity to perceive of itself as powerful agents able to work for good by restoring the ties of interconnectedness that consumerism has severed. Miller would likely agree with Sack that awareness is the basic and beginning tactic for countering commodification.[34] Sack's conceptualization, however, fails to account for the ritualized formation of human imaginative abilities by consumer culture itself; it also fails to provide a cohesive reorientation that would lead to action. Simple awareness or imaginative projections of both self and society do not necessarily lead to change. Both Miller and Sheldrake, on the other hand, look toward the liturgical formation of specific patterns and practices of Christian communal life as the framework in which the imagination is trained to pursue and embody alternatives to the disorientation of consumerism.

Second, while consumerism emphasizes the process of desire over the object itself, the sacramental sensibility of Sheldrake and Miller connects believers instead with material reality. Miller states that hallowing physical things endows them with importance because they become mediations of the divine.[35] By hallowing place and thing, we not only increase our enjoyment of them, we also open them to their transcendent potential. Places cease to be consumable commodities. Instead, places are infused with memory, expectation, and appreciation of their uniqueness and the lives they shape. They evoke an awareness that extends beyond the literal context.

Third, by their natures, consumerism and the Eucharist are topogenic. Both create place and pattern. God's actions in Christ, the Eucharist, and the church are place-creating realities. The Eucharist proclaims the death, resurrection, and return of the Lord and creates a space in which this mystery is embodied as an ever-present reality. Additionally, the Eucharistic institution by Jesus is a creative endeavor establishing the New Covenant as a saving presence with the meal. Likewise, those who gather in the Eucharist are created into a new corporate reality, greater than the sum of its parts, constituted and transformed into the body of Christ.

The prophetic nature of the Eucharist has the potential to un-mask consumerism's disorientation and hidden links by reconsti-tuting its catholic unity across time and space. The Eucharist can expose links to other places and people hidden by consumerism, allowing believers to be reunited across time and space. Places are reconnected to other places, communities with other communities, and individuals with other individuals. We become aware of our mutual participation in each other's lives and places both on our block and around the world. It is within these Eucharistic places that we experience true place and are also trained to replicate it within a broken world.

The Eucharist's essential topogenic and reconciliatory natures free participants to learn their identity.[36] The Eucharist is intended to incarnate and root a person in the particularity of place. With consumer places no longer severed from the world, in the Eucharist we can learn our identity as part of both local and global com-munities. With our identities rooted in God as an external *telos*,[37] our longings become fixed, thereby stabilizing place, meaning, and identity. The places in which we may dwell may regain a depth of memory and community.

Finally, emerging from this place-creating and re-creating directive, the body of Christ transforms both public and private spaces. The Eucharist trains its communities to be "well-formed practitioners of tradition who engage beliefs, symbols, and prac-tices in a manner informed by its logic."[38] Having been trained in these traditions, participants come to understand their agency by practicing and improvising place in transformative ways.

If cable programming presents place and thing as commodities of privilege and consumption, the Eucharist instead trains its fol-lowers in appropriate desires and affections. In turn, the spaces of our homes and travels become places of opportunity for hospitality where we might receive the other as Christ, rather than mere private space for entertainment and commodity-oriented existence. In so doing, we have the opportunity to re-imagine our travel practices by considering the ecological and social impact upon the host com-munity. The church can begin to transform both private and public places for the oppressed, marginalized, and excluded, so they are no longer based in societal boundaries, commercial sponsorship, or economic obligations. [39] We can challenge our towns and cities for more humane city planning, architecture, mixed-use zoning, neighborhood rehabilitation, and community development.

Conceiving place through a sacramental sensibility rather than a consumer culture should allow us to rightly desire and cultivate place in ways that make us aware of our global effects and to create places that transform and reconcile, places that facilitate community and traditions, and places that refuse to be homogenized by either commercialism or the exclusion of diversity. Through this sacramental sensibility the church is reminded of its missional nature to create places of memory that will evoke what is most precious.

Notes

[1] Vincent Miller, *Consuming Religion: Christian Faith and Practice in a Consumer Culture* (New York: Continuum, 2005), 7.

[2] Martin Parr, *Small World* (Stockport, England: Dewi Lewis Publishing, 2007). Many of Parr's images may be found on www.martinparr.com or through Magnum Photos at www.magnumphotos.com.

[3] Geoff Dyer, introduction to *Small World*, 5.

[4] See Robert David Sack, *Place, Modernity, and the Consumer's World: A Relational Framework for Geographical Analysis* (Baltimore: The Johns Hopkins University Press, 1992), 169-73. Sack draws attention to the postmodernist Baudrillard, suggesting the stages of simulation present within modern life: first, the image is a reflection of basic reality; second, it masks and perverts basic reality; third, it masks the absence of a basic reality; and fourth it bears no relation to any reality whatsoever (170).

[5] Parr, *Small World*, 5. Sack also suggests that the idea of place as commodity can easily be expanded to entire countries where the marketing of merry old England and romantic France becomes what the tourist expects to see. This perhaps is the most dangerous effect where the replica risks becoming the real (Sack, *Place, Modernity, and the Consumer's World*, 162).

[6] Parr, *Small World*.

[7] More of Nelson's work may be found on her website at www.jennifer anelson.com.

[8] Jennifer A. Nelson, interview by author, January 15, 2010, Grand Forks, North Dakota, e-mail.

[9] Ibid. They began searching for a historic two-story home and ended up with a 1960s ranch home. The process made her "aware of how the idea of home and the practical home are so far apart."

[10] Ibid.

[11]Ibid.

[12]Miller, *Consuming Religion*, 107-45.

[13]Ibid., 109.

[14]Ibid.

[15]Sack, *Place, Modernity, and the Consumer's World*, 149. Here the disorienting dichotomy between public and private is further cultivated where the subjective inward life of the self is perceived to be manifested in an "authentic" outward expression in mass-produced geographical segmentations of space. He reminds us that each commodity brought into and out of our home transforms the visible and physical nature of our home, but also alters its meaning, and the perception of our self identity. Likewise, Miller spends a considerable amount of time delineating the connections between the commodification of culture and the single-family home (Miller, *Consuming Religion*, 46-54).

[16]Miller, *Consuming* Religion, 107.

[17]Beldon Lane, *Landscapes of the Sacred: Geography and Narrative in American Spirituality* (Baltimore: The Johns Hopkins University Press, 2002), 39.

[18]Many scholars have commented on the placelessness of the post-World War II society. In 1970 Alvin Toffler published the first of many editions of his widely read *Future Shock*. The futurist Toffler commented on the nomadic experience of American life, suggesting that an increased transience in travel for work and pleasure as well as an increase in the familial relocation of home has caused a significant loss of commitment and roots. Toffler states, "Commitments are shifting from place-related social structures (city, state, nation, or neighborhood) to those (corporation, profession, friendship network) that are themselves mobile, fluid, and, for all practical purposes, place-less" (Alvin Toffler, *Future Shock* [New York: Random House, Inc., 1970], 93). Ideas of "placelessness" have also been picked up on by French anthropologist Marc Auge in his work *Non-Places*. Auge distinguishes between a place full of history and memory and that of the ephemeral non-places that reflect our cultural transience where people "coexist . . . without living together," such as airports, hotels, interstates, televisions, and computers (Marc Auge, *Non-Places: Introduction to an Anthropology of Supermodernity* [London: Verso, 1995], 110).

[19]Timothy Cresswell, *Place: A Short Introduction* (Malden, MA: Blackwell Publishing, 2004), 18-24.

[20]See Edward Casey, *The Fate of Place: A Philosophical History* (Berkeley: The University of California Press, 1997), 246. See also John Inge, *A Christian Theology of Place* (Hampshire, England: Ashgate, 2003), 18-19.

[21]Sack, *Place, Modernity, and the Consumer's World*, 21.

[22]Ibid., 177.

[23]Ibid., 22: "even though our actions in and through that place may be (accidentally) benign."

[24]Ibid., 3.

[25]Ibid., 204.

[26]Sack followed up on this project in 2003 with *A Geographical Guide to the Real and Good* (New York: Routledge, 2003).

[27]Philip Sheldrake, *Spaces for the Sacred: Place, Memory, and Identity* (Baltimore: The Johns Hopkins University Press, 2001).

[28]Ibid., 1.

[29]Sheldrake begins his project by aptly noting this inevitable tension between the local and universal dimensions of place where Christian theology tenuously balances *deus incarnatus* and *deus absconditus,* where God's action and presence is accessible to human experience and yet unbounded by the local and specific (Sheldrake, *Spaces for the Sacred,* 64). See also Lane, *Landscapes of the Sacred,* 248.

[30]Sheldrake, *Spaces for the Sacred,* 66-71.

[31]Ibid., 72, 74.

[32]Ibid., 168, 77: "The Body of Christ, which the Eucharist shapes, is thus a place that critiques human totalitarianism. It rejects a detached universalism. In this place, people are not opposed or juxtaposed but precisely allowed space to be identified as who they are. . . . The Body of Christ is truly catholic to the degree that each member is able to 'do' or 'practise' themselves in all their specificity."

[33]Ibid., 75.

[34]Miller, *Consuming Religion,* 192.

[35]Ibid., 189.

[36]Jeff Malpas, *Heidegger's Topology: Being, Place, World* (Cambridge: The MIT Press, 2006), 74-75. As noted earlier, Sheldrake's reliance upon Heidegger's *Dasein* emphasizes the character of being as "dwelling within" and carries connotations of care and cultivation.

[37]Miller, *Consuming Religion,* 138. Miller states, "The loss of *telos* brings a loss of self-critique . . . [where] the spiritual life becomes moored to a potentially deluded self and these practices cease to be transformative." Spirituality takes a utilitarian turn, de-emphasizing for formation and transformation, except as it is useful to the individual.

[38]Ibid. Miller makes a key point when he states, "The problem is that when people are trained to lift cultural/religious objects from their traditional contexts, they are less likely to be influenced by other logics, values, and desires mediated by the religious traditions" (210). This is one of the supreme problems with post-modernism and the consumer mentality. Culture trains its followers to sample and lift pieces from the traditions and reapply them in a useful manner. Miller suggests that one of the issues at stake for the church is balancing a sense of obligation to the tradition and its logic with appropriation and use.

[39]Sheldrake, *Spaces for the Sacred,* 81.

Part III

EXPANDING THE BOUNDARIES OF CONVERSATION

Christ of the Borderlands

Faith and Idolatry in an Age of Globalization[1]

Roberto S. Goizueta

The "border" has become a prominent theme in much contemporary scholarship, across a whole range of disciplines. As evidenced by the recent events in Arizona, the need to promote such scholarship gains increasing urgency with every passing year. Such scholarship can no longer be seen—if it ever was—as simply one among many options any more than scholarship on racism can be merely one option among others. In Christian theology, therefore, any preferential option for the poor as a context for doing theological reflection must today take the form of a preferential option for those who live and die on the border.

In this paper, I will offer some reflections on the reality of the border as a challenge to Christian theology and, more importantly, to Christian faith. My argument will examine four aspects of the reality of the border: (1) the preferential option for the poor as a precondition for Christian faith *as such*; (2) the "frontier myth" that promotes an idolatrous conception of the border and thus functions as an obstacle to the option for the poor in the United States; (3) alternative conceptions of the border emerging from those "on the other side" of the border; and (4) some Christological implications of a preferential option for the borderland as a condition of the possibility of doing Christian theology.

Underlying my argument will be the conviction that such a methodological option is more than an ethical imperative; it is indeed the decisive criterion that distinguishes Christian faith, *qua Christian*, from idolatry in the United States today. In addition to being a political, cultural, racial, economic, and ethical problem, the border is, above all, a *theological* problem.

In our contemporary context, Christian communities must come to view ongoing debates about so-called "illegal aliens" as, at bottom, a theological struggle between an idolatry that, like all idolatry, produces an untold number of innocent victims, and faith in the transcendent Christian God. Precisely because our God is transcendent, God will always be rejected as alien by those for whom borders are not places of mutually enriching encounter between different peoples but military garrisons for defending "civilization" against "savagery." In such a historical context, to say that God is transcendent is to say that God is illegal and is revealed in a special way among illegal persons. Conversely, to reject human beings from the other side of the border as illegal aliens while, simultaneously, eliminating virtually all barriers to the free movement of capital across those same borders is to reject the transcendent God in favor of an idol who demands human sacrifice.

I begin my reflections with three stories, three examples of the explicitly religious and theological character of the borderland. April 22 of this year (2010) marked the tenth anniversary of an event that as a Cuban-American I remember as if it had happened yesterday. Some of you may also remember. In the early morning hours of April 22, 2000, heavily armed agents of the U.S. Border Patrol stormed a house in Miami's Little Havana neighborhood. The house was occupied by a young Cuban boy, Elian González, and his relatives. They had taken him in after his mother, who fled Cuba with him, had drowned at sea. In what became an international incident, Elian's father, still in Cuba, was demanding his son's return against the wishes of Elian's Miami relatives. In order to force the return, U.S. Attorney General Janet Reno ordered the raid on the house and the removal of Elian.

The scene is seared in my memory. It was Holy Saturday morning, and I was spending the Easter weekend with my family in Miami, a city that had been turned upside down by the tug-of-war between Cuba and the Miami Cuban-American community. An early riser, I turned on the news at 5:00 a.m. and witnessed a live broadcast of the horrifying scene. I'll never forget the terrified face on the young boy as he was confronted and grabbed by a helmeted Border Patrol agent brandishing a machine gun.

Another image also still stands out in my mind, one that attracted little attention in the popular media. Strewn about the living room after the raid were the shattered pieces of the home altar the family had built, and which the agents had reduced to rubble as they had burst into the house: a scarred picture of the *Divino Rostro*, or the Holy Face of Christ on one corner of the floor; a mangled statue of *Nuestra Señora de La Caridad del Cobre*, Our Lady of Charity, in another corner; half-burned votive candles in yet another corner. In the midst of the tragic events of that day, few commentators seemed to have noticed the explicitly religious—or, perhaps more accurately, sacrilegious—character of that scene. Few, that is, beyond the González family members themselves, who repeatedly and painfully drew the cameraman's attention to the destroyed religious objects.

Moreover, few commentators seemed particularly troubled by the fact that the raid had taken place during the Paschal Triduum, the most sacred time of the year for Christians. In a world where such religious observances, home altars, religious statues, and the bloodied face of the Crucified Christ appear as little more than strange, at best "quaint" reminders of another time and place, these are too readily dismissed as but curious examples of those unsophisticated superstitions that we modern Christians have outgrown. Yet they give expression to a faith born on the border, a faith in a God whose love and presence are experienced most profoundly by the sacrificial victims of the border-as-idol.

The year 2010 also marks the quincentennial of a momentous event in the history of the Americas, this one reflecting a dramatically different, alternative understanding of the border—not as a place of sacrifice and sacrilege but as a locus of conversion. Five hundred years ago, the Spanish missionary Fray Bartolomé de Las Casas became the first priest ordained in the Americas. Arriving in the "New World" as an *encomendero* (or slaveowner), Bartolomé de Las Casas eventually joined the Dominican order and committed himself to the evangelization of the Indians.

Though known for his charitable treatment of the Indians in his care, Las Casas nevertheless did not initially see a contradiction between his Christian, priestly calling and his role as an *encomendero*. This changed when, while preparing to celebrate the eucharistic liturgy one day, the Spanish Dominican underwent a conversion that would dramatically alter his understanding of his Christian faith, his priestly vocation, his role as a missionary, and, especially, his relationship with the indigenous peoples of America. While studying the Scriptures in preparation for his homily, Las Casas came across a text from the Book of Sirach (34:18-22):

> Tainted his gifts who offers in sacrifice ill-gotten goods!
>   Mock presents from the lawless win not God's favor.
> The Most High approves not the gifts of the godless.
>   [Nor for their many sacrifices does he forgive their sins.]
> Like the man who slays a son in his father's presence
>   is he who offers sacrifice from the possessions of the poor.
> The bread of charity is life itself for the needy,
>   he who withholds it is a person of blood.
> He slays his neighbor who deprives him of his living;
>   he sheds blood who denies the laborer his wages.[2]

This text opened Las Casas's eyes to the meaning and import of the liturgical action he was about to undertake. As a slaveowner, he would be offering to God bread and wine that were the fruit of the labor of the Amerindians in his care, men and women who themselves remained poor and hungry. He would be offering to God the "objectivized lives" of his workers, now in the form of bread and wine; he would be sacrificing *their* lives on God's altar, thereby committing the worst kind of sacrilege and blasphemy. Any God who would countenance such a sacrifice could not be the transcendent just God of the Scriptures but a mere idol, a "god" who legitimates murder.[3]

This realization led Las Casas to his subsequent decision to release his slaves, and he himself became a tireless defender of the Amerindians. (One should note the tragic irony, however, that Las Casas did not condemn the practice of African slavery until the end of his life, initially seeing this as an alternative to the enslavement of the Amerindians.) If the Spanish conquistadores and missionaries condemned the Indians for their practice of human sacrifice, he argued, the Spanish Christians themselves were guilty of human sacrifice when, in the eucharistic liturgy, they presented offerings of bread and wine that were the products of exploited labor. What was offered up on the Spanish altars was not the body and blood of Christ but the body and blood of the Indians.

If the Amerindians did not accept the message preached by the Spanish missionaries, such recalcitrance was not only understandable but justifiable and, indeed, demanded. What the Amerindians rejected was not the God of love preached by the Spanish but the "god" of hatred and violence manifested in their actions. In that context, the Indians had not only a right to reject "Christianity" but a duty to do so, for what they were rejecting was not Christianity but an idolatry more destructive than the "idolatry" practiced by the indigenous peoples themselves.[4]

As Las Casas had so prophetically argued, if at the very heart of the Christian faith is the assertion that "God is love," a genuine respect for and love of "the other" is a condition of the possibility for any authentic evangelization. Such a respect and love is the fundamental criterion of the credibility and validity of the Christian faith. Eventually, Bartolomé de Las Casas would strive to interpret and judge the Spanish evangelizing efforts through the eyes of the indigenous people.[5] In his comparison of Las Casas' account of the conquest with the Amerindians' own accounts, the Las Casas scholar André Saint-Lu notes that:

> the viewpoint of Las Casas, a Spaniard, intimately takes on that of the indigenous people, as if he also had undergone their physical sufferings and their sorrow. But to the desperate pain of the martyred people there is added, in the defender of the Indians, the vehement denunciation of so many cruelties, judged as detestable crimes and deeds. The indigenous accounts constitute a pathetic lamentation; those of Las Casas, also heart-rending but full of indignation, are a cry of anguish and rebellion.[6]

In his study of Las Casas, Gustavo Gutiérrez makes the same point: "In his attempt to see things 'as if he were an Indian', Las Casas seeks to assume what today is called 'the viewpoint of the defeated.' . . ."[7] On the border between Spain and the "New World," Las Casas came to understand that it was he, the Spanish Christian, who needed to be converted—and the agents of that conversion would be the indigenous people.

This same message of the border as a place where, paradoxically, Christians themselves experience conversion was again affirmed only a few years later, on December 12, 1531. On that day, *la Virgen morena* ("the dark-skinned virgin") appeared to an indigenous man, Juan Diego, on a hill outside what is now Mexico City. The narrative recounts several encounters between *la Morenita* and Juan Diego, in the course of which she repeatedly assures him that, despite his own sense of worthlessness vis-à-vis the Spaniards, he is her most beloved, favored child. He refuses to believe that he is worthy of her trust. Nevertheless, as she continues to reassure him, Juan Diego gradually develops a sense of his own dignity as a child of God.

In their first encounter, she commanded Juan Diego to ask the Spanish bishop in Mexico City, Juan de Zumárraga, to build a church on the hill where she had appeared. Juan Diego resisted, arguing that he was not worthy to be charged with such a mission. The Lady insisted, so Juan Diego eventually went to the bishop's palace to make the request. At first, the bishop would not even receive the poor indigenous man. Later, the bishop received but did not believe him. Finally, the Lady gave Juan Diego a "sign" to take with him, a bouquet of flowers she had ordered him to pick from a nearby hilltop. Since all knew that such flowers could not grow at that time of the year, they would recognize the miraculous nature of the sign. So Juan Diego put the flowers in his *tilma*, or cloak. When the indigenous man arrived at the bishop's palace and opened the cloak to reveal the flowers, another miraculous sign appeared, an image of the Virgin, Our Lady of Guadalupe, imprinted on the cloak. Stirred and convinced by these signs, the bishop relented and ordered that the Lady's wish be granted. In the Guadalupe narrative, the traditional roles are thereby reversed: the dark-skinned Virgin and the indigenous man themselves become the messengers of God and evangelizers to the Spanish bishop, who is portrayed as the one in need of conversion.

In each of these three stories, the roles of believer and idolater are reversed: the presumptive representatives of the Christian faith are unmasked as, in fact, worshippers of idols. Each story illustrates the theological significance of the border as a privileged locus of conversion—not the conversion of the "heathen" but of the "Christian." The borderland is the privileged place for encountering the Christian God among the victims of a border that is itself worshipped as idol. I maintain that this reversal demands a reconceptualization of the border rooted in God's preferential love for the poor—in this case, God's preferential love for the people of the borderland, those persons who are excluded and exploited as heathen, barbarians, and savages.

God's Preferential Love for the Poor

Gustavo Gutiérrez contends that the two principal, overarching themes in Scripture are: (1) the universality and gratuity of God's love, and (2) God's preferential love for the poor. God's preferential love for the poor is the theological and methodological guarantee, or safeguard, of God's transcendence, sovereignty, and Mystery. If God is truly "Other" and thus irreducible to any human concept or construction, then *logically* God will take the side of the poor, the marginalized, the excluded. In other words, *if* God loves everyone equally and gratuitously, *then* God will love the poor preferentially. What, at first glance, appear to be mutually contradictory assertions are, in fact, mutually implicit.

Tragically, we live in a divided world and society. And the persons in the best position to acknowledge that fact are those who suffer the consequences of the division. Conversely, those of us who benefit—whether explicitly or implicitly—from social divisions are likely to either ignore these or deemphasize their significance. It is the hungry person, after all, who is in the best position to determine whether hunger exists in our society. In other words, the poor or powerless have a privileged epistemological perspective from which to evaluate "reality" (though such privilege in no way assumes infallibility or inevitability—only a greater likelihood of accuracy). In Jon Sobrino's words, the poor are in a privileged position from which to be "honest about reality."[8] And, if we believe that God becomes present to us in reality, such honesty is a fundamental precondition for recognizing God.

If we do indeed live in a divided world in which the victims of that division have an epistemological privilege, then, what is the *theological* significance of this reality? More specifically, what can it mean to say that God enters into and becomes incarnate in a world, society, and history beset by divisions between the powerful and the powerless? In such a world, what would it mean to say that God loves all people equally and gratuitously? In such a world, what would it mean to say that Jesus Christ is the perfect expression of God's love?

For two thousand years the Christian tradition has proposed an answer that, for many, has seemed inconceivable, if not scandalous. In such a world the perfect expression of God's love is found in the utter powerlessness of a condemned criminal who, having experienced abandonment by his closest friends and even God, hangs helplessly from a cross. God's love enters history in the person of an outcast tortured and crucified for befriending outcasts. God's love enters a divided society on the side of those who suffer the consequences of the division—not because God loves the outcast more, but because in the midst of division and conflict God's love for the victims and God's love for their victimizers must take different forms. Indeed, God's love for the powerful will not (at least initially) be experienced as love at all, since it will take the form of challenge, confrontation, and a call to conversion, to *metanoia*. To say that God's love is universal, then, is not to say that it is *neutral*. In fact, it is to say the very opposite: precisely *because* God's love is universal, it *cannot* be neutral.

The Crucified and Risen Christ is the historical incarnation of this logic, the logic of God's universal, gratuitous love. If the incarnate God is truly Other, truly Mystery, then God will be revealed most fully among those persons who themselves are most "other," most incomprehensible in our world—among those who do not belong. The God who is absolutely Other, and thus "makes no sense" in the context of merely human calculations and expectations, will be encountered most fully among those persons whose very existence makes no sense, such as among the hungry in a gluttonous world, among the powerless in a power-mad world, among the savages in a civilized society.

The Frontier Myth

The Argentine historian Enrique Dussel has suggested that what we today call "globalization" is founded, not on the relativization of borders but, on the contrary, on the establishment of borders between a "center" and a "periphery." From its very origins and of its very essence, the modern West needs and demands a center *and* a periphery, separated by a border. Conquest is not the consequence of but the origin of modernity. The "civilized" modern ego must conquer in order to establish a "barbarian other" against which the ego can define itself. The modern Christian ego defines itself over against the pre-modern, idolatrous savage.[9] The Cartesian individualism and rationalism so often identified as the origins of modernity are, conversely, merely derivative, legitimating consequences of this center-periphery global structure.

The need to construct an "other," however, manifested itself differently in the North and South among the British colonists and the Iberian conquistadores respectively. These historical differences yielded different conceptions of the border. To understand contemporary debates about the border in the United States one must understand the history of our country's conception of the border as a fundamental—perhaps *the* fundamental—characteristic of national identity. That is, in our history the border has functioned as much more than a geographical boundary; it has been perhaps the defining characteristic of everything we call "American." But to appreciate this fact we have to trace the roots of contemporary debates about the border to earlier conceptions of what we used to call the "frontier."

In June 1914 the great American historian Frederick Jackson Turner delivered the commencement address at the University of Washington, only a couple of hundred miles from where we gather here today. Turner ended that speech, entitled "The West and American Ideals," with a quote from Alfred, Lord Tennyson's poem "Ulysses":

> I am become a name/For always roaming with an hungry heart,/Much have I seen and known . . . /I am a part of all that I have met;/Yet all experience is an arch, where thro'/ Gleams that untravelled world, whose margin fades/Forever and forever when I move./How dull it is to pause, to make an end./To rust unburnished, not to shine in use!/And this gray spirit yearning in desire/To follow knowledge like a shining star/Beyond the utmost bound of human thought./ . . . Come my friends,/'Tis not too late to seek a newer world./Push off, and sitting well in order smite/The sounding furrows; for

my purpose holds/To sail beyond the sunset, and the baths/
Of all the Western stars until I die/To strive, to seek, to find
and not to yield.[10]

Tennyson's words evoked for Turner those frontier ideals that had
served the United States so well until the end of the nineteenth
century: "to seek a newer world . . . to sail beyond the sunset . . .
to strive, to seek, to find and not to yield."

Already by the second half of the nineteenth century, however,
new frontiers had seemingly been exhausted, the West had been
"won," and American civilization had extended its reach to the
continent's Pacific limits. Frederick Jackson Turner noted this fact
in his 1893 essay on "The Significance of the Frontier in American
History," which Yale historian John Mack Faragher has called "the
single most influential piece of writing in the history of American
history."[11] Observing that the closing of the Western frontier raised
troubling questions about our nation's future, Turner proposed
what came to be known as the frontier thesis:

> American social development has been continually begin-
> ning over again on the frontier. This perennial rebirth, this
> fluidity of American life, this expansion westward with its
> new opportunities, its continuous touch with the simplicity
> of primitive society, furnish the forces dominating American
> character. In this advance, the frontier is the outer edge of
> the wave—the meeting point between savagery and civili-
> zation. . . . And now, four centuries from the discovery of
> America, at the end of a hundred years of life under the
> Constitution, the frontier has gone. . . .[12]

By the end of the nineteenth century, the western frontier "finally closed forever, with uncertain consequences for the American
future."[13] How could our national self-understanding survive the
end of the frontier that had for so long defined the American character? Indeed, if the frontier myth was what *defined* the American
character, could it ever be completely left behind? "Long after
the frontier period of a particular region of the United States has
passed away," wrote Turner, "the conception of society, the ideals and aspirations which it produced, persist in the minds of the

people. . . . This experience has been wrought into the very warp and woof of American thought."[14] And Turner's very definition of the frontier myth explicitly articulated, with great precision, what that underlying conception of society was: the frontier, Turner wrote, is "the meeting point between savagery and civilization." Though hardly unique to the U.S. drive for expansion, that understanding of the frontier has defined the U.S. character in a particular way from the beginning.

From the time of the British colonies, the very drive to *extend* the frontier came to be seen as a constitutive feature of the United States itself, indeed, a constitutive feature of "American civilization": to be a civilized citizenry in the United States *is* to extend the frontier, to expand, to seek new opportunities, to dominate, to conquer (in Tennyson's words, "How dull it is to pause, to make an end"). Conversely, then, to accept limits to this expansion would be to undermine the very foundations of civilized society as we had come to know it: "once free lands were exhausted . . . the whole moral fabric would collapse and the land descend into the state of depravity and tyranny that overcrowded Europe already knew."[15] Thus, implicit in the frontier myth is the assumption that the only alternative to expansion is decline, or degeneration (including moral degeneration).

If, then, the frontier myth and its underlying conception of society have indeed been "wrought into the very warp and woof of American thought," how would that myth survive the closing of the western frontier? This was Turner's question, though he would not live to see its answer. A century later, at the beginning of the twenty-first century, I do think we can suggest a possible answer, an answer that lies not to the west but to the south. In retrospect, the turn of the twentieth century represented not so much the demise of the frontier as the replacement of the western frontier with a southern frontier. The westward territorial expansion, including the annexation of Mexican territory in the first half of the nineteenth century, was replaced by a southern expansion. Initially, this latter followed the earlier pattern of military, geographical, and political expansion. Thus, in the first half of the twentieth century, the U.S. frontier became the Caribbean and Central America. Just as the western frontier had expanded into "virgin territory," so too would the southern frontier. The United

States would expand its control into its "backyard," particularly the Caribbean and Central America.

The most prominent instruments for extending this new southern frontier would be economic enterprises seeking to expand their markets, often in conjunction with U.S. political and military interests. When territorial expansion proved impracticable, more benign forms of economic expansion would take its place, even if sometimes with the aid of political and even military intervention and occupation. During the first decade of the twentieth century, the United States began to export capital to a degree previously unequalled and by World War I had erased its trade deficits.[16] Moreover, U.S. activity on this fresh frontier to the south would bear the marks of the earlier westward expansion, drawing on the same historical myth. U.S. attempts to extend its southern frontier, argues historian Walter LaFeber, "rested on views of history, the character of foreign peoples ['savagery'], and politics that anticipated attitudes held by North Americans throughout much of the twentieth century. . . . North Americans seldom doubted that they could teach people to the south to act more civilized."[17] If, as Turner averred, the frontier myth has been "wrought into the very warp and woof of American thought," the end of the nineteenth century did not signal the end of the frontier myth, only its relocation. The savages would now be found not to our west but to our south.

If Turner and Faragher's suggestion concerning the foundational character of the frontier myth is accurate, we should not assume that simply because we now prefer the language of borders to the language of frontiers, the difference in terminology reflects a truly different understanding of history and identity. In 2010, the frontier myth still functions as the lens through which we as a society read the reality of our southern border. Indeed, the fact that it is *only* our southern border that is so viewed is further evidence of the enduring influence of the frontier myth. American civilization and identity are not threatened from the north, where there is no savagery. On our southern border, many miles of barbed wire-capped fences are erected to prevent the movement of *human beings* northward, even as trade agreements are signed to eliminate all limits to the free movement of *capital* across the border. Thus, in our twenty-first century version of the frontier myth, human labor is enslaved while capital is liberated.

The Border

As distinct from that of the United States, the Latin American conception of the border is rooted in the distinctive history of Latin America itself. It may be, therefore, that the victims of the frontier myth, the savages on the other side of the frontier, can offer an alternative conception of the border. While the modern drive for territorial expansion and domination is at the heart of both the Iberian and British colonization of the Americas, observes historian Justo González, the processes of expansion developed differently in the North and South:

> The difference was that in the north it was possible and convenient to push back the native inhabitants rather than to conquer and subdue them. What northern colonialists wanted was land [rather than slave labor]. The original inhabitants were a hindrance. So, instead of subjugating the Indians, they set about to push them off their lands, and eventually to exterminate them. If the myth in the Spanish colonies was that the Indians were like children who needed someone to govern them, the myth in the English colonies was that the Indians were nonpeople; they didn't exist, their lands were a vacuum. In north Georgia, in the middle of Cherokee County, there is a monument to a white man who was, so the monument says, "the first man to settle in these parts." And this, in a county that is still called "Cherokee"! This contrast in the colonizing process led to a "border" mentality in Mexico and much of Latin America, and a "frontier" mentality in the United States. Because the Spanish colonizers were forced to live with the original inhabitants of the land, a *mestizo* population and culture developed. . . . In contrast, in the lands to the north, the process and the myth were of a constantly moving frontier, pushing back the native inhabitants of the land, interacting with them as little as possible. There was civilization this side of the frontier; and a void

at the other side. The West was to be "won." The western line, the frontier, was seen as the growing edge; but it was expected to produce growth by mere expansion rather than by interaction.[18]

As violent as both were, the Spanish conquest ultimately generated borders, while the British conquest generated a frontier. González notes the difference: a frontier moves in only one direction, outward, while a border allows for movement in both directions. In the North, any movement back across the frontier is thus perceived as "an incursion of the forces of evil and backwardness into the realm of light and progress."[19] If, as Frederick Jackson Turner so explicitly declared, what lies on the other side of the frontier is mere "savagery," then any movement back toward the north must be prohibited as a threat to "civilization," a threat to national identity, a threat to national security. Above all, however, any movement north forces civilized society to confront its barbaric *alter ego*.

In other words, Turner was right: the frontier is indeed the "meeting point between savagery and civilization." What he failed to see was that the savagery we meet on the frontier is *our own*. And that is why we fear any movement back across the border toward the north. Ultimately this is not because our nation wants to deny the existence of "those" savages south of the border, but because, for its own sense of national identity, the United States *must* deny the truth of *its own* savagery. The faces of those "savages" are the mirrors of our nation's soul; they are the "dangerous memory" that is never quite fully repressed. The faces of the "savages" are what the German theologian Johann Baptist Metz has called "dangerous memories, memories which make demands on us."[20] And the most basic demand is that we surrender the illusion of innocence that feeds the frontier myth.

"It is precisely in that willful innocence," warns González, "that guilt lies."[21] "The reason why this country has refused to hear the truth in its own history," he continues, "is that as long as it is innocent of such truth, it does not have to deal with the injustices that lie at the heart of its power and its social order."[22] The reason why the myth of innocence, the frontier myth, must be exposed is that such honesty about our present and past reality is a precondition for justice and reconciliation. (After all, attacks against "illegal aliens" and anyone whose existence recalls those dangerous memories represent simply the violent surfacing of repressed memories.)

Yet a border need not function as a frontier that only expands and excludes; it need not be perceived as the boundary that protects civilization from savagery. Even if too-often denied in practice, an alternative understanding of the border is implicit in the *mestizo* history of Latin America:

> A border is the place at which two realities, two worldviews, two cultures, meet and interact. . . . At the border growth takes place by encounter, by mutual enrichment. A true border, a true place of encounter, is by nature permeable. It is not like medieval armor, but rather like skin. Our skin does set a limit to where our body begins and where it ends. Our skin also sets certain limits to our give-and-take with our environment, keeping out certain germs, helping us to select that in our environment which we are ready to absorb. But if we ever close up our skin, we die.[23]

A border may function to affirm differences while, at the same time, allowing for mutually enriching interaction. The *mestizo* history of Latin America is evidence that ambiguity can be the seedbed of new life, the border can be the birthplace of a new, reconciled human community. Such a recognition of the ambiguity of *all* human histories is a necessary precondition for an understanding of the difference between a frontier and a border. The possibility is no mere utopian illusion but is the lived reality of the borderland today. As Virgilio Elizondo notes:

> Today, the borderlands between the U.S. and Mexico form the cradle of a new humanity. It is the meeting ground of ancient civilizations that have never met before. Old cultural borders are giving way and a new people is emerging. . . . The borders no longer mark the end limits of a country, a civilization, or even a hemisphere, but the starting points of a new space populated by a new human group.[24]

If the frontier is, for Frederick Jackson Turner, the "meeting point between savagery and civilization," the border is, for Elizondo, the meeting ground of ancient civilizations.

Only such a conception of the border, moreover, can allow for a genuine encounter with a transcendent God, a God who irrupts in our world from the other side of the border, a God who can speak through an Elian González, a Juan Diego, or an indigenous slave. Conversely, a frontier that is perceived as the "meeting point between savagery and civilization" is but an idol that, like all idols, generates sacrificial victims. By definition, a frontier precludes the possibility of transcendence, or a revelation that unexpectedly and "illegally" breeches the frontier from the other side. It is for this reason—again, a profoundly theological reason—that the stranger and the alien play such a central role in both the Hebrew and Christian Scriptures. As the one from the other side, the stranger or alien is the privileged messenger of the God who, as transcendent, also approaches us from the other side. Again, the point is not that the believer *ought* to extend hospitality to the stranger and the alien. The point is that, *unless* one extends such hospitality, one is not a believer at all; one is an idolater.

The Crucified and Risen Christ

Consequently, a preferential option for the borderlands—more specifically, for those persons who live and die as victims of the frontier myth—is a precondition for an encounter with the Crucified and Risen Christ of the gospels, for the God of Jesus Christ takes flesh on the border "between savagery and civilization." As Virgilio Elizondo reminds us, Jesus Christ is a Jew from Galilee, from the borderlands of Palestine, far from the center of power in Jerusalem and contiguous with Greco-Roman populations; Jesus' ministry and mission, especially, begin and end in the borderland.[25] It is in the midst of the Jewish population of the borderland that the resurrected Christ, the now-glorified Witness to God's power and love, would be encountered: "he has risen from the dead, and behold, he is going before you to Galilee; there you will see him" (Mt 28:7). Jesus' ministry would end where it had begun: it is in Galilee that his disciples would see the resurrected Jesus.

In the Galilean borderland the new church is born from the

Pentecost that breeches the barriers of culture, race, and language. ("Are not all these people who are speaking Galileans? Then how does each of us hear them in our own native language?" [Acts 2:7-8]) In the gospels, then, the borderland reality takes on *theological* significance. Jesus Christ's social location is not merely accidental to the Christian *kerygma*; it is at the very heart of our Christian faith. In Galilee, the epistemological privilege of the poor becomes, even more specifically, the epistemological privilege of the alien, the stranger from the borderland. Conversely, insofar as the border functions to exclude, those persons who are excluded are in a privileged position to recognize the Crucified and Risen Christ, who himself was and continues to be excluded.

Jesus' resurrection, then, includes as an intrinsic element the reconstitution of the community that had been rent asunder when Jesus' friends abandoned him on the way to Calvary. This newly reconstituted community is born in Galilee, in the borderland. This fact is no mere coincidence, for it reflects the divine logic of transcendence, the logic of divine freedom and gratuitousness. If God is radically "other," or absolute Mystery, then God will be revealed especially among those persons who are most "other," those strangers and aliens who intrude illegally into our well-defended, ostensibly secure world. Thus, God's special love of the alien in no way limits God's love. On the contrary, that preferential love is the guarantee and safeguard of that radical gratuitousness and mercy that define the God who is Mystery.

Galilee is the final confirmation that God's preferential love for the poor is the safeguard of God's universal, gratuitous love. In his return to Galilee, the full ramifications of Jesus' crucifixion and resurrection become visible. The scandalous and inconceivable self-communication of God in the person of a crucified convict reveals the radical strangeness of God's love.

Equally strange is the command to "go to Galilee" in order to see the resurrected Jesus. *Because* God's love is most fully revealed in the person of a convict hanging from a cross, God's love can be revealed to everyone. *Because* the Crucified and Risen Christ will be seen first in Galilee among those people living dangerously close to "the other side," he can be seen everywhere and in everyone. *Because* the church is the church of the borderland and its inhabitants, the church can be—and must be—universal, welcoming everyone. Far from implying any exclusivity that undermines the universality and gratuity of God's love, God's preferential love for the poor is the only credible guarantee of that universality and gratuity.

Insofar as borders become frontiers, barriers that separate "us" from "them," they become barriers to the God who, because God is Mystery, is revealed first among the strangers and aliens. In the words of Gustavo Gutiérrez, "[T]he world outside the fence [i.e., the border] is the world of gratuitousness; it is there that God dwells and there that God's friends find a joyous welcome."[26] It is there that the Crucified and Risen Christ will be seen and will find a joyous welcome. Not coincidentally, the most vibrant, thriving Christian churches in our "globalized" world are to be found not among civilized people but among the savages and barbarians. For it is there that the idolatry of the frontier is unmasked and the Crucified and Risen Christ is revealed.

Notes

[1]Sections of this essay appear in different form in my recent book *Christ Our Companion: Toward a Theological Aesthetics of Liberation* (Maryknoll, NY: Orbis Books, 2009) and in my forthcoming essay "The Preferential Option for the Poor: Christ and the Logic of Gratuity" in *Jesus of Galilee: Contextual Christology for the 21ˢᵗ Century*, ed. Robert Lasalle-Klein (Maryknoll, NY: Orbis Books).

[2]Quoted in Gustavo Gutiérrez, *Las Casas: In Search of the Poor of Jesus Christ* (Maryknoll, NY: Orbis Books, 1993), 47.

[3]Ibid., 46-61.
[4]Ibid., 154-89.
[5]Ibid., 87-90.
[6]Quoted in ibid., 88-89.
[7]Ibid., 89.

[8]Jon Sobrino, *Spirituality of Liberation* (Maryknoll, NY: Orbis Books, 1988), 14-16.

[9]Enrique Dussel, *The Invention of the Americas: Eclipse of "the Other" and the Myth of Modernity* (New York: Continuum, 1995), 17.

[10]Alfred, Lord Tennyson, quoted in Frederick Jackson Turner, *Rereading Frederick Jackson Turner*, with commentary by John Mack Faragher (New York: Henry Holt and Co., 1994), 158.

[11]John Mack Faragher, Introduction, in *Rereading Frederick Jackson Turner*, with commentary by John Mack Faragher (New York: Henry Holt and Co., 1994), 1.

[12]Turner, *Rereading Frederick Jackson Turner*, 32, 60.

[13]Faragher, Introduction, 1.

[14]Turner, *Rereading Frederick Jackson Turner*, 96.

[15]Ray Allen Billington, *The Genesis of the Frontier Thesis: A Study in Historical Creativity* (San Marino, CA: The Huntington Library, 1971), 72.

[16]Walter LaFeber, *Inevitable Revolutions: The United States in Central America* (New York: W. W. Norton and Company, 1983), 35.

[17]Ibid., 39.

[18]Justo González, *Santa Biblia: The Bible Through Hispanic Eyes* (Nashville: Abingdon Press, 1996), 85-86.

[19]Ibid., 86.

[20]Johann Baptist Metz, *Faith in History and Society: Toward a Practical Fundamental Theology* (New York: Seabury Press, 1980), 109.

[21]Justo González, *Mañana: Christian Theology from a Hispanic Perspective* (Nashville: Abingdon Press, 1990), 39.

[22]Ibid.

[23]González, *Santa Biblia*, 86-87.

[24]Virgilio Elizondo, *The Future Is Mestizo: Life Where Cultures Meet* (Bloomington, IN: Meyer-Stone, 1988), x-xi.

[25]Virgilio Elizondo, *Galilean Journey: The Mexican-American Promise* (Maryknoll, NY: Orbis Books, 1983).

[26]James Nickoloff, ed., *Gustavo Gutiérrez: Essential Writings* (Maryknoll, NY: Orbis Books, 1996), 172.

Expanding Catholic Ecological Ethics

Ecological Solidarity and Earth Rights

Daniel P. Scheid

While the common good has become an important component of Catholic reflection on ecological ethics,[1] two other related and vital themes of Catholic social thought have received less attention: (1) the virtue of solidarity, which develops in people a resolute commitment to the common good; and (2) rights discourse, which emphasizes the importance of an intrinsic dignity that others are bound to respect. As all three components have generally referred to human relationships, a reformulation is necessary for them to include and express direct concern for nonhuman nature.

Such expansions of ethical terms are not unprecedented. Indeed, they have already begun for the principle of the common good. For example, in 1992 the U.S. Catholic bishops introduced the idea of a "planetary common good,"[2] and theologian John Hart argued that " 'common good' understandings should be extended to nonhuman creation."[3] Hart helpfully broadened the common good tradition by parsing out various aspects of the common good while continually incorporating the good of nonhuman nature.[4] These trends continue and extend the tradition of Pope Paul VI, who witnessed a growing interdependence among nations and therefore urged a reconsideration of the common good to include not just the good of a particular society but now the entire human family. Espousing a "planetary common good" recognizes that interdependence characterizes not only human communities but the entire Earth. A common good that includes nonhuman nature challenges us to see creation as more than a resource to sustain human life and to broaden our perspective to see human beings as one creature among many who glorify God.

While Hart and others explain well the idea of a "planetary common good" that incorporates more than human well-being, the ramifications of this for solidarity and rights have not been articulated: if nature is to be considered part of the common good, what reformulations are possible or desirable for the concepts of solidarity and human rights, since the common good is fulfilled at least in part through solidarity and the observance of rights and duties?[5] All three of these themes from Catholic social thought are important in providing a moral response to globalization and the increasing interdependence among humans. They thus seem fitting to address the undeniable interdependence between humans and the Earth and the ecological effects of globalization. Just as the common good can now entail the good of nonhuman nature, I propose considering a similar expansion wherein solidarity becomes "ecological solidarity" and rights discourse includes "rights for the Earth."

Expanding solidarity and rights discourse represents a challenge to conventional Catholic social thought in two general ways.[6] First, doing so suggests the insufficiency of couching ecological ethics only in reference to human well-being. As theologians begin to describe a common good beyond the human community, concepts such as "stewardship" or "care of creation" do not adequately challenge the typical presumption in theological ethics that the goods of the Earth exist solely for humanity. Ecological solidarity and rights for the Earth better correlate to this developing notion of the common good.

Second, the critique can be made that broadening solidarity and rights to include nonhuman creation dilutes the meaning of these concepts to the point that they no longer provide clarity on moral issues related to inter-human ethics. I sense two hesitations in this critique. First is the fear that investing nonhuman nature with dignity could undermine the primacy of human dignity that theologians have worked tirelessly to establish. Second, to apply characteristics of human relationships to our interactions with nature seems naïve because doing so is unscientific, and legally and economically impractical.

While these are legitimate hesitations, I contend that there are three reasons why we may and should promote ecological solidarity and Earth rights. First, theologians can still articulate distinctions between human and nonhuman relationships so that our duties to humans are not conflated with our duties to nonhuman nature. Second, one could propose analogous concepts of solidarity and rights that apply to nonhuman creation and bear different names. My reason for not taking this approach is that creating terms applicable only to nature serves to reinforce the sharp divide between humans and nature that ecological theologians have been striving to deconstruct.[7] Third, drawing on concepts deeply rooted in Catholic social thought gives the reformulated terms (ecological solidarity, Earth rights) a gravitas that they might not otherwise have. This additional moral weight is deserved, based on the scope and severity of the ecological crisis. Growing industrial economic development puts the planetary common good under increasing threat. This danger justifies retrieving and revising the traditions of solidarity and rights so as to increase protections for the planetary common good.

To give credence to my third point, I turn at the end of this essay to two pressing ecological concerns that epitomize the ill effects of industrial, economic globalization: anthropogenic climate change, and the oil spill in the Gulf of Mexico caused by the collapse of the Deepwater Horizon drilling rig on April 20, 2010. Climate change exemplifies the fact of interdependence between humans and the Earth and prompts us to reconsider the demands of the planetary common good. The Gulf oil spill, the largest in U.S. history, becomes a case study in the links among economics, globalization, and ecological vulnerability. While solidarity with humans is not identical to solidarity with nonhumans, nor are Earth rights the same as human rights, solidarity must be ecological rather than merely human, and some form of rights must be extended to non-human nature to address climate change and to respond to catastrophes such as that in the Gulf.

The contexts of climate change and the Gulf oil spill suggest two reformulations of Catholic social thought. The first, ecological solidarity, includes a threefold solidarity with all human beings, especially those most affected by climate change; all plant and animal species, especially those most imperiled; and the ecosystems themselves that sustain and support a diversity of creatures. The second, Earth rights, lifts up the goodness of nonhuman nature and imposes human duties.

Extending Solidarity

Solidarity was first introduced as a moral virtue by John Paul II in 1987 to acknowledge the fact that one may recognize interdependence without working for the common good.[8] As Charles Clark explains, solidarity challenges modern Western approaches to economics and culture that privilege individual happiness over the common good: "[Solidarity] is the opposite of the attitude of extreme individualism that underlies neoclassical economic theory and its strictures that all interpersonal interaction must be based on individual self-interest."[9] Instead, Christians are called to cultivate a disposition whereby they commit themselves to improve the quality of global interdependence and enhance the good of the whole.

John Paul II observed "the positive and moral value of the growing awareness of interdependence among individuals and nations. . . . [M]en and women in various parts of the world feel personally affected by the injustices and violations of human rights committed in distant countries" (*Sollicitudo Rei Socialis*, §38). The virtue of solidarity is meant to direct these emotional responses to injustices toward proper action. Thus solidarity

> is not a feeling of vague compassion or shallow distress at the misfortunes of so many people, both near and far. On the contrary, it is *a firm and persevering determination* to commit oneself to the *common good*; that is to say to the good of all and of each individual, because we are all really responsible *for all* (*Sollicitudo Rei Socialis*, §38).

The virtue of solidarity includes both the feeling of being personally affected by the injustices suffered by others and a commitment to end that misery by contributing to the common good.

Though John Paul II never explicitly included the Earth within his notion of solidarity, one might argue that the growing interdependence of humans with the Earth coupled with our distress at injustices done to the Earth demand some kind of commitment to this order. Indeed, in Donal Dorr's assessment of John Paul II, "The moral dimension of genuine human development involves a sense of responsibility for the whole cosmos; such moral responsibility is either a part of the virtue of solidarity itself or else it is a sister virtue that has very much in common with it."[10] I contend that ecological solidarity should be considered a part of the virtue of solidarity. Referring to solidarity as "ecological" highlights the fact that commitment to the Earth is done in light of humanity's interdependence with the Earth but for the benefit of nonhuman nature. Solidarity with the Earth is the virtue that converts our distress into concrete moral action for the planetary common good.[11]

Still, the concern remains that solidarity, as envisioned by John Paul II, presumed the potential for a mutual and transformative relationship between equals. The heart of John Paul II's social vision is the dignity of the human person, made in the image of God. Solidarity between human beings is modeled after the interpersonal communion of the divine Trinity. As such, solidarity connotes a mutuality that is open to transformation and interpersonal love and care.[12] Since nonhuman nature cannot love us in return in the same way that humans can, does solidarity apply?

I submit that solidarity can be applied to creation because solidarity is first and foremost a virtue that channels into action our feelings of compassion at the suffering of others with whom we are interdependent, and this dynamic also characterizes our relationship to the Earth. Moreover, solidarity enables people to recognize those upon whom they are dependent as more than simply resources that can be abandoned when they have served their purpose. In his understanding of solidarity, John Paul II highlights "the importance of reawakening the religious awareness of individuals and peoples" so that "the exploitation, oppression and annihilation of others are excluded" (*Sollicitudo Rei Socialis*, §39).

Ecological solidarity does not indicate that humans are meant to share our lives as equals with nonhumans. There remains a unique potential for mutual love between humans that does not apply to nonhuman creatures. Yet ecological solidarity reminds us of the goodness of all Earth's creatures apart from human use. It is the virtue that corresponds to the efforts of many theologians to "reawaken the religious awareness" of the goodness of creation. John Paul II even suggests that such an extension may be a natural part of solidarity when he highlights the "urgent need to change the spiritual attitudes which define each individual's relationship with self, with neighbor, with even the remotest human communities, *and with nature itself*; and all of this in view of higher values such as the common good" (*Sollicitudo Rei Socialis*, §38; emphasis added).

Thus ecological solidarity is one of the ways in which humanity should redefine our relationship to nature and our shared orientation to the planetary common good. As John Paul II realized, a simple recognition of interdependence does not necessarily lead to a transformation of moral choices. Solidarity with the Earth and especially its most threatened species must not be some "feeling of vague compassion or shallow distress at the misfortunes" of non-humankind, such as when we see the extent of oil spills like that in the Gulf of Mexico that endanger and may extinguish whole species. Rather, on behalf of the planetary and cosmic common good, it must be marked by a "firm and persevering determination" to preserve the various sensitive and interconnected ecosystems that support manifold species. As a virtue, solidarity leads to practices that embody these norms in all dimensions of human life.

Ecological Solidarity

Ecological solidarity has three foci: solidarity with human beings, with plants and animal species, and with whole ecosystems. Though the planetary common good demands solidarity with nonhuman animals and the ecosystems we all rely on for life, the first focus for Catholic social thought is solidarity with human beings. Ecological solidarity affirms differing values for different creatures; the death of a bird is not morally equivalent to the death of a human being. Often it is the poor and vulnerable who suffer most from human-induced ecological disaster, and solidarity and the preferential option for the poor demand a response. While this point may be controversial from an economic or political vantage point, I consider it uncontested from the perspective of Catholic social thought. In this essay I mean only to challenge those who might see solidarity in the context of ecological harm applying only to fellow human beings, whether those presently threatened or future generations.

Solidarity that is truly ecological includes two other foci: solidarity with plants and animals, and solidarity with the ecosystems they inhabit. This is typical of a Catholic "both/and" theological approach: it includes both a concern for holistic systems as well as for the individual creatures that populate them. Ecological solidarity attempts to balance what at times are two conflicting and divergent camps within ecological ethics: those concerned with "ecocentric holism," which focuses on the common good of the whole, such as Aldo Leopold's "land ethic"[13]; and those who advocate a "biocentric individualism," which pays attention to the well-being of individual living creatures.[14] As with Catholic teaching about the human person and the common good, ecological solidarity must strive to balance both poles of these concerns.

Ecological solidarity suggests that it is no longer acceptable to separate the human common good from that of other creatures. Human activity reaches to every corner of the planet, attenuating any sense of a "nature" untamed and untouched by human beings. Citing evidence of DDT in penguins in Antarctica, Holmes Rolston III argues that "nature, at least in the pristine sense, is at an end. We shall increasingly have managed nature, or none at all. Global warming proves that. There are no unmanaged systems, just varieties and degrees of management."[15]

Ecological solidarity demands a commitment to the well-being of individual creatures and species but does not presume to trust in humanity's superior skill and wisdom in managing nature. On the contrary, it acknowledges the interdependence of humans with the Earth and sees that the good of plants and animals requires the responsible action of human beings who, by and large, have demonstrated a paucity of prudential judgment and humility when it comes to assessing the ecological impact of economic, political, and social decisions.

Third, ecological solidarity must also include a concern with ecosystems.[16] Similarly to John Paul II, who emphasized that the common good of all human beings transcends the good of individuals and individual nations, we may now recognize that solidarity with both human and nonhuman creatures demands solidarity with the ecosystems they rely on for survival. Interconnections among creatures and the importance of the whole is a theme prominent throughout Christian theology. Thomas Aquinas taught that the greatest aspect of creation is not a single species but "the order of the universe, wherein the good of the universe consists."[17] Sallie McFague expounds a similar theme, but she draws on the new story of the evolving universe as articulated by modern science to argue for an even more radical interconnectedness and interrelatedness of all creatures. This "common creation story" emerging from the sciences suggests a universe marked by interrelationship, interdependence, openness, change, and novelty.[18]

Ecological solidarity calls humans to develop solidarity for the Earth in all these dimensions—humans, plants, and animals, and whole ecosystems—in service of the planetary common good. In fact, ecological solidarity is a way of acting in solidarity with the entire universe, suggesting a broader cosmic common good. To our knowledge, Earth is the only planet that contains life, let alone intelligent life. If Aquinas is right that it requires a diversity of creatures to best imitate the divine goodness,[19] then the Earth is absolutely essential for the well-being of the cosmos as a whole and for creation's ability to praise God. Human beings do well to cultivate solidarity with the Earth not only for human benefit, and not just for the well-being of the human poor, but indeed on behalf of the entire universe.

Extending Rights

I have proposed the expansion of solidarity in light of the interdependence between humans and the Earth, but an equally important extension of Catholic social thought is the discussion of Earth rights. As a virtue directed to the common good, solidarity is bound up with justice,[20] and justice is intricately bound up with the notion of rights.[21] Pope John XXIII offered a Catholic conception of human rights in *Pacem in Terris*, arguing that "the common good is chiefly guaranteed when personal rights and duties are maintained" (§60). Thus an important corollary to solidarity is to demonstrate and codify commitment to the common good through the bestowal of rights.[22] As we saw in our discussion of solidarity, compassion with nonhuman nature must become a disposition to act. Rights inform this action by establishing a negative barrier that makes violations of the planetary common good more difficult to justify. Ecological solidarity calls us to embody our solidarity with the Earth and the most vulnerable of her creatures, and rights have a way of specifying whether we have embodied that solidarity or not.

Some theologians[23] and philosophers[24] oppose such a move, and while ecological solidarity finds resonance in Catholic social thought, the notion of Earth rights challenges Catholic social thought more fundamentally. As with solidarity, there is a reasonable concern that extending the notion of rights to nature will weaken the commitment to human rights. In addition, one may plausibly argue, as John XXIII does, that rights are accorded because of duties. Some would argue that animals and plants cannot fulfill duties as humans can and so cannot possess rights.

While I am sympathetic to concerns of undermining human dignity and the tradition that links rights to duties, I argue that rights language is important if we are to perceive the real demands of what solidarity entails. Rights language becomes a practical formulation of human duties to the Earth. To explore how Catholic social thought could benefit from a consideration of Earth rights, I look to the work of theologians Larry Rasmussen and James Nash. Rasmussen and Nash argue that ecological ethics need some form of rights for nonhumans. Rights language is grounded in the affirmation of value in nature apart from its benefit to humans. Thus attributing rights is a way of identifying and acknowledging the various kinds of value we discover in nature. Just as human rights draw attention to the intrinsic dignity of human beings and to the particular instances when this dignity is violated, so rights for nonhuman creatures can direct us to their intrinsic value and engender sanction when this value is denigrated.

Rasmussen suggests that biotic rights—rights for all living beings—seems odd in the West because rights language grew out of a vision of the human person as autonomous and separate from the rest of creation.[25] Our moral terms reflect this: we speak of two classes of creatures, humans and nonhumans, as if stars, bacteria, mollusks, and chimpanzees can adequately be contained by one category that describes what they are not. Rasmussen poignantly characterizes this as "apartheid habits," whereby the value of creatures is organized according to human standards, and nonhumans are implicitly less than us: "Such apartheid thinking leaves us imagining we are an ecologically segregated species. Such thinking violates the integrity of creation and puts it at risk."[26]

Contemporary science, however, rejects apartheid thinking. The evolutionary history of the universe describes an intimate connection and shared past between humans and other creatures, from fellow mammals to single-celled bacteria and even stars in galaxies thousands of light years away.[27] The ecological sciences also demonstrate that the Earth and human beings are interdependent, and that each has great power to influence the well-being of the other. The Earth is a network of various forces and values, cultural, biological, and geological. This history suggests a new narrative of what it means to be human, and it is only in the context of a new narrative framework that biotic rights are possible. Rasmussen wonders, "What would have been the case if the organic assumptions of dynamic, interrelated reality as a comprehensive community had framed the discussion of rights?"[28] Considering the cosmological and ecological interdependence between humans and other creatures within a "comprehensive community," rights language begins to seem less alien.

Rasmussen underscores the importance of rights as a central component of caring for nonhuman creatures and counteracting human presumption. To treat the Earth as a bottomless sewer ordained to contain and process all our human garbage "is only to indulge a hubris" against which all religions warn.[29] Bestowing rights to nonhumans enables humanity to accept its dependence on the Earth and calls human beings to a more realistic and respectful acknowledgment of our place on Earth: "Universally binding environmental rights are one medium for such an ethos of appropriate humility and the recognition of limits and proper human reach."[30] "Care" and "respect" are too weak to call forth the kind of steps and provisions that need to be made. Rasmussen's approach suggests that for the planetary common good and solidarity to have real implications, Catholic social thought requires more than a mere moral exhortation to care for the Earth: "Without rights [and strong legal foundation], there are insufficient means for engendering and enforcing human responsibility."[31]

James Nash concurs that biotic rights are indispensable in

discussing environmental ethics. Nash provides a helpful definition of biotic rights: *"Morally justified and prima facie claims or demands on behalf of nonhuman organisms, as individuals and collectives (populations and species), against all moral agents for the vital interests or imperative conditions of well-being for nonhumankind."*[32]

Nash distinguishes loving nature from doing justice to nature. Love and benevolence toward creatures are important, but he argues they describe only an internal command, such as arises from the dictates of one's conscience. In this way, Nash describes the dispositions that ecological solidarity might develop in people. More is needed, however. Justice entails an external dimension. Rights become part of the moral landscape outside of the agent's interests or concerns. As opposed to love or solidarity, which can only be requested, justice can be demanded, since it is owed to the other. Like Rasmussen, Nash connects the fact of interdependence and human relatedness to nonhuman creatures to the need for rights language: "God has created a moral order of universal interdependence and biotic kinship, which entails human obligation."[33] Biotic rights redefine the boundaries of human responsibility to the Earth. Moreover, they are necessary because they are grounded not in human self-interest[34] or charity but in the demands of justice.

Nash does not mean to equate human rights with biotic rights. The former are grounded in the fact of human equality, while biotic rights operate according to a descending scale of value. Biotic rights are meant to "deny exclusivity of human values and rights" while acknowledging a different degree of value.[35] Rather than grounding rights in some characteristic that humans find valuable, Nash links biotic rights to the principle of conation, "a striving to do and to be."[36] Whether or not living creatures provide a benefit to human beings, they are also valuable in themselves because *"the valuer is the nonhuman lifeform itself for itself."*[37] While Nash's defense of intrinsic value is lengthy,[38] the foundation for it is an estimation of what God loves and therefore values: "Respect for biotic interests, therefore, is theocentric respect for the biotic values of God."[39] Nash's understanding of biotic interests affirms the possibility of Earth rights that do not diminish human rights because his understanding allows for differing values of creatures while upholding the worth of all creatures and the ecosystems they inhabit.

Since Nash recognizes differing degrees of value among creatures, with human value supreme among Earth's creatures, Nash admits that biotic rights can be overridden for significant purposes. Biotic rights are "prima facie," meaning one must have a good reason to contravene them, and Nash invokes the principles of proportionality and discrimination to guide choices in individual cases.[40] Nash even allows the possibility that particular diseases or pathogens may drive an entire species into extinction. Yet, in general, as human activity nears destroying a species, let alone whole ecosystems, a violation of biotic rights becomes nearly impossible to justify. Nash qualifies and expands considerably on the extent and meaning of biotic rights,[41] but my purpose is to challenge Catholic social thought in a more general way: without a discussion of Earth rights, calls to care for the Earth may remain anemic moral claims, individualistic and unnecessarily anthropocentric.

Earth Rights

Nash and Rasmussen make a compelling case for specifying the character of ecological solidarity in terms of rights, yet I wish to press both of them further. First, Rasmussen contends that the terminology of these rights—whether we call these "biotic rights" or "human environmental rights"—does not matter. If humans saw themselves as an integral part of the community of life, these two terms would have the same force in terms of directing humans to take responsibility for nonhumans.[42] I suggest, however, that justice leads us to Earth rights rather than human environmental rights. Rights designate beings worthy of moral consideration and care, and the purpose of these rights is to expand our understanding of what has value and deserves protection. The theological import of extending solidarity and rights to include nonhuman nature is that it may broaden our capacity to love so that we love as God loves, which is to say we love all. "Human environmental rights" maintains an unnecessary focus on only human well-being.

Second, Nash limits rights to biota due to conation. Abiota

(nonliving creatures), he argues, cannot have rights and are only the setting for living creatures. He defines the ecological common good, which I characterize in terms of solidarity with ecosystems, as the "total constellation of all creatures' biotic rights blended and balanced."[43] By excluding abiota as merely the blended rights of biota, Nash threatens to lose the both/and approach of ecological solidarity that balances ecocentric holism and biocentric individualism.

Instead, I propose expanding the category of rights to include ecosystems as well. In particular, the examples of climate change and the Gulf spill remind us that we must not focus solely on living creatures but also on the conditions of the habitat on which they depend. Ecological solidarity affirms that the greatest aspect of creation is its interconnections and the order among its mutual parts. Therefore Earth rights should include the right of ecosystems to participate in the natural dynamics of existence, evolving in ways that may bring an end to particular species, or even to the ecosystem itself.[44] There is a good not only in the diversity of creatures that occupy a particular place, but also to the nonliving elements that provide their space and nutrients. There is an intangible good in their common living together, and rights language must identify this as well. As Holmes Rolston argues, the intrinsic value of a creature cannot be separated from the holistic web in which it lives. Intrinsic value "requires a corporate sense where value can also mean 'good in community.' "[45] Thus Nash's Bill of Biotic Rights must be expanded to be a Bill of Rights for the Earth, highlighting the interconnected webs of life, from individual creatures, to ecosystems, to Earth as a whole. This is the planetary common good to which ecological solidarity directs us.

Ecological Solidarity and Earth Rights in the Context of Climate Change and the Gulf Oil Spill

I have argued that because of humanity's interdependence with the Earth, and the vision of a planetary common good extending solidarity and rights to include nonhuman nature is worthwhile. While other terms could be used to describe concern for the Earth, one reason to expand solidarity and rights is the scope and severity of ecological degradation. To see why ecological solidarity and Earth rights are worthy moral concepts to address ecological degradation, I turn briefly to climate change and the Gulf oil spill. These eco-disasters should convince us that ecological solidarity and Earth rights are important terms that provide further impetus to reform our cultural and economic choices in light of the planetary common good.

Ecological solidarity and Earth rights support those human beings suffering the negative impact of climate change. As the United States Catholic Bishops write, "Working for the common good requires us to promote the flourishing of all human life and all of God's creation. In a special way, the common good requires solidarity with the poor who are often without the resources to face many problems, including the potential impacts of climate change."[46] The various effects of climate change—including, among others, flooding, more intense storms, and a widening range of infectious diseases—will disproportionately affect indigenous populations and those in poverty[47] and solidarity alongside the preferential option for the poor demands our response.

One example that deserves special attention is how climate change will impact an already troubling refugee crisis. Some statistics may give us a better sense of the problem as well as invite us to feel distressed by the suffering of distant others. Rising sea levels have already forced some populations to leave their homes, introducing the world to the concept of "climate refugees."[48] In 2008, approximately twenty million were displaced by extreme weather, while over four and a half million were displaced due to violence.[49] Estimates of permanent or temporary refugees due to climate change in the twenty-first century vary, "with 200 million being the most widely cited estimate."[50] Ecological solidarity demands keeping the flourishing of such peoples in our view at all times. As we acknowledge that solidarity with the Earth will look different than solidarity with the human poor, we must continue to accent a preferential option for humans as a critical component of a full ecological solidarity.[51]

Solidarity with plants and animals entails a preferential option for those species directly imperiled by climate change. Again, some statistics can help stoke a sense of distress at what is happening. Among the myriad challenges facing nonhumans, perhaps none is more important that the threat of species extinction. In addition to humans who suffer "will be the 1.25 million species of living creatures—24% of all in existence today—predicted to become extinct by 2050 if temperatures rise as expected."[52] The rapidity with which climate changes occur means that animals and plants will have much less time to adapt than in a natural evolutionary cycle.[53] This is significant because the current high rate of extinctions, even aside from climate change, is exceptionally rare. While the loss of species is anticipated in an evolutionary worldview, today's levels are at least one hundred times higher than the normal base rate, and some estimates suggest it may be one thousand to ten thousand times higher.[54] In this light, the additional burdens of climate change make the rate of extinction that much more pernicious.[55]

Moreover, current extinctions are unusual in their scope and cause. First, this is a period of mass extinctions, only the sixth of such magnitude that the Earth has ever witnessed. It takes ten million years for the Earth to recover from periods of widespread species loss, meaning that "today's anthropogenic extinctions will diminish biodiversity for millions of years to come."[56] Observers are struggling to realize the magnitude of what is happening and properly name this new moment in the Earth's history. Some geologists propose declaring an end to the Holocene epoch (roughly the last 11,000 years) and renaming our present time as the "Anthropocene" epoch, to take its place among other time periods of massive planetary scale.[57] For the first time, a distinct geological timeframe would be the result of choices made by a particular species rather than natural forces. Similarly, climate change is altering the planet, with repercussions that will last for millions of years to come. Though solidarity will not reverse the tide, it offers the impetus to act on behalf of those species whose survival depends greatly on human intervention.

The second great difference about current mass extinctions, as well as contemporary shifts in the climate, is the cause. Neither is the result of an inanimate chance event like a meteor landing, or the simple outworking of natural processes such as an ice age. Instead, they are caused by a single species, human beings, a single species that has the power of evaluation and choice. Ecological solidarity and Earth rights attempt to reflect morally on the scope and significance of the ways in which humanity is reshaping the planet. They are ethical terms that adequately address the scale of human activity and the interdependence between humans and other living creatures.

Finally, ecological solidarity and Earth rights must dispose us to safeguard Earth's various ecosystems. The Gulf spill demonstrates the potential for ecological solidarity not only with individual creatures and populations of species but also with their ecosystems. Anger at BP has focused not only on the impact on local economies or the threat to species of animals but also on the Gulf as a whole and its ability to sustain diverse forms of life. Public concern for the Gulf and the creatures that depend on it, human and nonhuman alike, represents a kind of implicit ecological solidarity. Moved by compassion at the suffering induced by this spill, thousands of Americans made donations and volunteered to clean beaches, all in an attempt to protect the Gulf. Expanding solidarity to include nonhuman nature helps clarify a moral response already present and justifies the feeling of distress engendered by the Gulf spill. Indeed, ecological solidarity may alert Christians to the validity of such distress. Commitment to the common good of nonhuman nature *for its own sake* is theologically justified and encouraged by the virtue of ecological solidarity.

Moreover, this outrage—a manifestation of ecological solidarity—illustrates a consensus that the Gulf and the many creatures it supports have suffered an injustice. As of September 2010, BP faces about four hundred lawsuits over the Gulf spill.[58] The lawsuits are brought on behalf of a variety of affected parties in the United States and Mexico, including Gulf Coast fishers and shrimpers, property owners, restaurants, and owners of tourism businesses. Earth rights suggest that perhaps what is needed is a lawsuit on behalf of the Gulf of Mexico itself; its variety of fish and amphibian life; and on behalf of the rest of the planet, which may be affected in ways not yet imagined. Earth rights support the claim that these other parties truly have interests of their own, and the violation of those rights demands redress.

Conclusion

Solidarity and human rights are important categories for Catholic social thought, and each draws on a critical dimension of our moral lives: rights evoke our sense of justice, and solidarity is a highly affective virtue that inspires us to see the depth and meaning of our relatedness to others. Solidarity and rights address the fact of interdependence and orient us to the common good.

Ecological solidarity and Earth rights call for the inclusion of the Earth as a whole, its sundry ecosystems, and the myriad plants, animals, and creatures that live in them within the circle of moral consideration. I do not impose a rigidly egalitarian solidarity or sense of rights, where humans are equated with any and all living creatures. I do challenge, however, a construal of Catholic ethics where concern for environmental degradation flows simply and merely from a concern for its effects upon human beings. This is too narrow an interpretation of the planetary common good, and it hides from view the real and lasting effects of human activity on the living systems of the Earth.

Climate change threatens to present permanent and dramatic effects to the condition of life on the planet. The Gulf oil spill has become an immediate lesson in the interdependence of humans and the Earth and the ramifications of human choices on plants, animals, and the interconnected whole of an ecosystem. The virtue of ecological solidarity and the affirmation of Earth rights help us to name the suffering that many already feel in the light of ecological injustices, and they call forth our energies to reenvision our ethical commitments anew for the good of human and nonhumankind together.

Notes

[1] For background on this development, see Drew Christiansen, "Ecology and the Common Good: Catholic Social Teaching and Environmental Responsibility," in *And God Saw That It Was Good: Catholic Theology and the Environment*, ed. Drew Christiansen and Walter Glazer (Washington, DC: United States Catholic Conference, 1996), 183-95; and Russell Butkus and Steven Kolmes, "Ecology and the Common Good: Sustainability and Catholic Social Teaching," *Journal of Catholic Social Thought* 4, 2 (2007): 403-36.

[2] United States Catholic Bishops, *Renewing the Earth* (Washington, DC: United States Catholic Conference, 1992).

[3] John Hart, *Sacramental Commons: Christian Ecological Ethics* (Lanham, MD: Rowman & Littlefield, 2006), 68.

[4] For more see Hart, *Sacramental Commons*, 139-58.

[5] I am grateful to an anonymous reviewer for this formulation.

[6]I shall deal with objections more specific to ecological solidarity and Earth rights below.

[7]See, for example, Sallie McFague's *The Body of God* (Minneapolis: Fortress Press, 1993).

[8]Kenneth Himes points out that the fact of interdependence need not lead to any commitment to the common good nor does it "rule out domination or exploitation" (Himes, *101 Questions on Catholic Social Thought* [New Jersey: Paulist Press, 2001], 38).

[9]Charles M. A. Clark, "Greed Is Not Enough: Some Insights on Globalization from Catholic Social Thought," *Journal of Catholic Social Thought* 2, 1 (2005): 37.

[10]Donal Dorr, "Concern and Consolidation," in *John Paul II and Moral Theology*, ed. Charles E. Curran and Richard A. McCormick (Mahwah, NY: Paulist Press, 1998), 301.

[11]Other Catholic sources suggest a similar shift. Cardinal Peter Turkson, currently president of the Pontifical Council for Justice and Peace, also thinks that John Paul II's teaching on solidarity evolved to include ecological solidarity. That human beings have bodies drawn from the Earth, he argues, is "the basis of Pope John Paul II's teaching on ecological solidarity." Turkson defends this idea, commenting that humans "are not complete as a family without the earth and the rest of creation. . . . We make a family only if we accept our interrelatedness and interconnectedness to the whole. Indeed, we must not only accept them; we must love and respect them" (Address of Cardinal Peter Turkson to the General Assembly of Unum Omnes in Ghana in September 2006; http://www.unum-omnes.com (accessed 16 September 2010).

[12]I thank an anonymous reviewer for this formulation.

[13]Aldo Leopold, *A Sand County Almanac* (New York: Ballantine Books, 1970).

[14]These terms are Peter Wenz's. See Peter Wenz, *Environmental Justice* (Albany: State University of New York Press, 1988).

[15]Holmes Rolston, III, "Ecology: A Primer for Christian Ethics," *Journal of Catholic Social Thought* 4, 2 (2007): 293-312, at 305.

[16]While scientists debate the legitimacy of the term "ecosystem," it remains an important term both politically and ethically. The Convention on Biological Diversity, an international treaty signed by nearly two hundred countries, defines an ecosystem as "dynamic complex of plant, animal and micro-organism communities and their non-living environment interacting as a functional unit" (Convention on Biological Diversity, Art. 2, "Use of Terms"; http://www.cbd.int/convention/articles (accessed 16 September, 2010).

[17]Thomas Aquinas, *Summa Contra Gentiles*, trans. Fathers of the English Dominican Province (Chicago: Benziger Brothers, 1924), 2.42.3.

[18]See McFague, *The Body of God*, esp. chap. 2.

[19]Thomas Aquinas, *Summa Theologiae*, trans. Fathers of the English Dominican Province (Chicago: Benziger Brothers, 1948), 1.47.1.

[20]"Solidarity rises to the rank of fundamental social virtue since it places itself in the sphere of justice. It is a virtue directed par excellence to the common good" (*Compendium of the Social Doctrine of the Church*, #193).

[21]Brian Tierney argues that the Catholic Church has long defended the rights of individual persons. See his *The Idea of Natural Rights: Studies on Natural Rights, Natural Law, and Church Law 1150-1625* (Atlanta: Scholars Press, 1997).

[22]Roderick Nash's comprehensive analysis of the development of rights language applied to nature demonstrates that there has been a strand in Western philosophical thought that has sought to do this. See Roderick Frazier Nash, *The Rights of Nature: A History of Environmental Ethics* (Madison: The University of Wisconsin Press, 1989).

[23]Thomas Sieger Derr, for example, argues that rights are "applicable only to human society" (Thomas Sieger Derr, "Environmental Ethics and Christian Humanism," in *Environmental Ethics and Christian Humanism*, ed. Thomas Sieger Derr with James A. Nash and Richard John Neuhaus [Nashville: Abingdon Press, 1996], 30).

[24]For example, renowned environmental philosopher Holmes Rolston III dismisses the idea of biotic rights, urging instead "universal human benevolence" (Holmes Rolston III, *Environmental Ethics: Duties to and Values in the Natural World* [Philadelphia: Temple University Press, 1988], 52.

[25]Larry Rasmussen, "Human Environmental Rights and/or Biotic Rights," in *Religion and Human Rights: Competing Claims?* ed. Carrie Gustafson and Peter H. Juviler (Armonk, NY: M. E. Sharpe, Inc., 1999), 38.

[26]Larry Rasmussen, *Earth Community, Earth Ethics* (Maryknoll, NY: Orbis Books, 1996), 32.

[27]A number of theologians vividly expand on this evocative theme. See, for example, Thomas Berry and Brian Swimme, *The Universe Story: From the Primordial Flaring Forth to the Ecozoic Era—A Celebration of the Unfolding of the Cosmos* (San Francisco: HarperSanFrancisco, 1992).

[28]Rasmussen, "Human Environmental Rights," 46.

[29]Ibid., 46.

[30]Ibid.

[31]Ibid., 47.

[32]James Nash, "Biotic Rights and Human Ecological Responsibilities," *The Annual of the Society of Christian Ethics* (1993): 137-162, at 145.

[33]Ibid., 147.

[34]While arguments aimed at people's self-interest may carry more force politically than arguments from rights, in ethical reflection, they denote the weakest form of ethical justification.

[35]James Nash, "In Flagrant Dissent: An Environmentalist's Contentions," in *Environmental Ethics and Christian Humanism*, ed. Thomas Sieger Derr with James A. Nash and Richard John Neuhaus (Nashville: Abingdon Press, 1996), 111.

[36]James Nash, *Loving Nature: Ecological Integrity and Christian Responsibility* (Nashville: Abingdon Press, 1991), 178.

[37]Nash, "In Flagrant Dissent," 110. Italics in original.

[38]See Nash's *Loving Nature* for a more thorough theological exposition.

[39]Nash, "In Flagrant Dissent," 109.

[40]Nash, *Loving Nature*, 189-91.

[41]For the specific rights Nash outlines, see "Biotic Rights and Human Ecological Responsibilities," 154-57.

[42]Rasmussen, "Human Environmental Rights," 44.

[43]Nash, "Biotic Rights and Human Ecological Responsibilities," 155.

[44]This must always be understood, however, in the context of the enormous and unprecedented activity of human beings. The projected effects of climate change pose a threat to species, ecosystems, and the well-being of the Earth as a whole.

[45]Rolston, "Ecology," 307.

[46]United States Catholic Bishops, *Global Climate Change: A Plea for Dialogue, Prudence, and the Common Good* (Washington, DC: United States Catholic Conference, 2001).

[47]See Juliet Eilperin, "Climate Shift Tied to 150,000 Fatalities: Most Victims Are Poor, Study Shows," *The Washington Post* (November 17, 2005), A20.

[48]The Environmental Justice Foundation defines the term as "people forced from their homes and land—by rising temperatures, sea-level change and extreme weather events" (Environmental Justice Foundation, "What Is a Climate Refugee?" http://www.ejfoundation.org/page563.html [accessed 16 September, 2010]).

[49]The International Organization for Migration, "Migration, Climate Change, and Environmental Degradation: A Complex Nexus," http://www.iom.int/jahia/Jahia/complex-nexus#estimates (accessed 16 September, 2010). The Environmental Justice Foundation states that currently 12 million people live in poverty because of climate change; 26 million people have been displaced as a direct result of climate change; 250 million people are affected by desertification; 508 million people live in water-stressed or water-scarce countries; 2.8 billion people live in areas of the world prone to more than one of the physical manifestations of climate change: floods, storms, droughts, sea level rise (EJF, "What Is a Climate Refugee?").

[50]The International Organization for Migration, "Migration, Climate Change, and Environmental Degradation."

[51]Much more could be said on the forms of solidarity between human beings necessary due to climate change, but my focus is to explore what other forms of solidarity are required.

[52]Gerald Braun, Monika Hellwig, and W. Malcolm Byrnes, "Global Climate Change and Catholic Responsibility: Facts and Faith Response," *Journal of Catholic Social Thought* 4, 2 (2007): 373-401, at 380.

[53]Ibid., 384.

[54]See Millennium Ecosystem Assessment, *Ecosystems and Human Wellbeing: Biodiversity Synthesis* (Washington, DC: World Resources Institute, 2005), 42.

[55]"The Intergovernmental Panel on Climate Change concludes that approximately 20-30% of plant and animal species are likely to be at increasingly high risk of extinction as global mean temperatures exceed warming of 2-3° C above preindustrial levels," while "another synthesis study predicts 15-37% 'commitment to extinction' by 2050 of the wide range of regionally endemic

and near-endemic species examined" (J.-C. Vié, C. Hilton-Taylor and S. N. Stuart, eds., *Wildlife in a Changing World—An Analysis of the 2008 IUCN Red List of Threatened Species* [Gland, Switzerland: IUCN, 2009]).

[56]James W. Kirchner and Anne Weil, "Delayed Biological Recovery from Extinctions throughout the Fossil Record," *Nature* 404 (March 9, 2000): 177-80.

[57]Jan Zalasiewicz, Mark Williams, Will Steffen, and Paul Crutzen, "The New World of the Anthropocene," *Environmental Science & Technology* 44, 7 (2010): 2228-31.

[58]Margaret Cronin Fisk and Laurel Brubaker Calkins, "BP Sued by Mexican States over Gulf Oil Spill Damage," *Bloomberg Businessweek*, http://www.businessweek.com (accessed 16 September 2010).

Peter Singer and *Caritas in Veritate*

Room for Mutually Critical Correlation?

Charles C. Camosy

Peter Singer, the well-known atheist philosopher at Princeton, has been called the world's most influential living philosopher.[1] But many Christians label him a leader of "the culture of death"; indeed, this is a man who notoriously argues that not only should we be pro-choice for adult euthanasia and abortion, but also infanticide.[2] He in turn rarely hesitates to criticize a typical Christian sanctity of life framework as a foreign and misguided import into the Western world from which we must extricate ourselves. After all, Singer claims, it was Christianity that set us along our "speciesist" path, which has led not only to strange conclusions about the value of embryos and brain-dead individuals, but also to the horrible practices directed toward non-human animals in factory farms.[3]

But this essay will argue that most of those who identify with a sanctity of life or a Singer-like approach, and even those who most publicly argue for these positions (such as the current Roman Catholic pontiff and Singer himself), are too quick in dismissing each other without making an attempt at good-faith engagement. Indeed, we are too often distracted by simplistic binaries like culture of life/death, religious/secular, theological/philosophical, liberal/conservative, and so forth. This dualistic approach falls prey to "defining by opposition": a practice that, all too common today, dramatically limits one's ability to see fruitful areas of overlap.

If both approaches would instead engage in the spirit of intellectual solidarity,[4] each would find that what they have in common with the other is far broader than almost anyone supposes and that the disagreements are actually quite narrow. The relationship between Singer's philosophical ethics and the moral tradition of the Roman Catholic Church, properly understood, can instead be one of broad-based, mutually critical correlation. This method was made famous by the theological giant David Tracy, but several modern Roman Catholic feminist theologians also use this method when trying to incorporate insights from contemporary feminist critical theory with the broader tradition of the church.[5] This method can at once critically acknowledge differences between two distinct approaches while *at the same time* examining areas of overlap that may provide fertile opportunities for insight and cooperation. This essay will attempt the show that, for Peter Singer and the Roman Catholic Church at least, such overlap is fertile ground indeed.

In selecting Pope Benedict XVI's most recent encyclical *Caritas in Veritate* as Singer's conversation partner, this essay will necessarily be limited in the issues it can address.[6] It will begin by exploring some objections to the whole premise of the argument: aren't there just sweeping levels of incompatibility (especially on matters of ethical method and moral anthropology) that make such correlation impossible? Having shown that these differences, when properly and systematically explored, actually point the way toward fruitful exchange, the essay will then explore the dramatic overlap present between Singer and the pope on two important topics: duties to the poor and ecological ethics.[7] The essay will conclude by suggesting some cultural and theological implications of this kind of engagement.

Understandable Objections

There are some good reasons why this argument might seem so counter-intuitive at first glance—and one of them undoubtedly has to do with ethical method. Singer is a famous utilitarian: that is, someone who believes that the foundation of moral theory lies not in the agent (virtue) or the act (rules), but instead focuses on the consequences. This is a method traditionally thought of as wholly incompatible with Christian ethics and perhaps especially a Roman

Catholic moral tradition that speaks of "intrinsically evil" acts. But in the way that official church teaching currently articulates its ethical theory, there are wide areas of overlap. Given that Singer is a kind of rule-consequentialist,[8] both approaches have moral rules—though they (at least appear to) have differently articulated reasons for touting them. And given that in many situations both Singer and the church have a rule in common, there can therefore be a fruitful discussion or argument about how to apply such a rule consistently in various specified situations.

Importantly, both also consider the proportionality of an act's consequences in many situations. Singer of course does so naturally as a consequentialist: nearly every moral judgment (even about what kinds of food to eat) is weighed based on the interests of those creatures the act affects. But the church does so in many instances as well—especially when proportionality is used to decide whether or not to remove life-sustaining medical treatment (a weighing of the "benefits" of the treatment against its "burdens") and in just-war theory (one needs a weighty "proportionate reason" to justify the unintended but foreseen deaths of civilians, for instance).

But in addition to this overlap, Roman Catholic theology has a "proportionalist" tradition that is even *more* like Singer's ethical theory.[9] This aspect of the tradition is complicated, controversial, and many church officials and theologians disagree about how to interpret it; but I want to claim (though the argument for this position goes beyond the scope of this paper[10]) that a certain interpretation of proportionalism is perfectly consistent with what the church is currently teaching and is strikingly similar to Singer's rule-consequentialism. So though there are clearly differences in method, they are not as pronounced as one might think, and they leave plenty of room for mutually critical correlation.

But what about moral anthropology? The church teaches that a tiny ball of cells should be treated as if she has the same moral value as any human person reading these words. By contrast, Singer thinks that not only can we kill human embryos and pre-sentient fetuses for virtually any reason at all, but even newborn babies—because they are not yet rational and self-aware creatures—can be killed without killing a person. How can two points of view, so diametrically opposed on fundamental issues like these, engage in meaningful conversation? I have argued elsewhere[11] that their opposition is not as fundamental as one might think. Consider that Singer and the church agree with the following five statements:

1. If the fetus is a person, it would be wrong to say that the choice to kill her should be a private decision of her mother.
2. If the fetus is a person, it would be wrong to say that the state cannot or should not impose legal protections on her life.
3. If the fetus is a person, it would be wrong to say that a mother does not have the duty to sustain her for nine months.
4. The morality of abortion is directly and logically connected to the morality of infanticide.
5. The moral status of a person is not constituted by belonging to the species *homo sapiens*—but rather consists in having a rational nature.

This last statement hints at where the actual (but narrow) disagreement lies: the church thinks that embryos, fetuses, and infants have a rational nature, but Singer does not.[12] The argument between them is complex and comes down to a quite technical Aristotelian distinction between active and passive potentiality. But, once again, there is much room for mutually critical correlation.

Having briefly considered the issues of method and abortion, perhaps this can clear some conceptual space for thinking in more detail about other areas for conversation. In the remainder of this essay I will focus attention on duties to the poor and ecological ethics, especially as they are present in Pope Benedict's recent encyclical *Caritas in Veritate*.

Duties to the Poor

In making their arguments about duties to the poor, both Singer and the Christian traditions have appealed strongly to a central narrative analogy. This is Singer's famous "shallow pond" thought experiment:

On your way to work, you pass a small pond. On hot days, children sometimes play in the pond, which is only about knee-deep. The weather's cool today, though, and the hour is early, so you are surprised to see a child splashing about in the pond. As you get closer, you see that it is a very young child, just a toddler, who is flailing about, unable to stay upright or walk out of the pond. You look for parents or a babysitter, but there is no one else around. The child is unable to keep his head above water for more than a few seconds at a time. If you don't wade in and pull him out, he seems likely to drown. Wading in is easy and safe, but you will ruin the new shoes you bought only days ago, and get your suit wet and muddy. By the time you hand the child over to someone responsible for him, and change your clothes, you'll be late for work. What should you do?[13]

And this is Jesus' well-known parable of the Good Samaritan—a story one recalls many times when reading in *Caritas in Veritate* with its frequent discussion[14] of the concept of neighbor:

A man was going down from Jerusalem to Jericho, when he fell into the hands of robbers. They stripped him of his clothes, beat him and went away, leaving him half dead. A priest happened to be going down the same road, and when he saw the man, he passed by on the other side. So too, a Levite, when he came to the place and saw him, passed by on the other side. But a Samaritan, as he traveled, came where the man was; and when he saw him, he took pity on him. He went to him and bandaged his wounds, pouring on oil and wine. Then he put the man on his own donkey, took him to an inn and took care of him. The next day he took out two silver coins and gave them to the innkeeper. "Look after him," he said, "and when I return, I will reimburse you for any extra expense you may have." Which of these three do you think was a neighbor to the man who fell into the hands of robbers? (Lk 10: 30-36)

Both of these stories are told in order to elicit the following intuition in the reader/listener: one should provide aid to those who need it. But both Singer and the church go even farther: they claim that it is *morally wrong not to provide aid*. Let us look at Singer's argument and then the features it has in common with the church.

In order to get from this moral intuition to a rational conclusion, Singer makes the following argument:

1. Suffering and death from lack of food, shelter, and medical care are bad.
2. If it is in your power to prevent something bad from happening, without sacrificing anything nearly as important, it is wrong not to do so.
3. By donating to aid agencies, you can prevent suffering and death from lack of food, shelter, and medical care, without sacrificing anything nearly as important.
4. Therefore, if you do not donate to aid agencies you are doing something wrong.[15]

When applied to the drowning child thought experiment above, we find that this argument supports the moral intuition that not only is it a good idea to aid the child, but one is morally *blameworthy* for not doing so. The phrase "anything nearly as important" is vague, but virtually no one could argue that ruining one's shoes, getting one's suit dirty, and being late to work could be nearly as important as the life of the drowning child.

Perhaps this argument doesn't even appear to be all that controversial. Yet, Singer rightly points out that:

> if we were to take it seriously, our lives would be changed dramatically. For while the cost of saving one child's life by a donation to an aid organization may not be great, after you have donated that sum, there remain more children in need of saving, each one of whom can be saved at a relatively small additional cost. Suppose you have just sent $200 to an agency that can, for that amount, save the life of a child in a developing country who otherwise would have died. You've done something really good, and all it has cost you is the price of some new clothes you didn't really need anyway.

Congratulations! But don't celebrate your good deed by opening a bottle of champagne, or even going to a movie. The costs of that bottle or movie, added to what you could save by cutting down on a few other extravagances, would save the life of another child. After you forgo those items, and give another $200, though, is everything else you are spending as important, or nearly as important, as the life of a child?[16]

The answer to the question, of course, is obvious. It looks like we must radically rethink how we use our resources—not simply because we want a feather in our cap for being charitable but because it is our moral *duty* to do so. We are morally blameworthy if we do not sacrifice things and interests of lesser value in order to save the lives of children in this way. For the vast majority of those in developed nations—including surely almost everyone reading this essay—Singer points that we have income we can dispose of without giving up the basic necessities of life; and this income should be donated to aid agencies serving the needy. Of course, just how much we will think ourselves obligated to give will depend on what we consider of being as "nearly morally important" compared to the lives we could save—but, for most of us, it would mean a radical rethinking of our lives.

We have already seen above that Jesus' parable about what it means to be neighbor—a central story for every Christian (and even for many outside the faith)—claims that we should aid those in need. But could a Christian agree with Singer that it is morally *wrong* not to aid? The answer appears to be yes. Mass-going Catholics, for instance, will recall the following Penitential Act of Contrition: I confess to Almighty God, and to you, my brothers and sisters, that I have sinned through my own fault, in my thoughts and in my words, in what I have done *and in what I have failed to do.*

Caritas in Veritate[17] reinforces our strict duty to help those in need: the Christian call to feed the hungry is "an ethical imperative" (27) and the principle of solidarity "imposes a duty" on us to support "other people's integral development" (43). This is not merely about giving money or other resources to charities (though it is about that), but also about "a specific social responsibility" of the consumer (66). Indeed, in a claim that would absolutely delight a preference utilitarian like Singer, *Caritas in Veritate* makes the dramatic claim that, "every economic decision has a moral consequence" (37).

But to whom do we specifically have such a duty? Singer suggests that the supposed community on which we generally focus, that which we describe as the nation-state, is really imagined rather than real—and therefore cannot ground a moral argument for unduly favoring our fellow citizens.[18] Based on the extreme need in communities outside our nation's borders—and "the complex set of developments we refer to as globalization"—he argues we should "begin to consider ourselves as the imagined community of the world. . . . Our problems are now too intertwined to be well resolved in a system of nation-states in which citizens give their primary, and near exclusive, loyalty to their own nation-state rather than to the global community."[19]

Giving preference to our nation-state is fine, for Singer, when it furthers the goal of broadening our concern (say, beyond our affluent areas to those of the American poor), but insofar as it turns us away from the dramatic need of the developing world such preferences should be rejected. He warns us by claiming that, "When subjected to the test of impartial assessment, there are few strong grounds for giving preference to the interests of one's fellow citizens, and none that can override the obligation that arises whenever we can, at little cost to ourselves, make an absolutely crucial difference to the well-being of another person in real need."[20]

The church agrees with Singer that we need to imagine ourselves as a world community; and not just for the reasons Singer advocates (though they are good ones), but also because *we really are* part of a world community. Indeed, *Caritas in Veritate* points to the "universal fraternity" (11) of humankind—such that we hold "the whole of humanity" (18) as our focus. The pope even goes so far as to claim that, "The development of peoples depends, above all, on a recognition that the human race is a single family working together in true communion" (52).

Whether in the Bronx, Botswana, or Bolivia, all human beings are our brothers and sisters and "all really are responsible for all."

The recent "explosion of worldwide interdependence" (33) simply reflects an already existing ontological connection. And this is why the church, agreeing with Singer, insists on the importance of international organizations. Indeed, one of the central tasks of the encyclical, especially in light of our worldwide financial crises,[21] is to rethink the role of the state in light of the challenges of today's world—calling for "new forms of political participation, nationally and internationally" (24).

But perhaps if we press deeper into the question of "to whom we have such a duty," we see that Singer and the church have a serious disagreement. Singer complains that evolution has produced disproportionate concern for our kin, those with whom we engage in social cooperation, and members of our "tribal group." But this "does not necessarily mean that it cannot be changed, nor does it mean that it should not be changed."[22] He cites Adam Smith's claim that this kind of bias "seems wisely ordered by nature" since those far from us are people "we can neither serve nor hurt." Singer pulls no punches in responding:

> Today these words are as obsolete as the quill with which Smith wrote them. As our response to the tsunami vividly demonstrated, instant communication and rapid transport mean that we *can* [original emphasis] help those far from us in ways that were impossible in Smith's day. In addition, the gap between the living standards of people in developed nations and those living in developing nations has increased enormously, so that those living in industrialized nations have greater capacity to help those far away, and greater reason to focus our aid on them: far away is where the vast majority of extremely poor are.[23]

But it might seem that our preferences for those we love, and with whom we are friends and kin, is not only *de facto* morally acceptable, but it would be near impossible to counteract. Singer quotes the philosopher Bernard Williams as an example of those who claim that a rational defense of love and friendship demands "one thought too many." Such preferences are self-justifying at the level of intuition. Singer concedes that while this is perhaps correct for "everyday decision-making" it is not correct at the critical level at which people should be examining their biases. Indeed, he claims preferences for friends or kin can be analogically connected to preference for race: an idea that had, in its time, "an intuitive appeal similar to the intuitive appeal of the idea that we have obligations to favor family and friends."[24] However, as we now know all too well:

> In a multiracial society, preferences for members of one's society often lead to strife, and in many countries it is now considered wrong to prefer those of one's own race or ethnic group in employment, education, or housing. Sanctions are invoked against those who do it. These efforts toward racial equality meet strong resistance, as one would expect from any attempt to counter a deep-seated bias, but they have generally been successful in changing people's attitudes, as well as their actions, toward fellow citizens of different races and ethnic backgrounds.[25]

Thus, Singer claims, if we let our intuitions go unchallenged we risk the result of a bad moral outcome and have one thought *too few*. That our intuitions are shared by others or come naturally "is not evidence that they are justified."[26]

But can Singer seriously mean that *no* partial preferences are justified? What kind of friend, parent, lover, spouse, or employer would we be without showing partial preference for those to whom one finds one's self in a particular kind of relationship? In some ways, the very definition of the relationship *presupposes* that one will have preferences for some over others. What would it mean to say that "*x* is the mother of *y* but not of *z*" if *x* must treat *y* and *z* exactly the same? Does this mean that the *relationships themselves* are immoral? Singer answers in the negative: we do not need to be impartial in every aspect of our lives. Indeed, acting partially toward some—like our spouse or child—can actually help us develop the virtues of compassion and service that prepare us for more impartial preferences at other times. They help us become other-centered rather than self-centered.

The Roman Catholic tradition claims that these relationships are more than simply tools for broadening our concern: they also reflect naturally given priorities that we are bound to respect morally. Thomas Aquinas articulated this in his conceiving of the "order of charity" that claims, all things being equal, that we have a stronger duty to our children, our parents, and our spouse than we do to a stranger.[27] This point of view is also expressed in *Caritas in Veritate*'s discussion of subsidiarity, which is defined as "first and foremost a form of assistance to the human person via the autonomy of intermediate bodies" (57). Why focus on more local, intermediate bodies? Because, though they should not do so in isolation, "peoples themselves have the prime responsibility to work for their own development"[28] (47). That is, we have a stronger moral duty to aid those in our more local groups and communities.

Ecological and Environmental Ethics

The interesting emphasis that *Caritas in Veritate* places on ecological ethics mirrors a broader emphasis that its author has given to these issues—so much so that he is being called the "Green Pope." Indeed, under Benedict XVI's watch the Vatican has become the first carbon neutral state—and has installed infrastructure (including a massive array of solar panels) such that it will garner 20 percent of its energy from renewable energies within the next decade.[29]

The reasons for focusing on these kinds of ecological practices are often human-centered: *Caritas in Veritate*, for instance, claims that, "the environment is God's gift to everyone" (48). Singer agrees that "a human-centered ethic can be the basis of powerful arguments for what we might call 'environmental values.'"[30] Indeed, he dramatically claims that in such a framework "preservation of our environment is a value of the greatest possible importance."[31] And one of the reasons such preservation is so important is because of the interests of *future generations*. He says, "It is for this reason that environmentalists are right to speak of wilderness and a 'world heritage.' It is something that we inherited from our ancestors, and that we must preserve for our descendants if they are to have it at all."[32]

This does not mean that we have any absolute duty to, say, refrain from cutting down a forest, but "it does mean that any such justification must take full account of the value of the forests to the generations to come in the more remote future, as well as the more immediate future."[33] Interestingly, something called "inter-generational solidarity" has been a theme of Pope Benedict's for the last several months (especially as related to the financial crisis) and it is therefore no surprise that *Caritas in Veritate* agrees with Singer on this point when it specifically mentions future genera-tions (48) as part of the reason why we have an ethical duty to use our resources responsibly.

But is it just the interests of *humanity* (both present and future) that must be considered in thinking about environmental ethics? Singer's answer is a qualified no. Non-human sentient animals, as long as they have conscious lives (that is, they are able to feel things like pleasure or pain), have intrinsic moral value that we are bound to respect.[34] As we will see below, the church agrees that non-human animals have intrinsic value. Where the two dis-agree, however, is on the matter of intrinsic value of *non*-sentient entities. And it is to this key topic we now turn.

Singer on Intrinsic Value

Singer admits that "in any serious exploration of environmental values a central issue will be the question of *intrinsic* value."[35] Should we give weight not only to the suffering and death of individual sentient animals, but also to the fact that an entire species of non-human animal may disappear? What about the loss of ancient trees and forests that have existed for hundreds of years? How much—if any—weight should we give to, say, a val-ley's ecosystem independent of the interests of sentient creatures? Singer's answer to these questions arises from an ethic that he sees as "an extension of the ethic of the dominant Western tradition"[36]: intrinsic moral value should be extended beyond human beings to all sentient creatures, but no further. After all, if we ask the question "What is it like for a possum to drown?" such a question not only makes sense, but we can rightly speculate that it must be horrible. However, he says that "there is *nothing* that corresponds to what it is like to be a tree dying because its roots have been flooded. Once we abandon the interests of sentient creatures as our source of value, where do we find value?"[37]

One answer might simply be that we can find value in non-sentient *living* things. Such entities seem to have interests: they do well or poorly based on, say, getting the proper energy and temperature in which to grow. Why shouldn't their interests be a source of intrinsic moral value? Singer's answer is the following:

> If we cease talking in terms of sentience, the boundary be-tween living and inanimate natural objects becomes more difficult to defend. Would it really be worse to cut down an old tree than to destroy a beautiful stalactite that has taken even longer to grow? . . . We may often talk about plants "seeking" water or light so that they can survive, and this way of thinking about plants makes it easier to accept talk of their "will to live," or of them "pursuing" their own good. But once we stop to reflect on the fact that plants are not conscious and cannot engage in any intentional behavior, it is clear that all this language is metaphorical; one might just as well say that a river is pursuing its own good and striving to reach the sea, or that the "good" of a guided missile is to blow itself up along with its target.[38]

The Church's Response

Christians have the advantage of talking about the sacramental value afforded to creation having been created "good" by God independent of human beings or other sentient creatures. *Caritas in Veritate*, though careful not to speak of nature as a divine be-ing like Gaia (another thing it shares with Singer), does speak of the Creator giving creation an "inbuilt order" and of our duty to respect "the intrinsic balance of creation" (48). The natural world is not made merely for our pleasure, but "it is a wondrous work of the Creator containing a 'grammar' which sets forth ends and criteria for its wise use, not its reckless exploitation" (48). But this "responsibility toward creation" (51) cannot ultimately be reduced to the interests of human beings or even sentient creatures. For we are asked to make "decisions aimed at strengthening that *covenant between human beings and the environment*, which should mirror the creative love of God, from whom we come and towards whom we are journeying" (50).

Unsurprisingly, Singer does ultimately disagree with an ethic that invokes this kind of sacramental or spiritual reality—but he does come close to straying from this path on multiple occasions. He says, for instance, that, "From the standpoint of the priceless and timeless values of the wilderness, however, applying a discount rate gives us the wrong answer. There are some things that, once lost, no amount of money can regain."[39] And this "timeless and priceless value" is something that produces in Singer something similar to the wonder cited by *Caritas in Veritate*. Consider this poetic recounting of his own experience of nature:

> [Y]et I have not had, in any museum, experiences that have filled my aesthetic senses in the way that they are filled when I walk in a natural setting and pause to survey the view from a rocky peak overlooking a forested valley, or sit by a stream tumbling over moss-covered boulders set amongst tall tree-ferns, growing in the shade of the forest canopy. I do not think I am alone in this; for many people, wilderness is the source of the greatest feelings of aesthetic appreciation, rising to an almost spiritual intensity.[40]

If one didn't know any better, one might suspect that the author of the above quote also had a covenant with creation. Indeed, he describes himself as reacting in an "almost spiritual" way to what Christians would describe as the intrinsic sacramental value of creation.

Population

Many environmental ethicists, seeing human beings primarily as polluters and destroyers of nature, imply or directly call for a reduction in the human population. Singer is no population growth alarmist, but he is clearly concerned about the population growth of human beings—especially as it affects the environment. Indeed, he argues that proliferation of human beings, coupled with our unethical use of resources, could even mean the end of the human race. His environmental ethic therefore "discourages large families" and "forms a sharp contrast to some existing ethical beliefs that are relics of an age where the earth was far more lightly populated." Though in context he is primarily attempting to show how our environmental crisis is significantly caused by the overpopulation of farm animals, he introduces this point by apparently affirming the proposition that "we look darkly at the number of babies being born in poorer parts of the world."[41]

But one of the most unique and interesting features of the ecological ethic of *Caritas in Veritate* is that it utterly rejects this way of thinking. Instead it brings to bear a concept called "integral development" and this particular section is worth quoting in its entirety:

The deterioration of nature is in fact closely connected to the culture that shapes human coexistence: *when "human ecology" is respected within society, environmental ecology also benefits.* Just as human virtues are interrelated, such that the weakening of one places others at risk, so the ecological system is based on respect for a plan that affects both the health of society and its good relationship with nature. In order to protect nature, it is not enough to intervene with economic incentives or deterrents; not even an apposite education is sufficient. These are important steps, but *the decisive issue is the overall moral tenor of society.* If there is a lack of respect for the right to life and to a natural death, if human conception, gestation and birth are made artificial, if human embryos are sacrificed to research, the conscience of society ends up losing the concept of human ecology and, along with it, that of environmental ecology. It is contradictory to insist that future generations respect the natural environment when our educational systems and laws do not help them to respect themselves. The book of nature is one and indivisible: it takes in not only the environment but also life, sexuality, marriage, the family, social relations: in a word, integral human development. Our duties towards the environment are linked to our duties towards the human person, considered in himself and in relation to others. It would be wrong to uphold one set of duties while trampling on the other. Herein lies a grave contradiction in our mentality and practice today: one which demeans the person, disrupts the environment and damages society (44).

Indeed, an "alarming decline in the birthrate in the West" (44) has accompanied ever more consumerism, waste, and ecological degradation. *Caritas in Veritate* claims that "responsible procreation" actually "makes a positive contribution to positive human development" (44). Indeed, perhaps the best way to get a strong sense of what we owe future generations is to have children. Is it any wonder that the West is losing its sense of solidarity with the future as we continue to have fewer and fewer close relationships with people who will inhabit this future?

No, instead of focusing on further depopulating ourselves, our ecological problems instead invite the West to:

> a serious review of its life-style, which, in many parts of the world, is prone to hedonism and consumerism, regardless of their harmful consequences. What is needed is an effective shift in mentality which can lead to the adoption of *new life-styles* "in which the quest for truth, beauty, goodness and communion with others for the sake of common growth are the factors which determine consumer choices, savings and investments" (51).

This is a call that Singer would support wholeheartedly. Indeed, he spends a good amount of energy attempting to get us to re-assess our notion of extravagance. It should no longer be limited to chauffeured limousines and Dom Perignon champagne. Instead, timber that has come from rainforests, disposable paper products, going for a drive in the country—*these* are all extravagances in Singer's view in light of environmental degradation. Especially given the methane gas produced by energy-intensive factory farms—and the radical inefficiency of such farms (we end up feeding 40 percent of the world's grain to animals when we could simply use the land to grow vegetables for ourselves)—he even insists that eating meat is a luxury that we can no longer afford.[42]

Moving Forward Together

It would be disingenuous to gloss over the very real differences between Peter Singer and the Catholic Church on many ethical issues. This paper has shown that, though narrow, they certainly exist and many are important. But until recently these differences have kept virtually anyone from exploring all that we have in common with each other. Given the immense overlap that exists between the two approaches, coupled with the massive influence that each wields in the modern West, this is something close to a tragedy. This essay has shown that both could marshal impressive resources in leading, together, massive campaigns to dramatically change our autonomy and privacy-centered consumerist life-styles—for they have led to both the abandoning of the global poor and to serious ecological devastation. People who likely never thought they could agree on much of anything (and who often find themselves on opposite sides of the often-polarized binaries mentioned above: life/choice, religious/secular, theologi-cal/philosophical, conservative/liberal) would find common cause on some of the most important issues of our time: poverty and ecological devastation. Indeed, perhaps the relationships formed through such personal encounters and practices could lead to new discoveries and common efforts on other issues.[43]

Peter Singer, far from having the "heart of stone" characteristic of a supposed culture of death, instead clearly has the compas-sionate "heart of flesh" that *Caritas in Veritate* calls all of us to cultivate in ourselves. As such, Christian engagement with Singer is a paradigmatic example of something else for which Pope Benedict XVI calls: "fraternal collaboration between believers and non-believers in their shared commitment to working for justice and peace in the human family" (57). Too much is at stake to let artificial, uninformed divisions keep us from this goal.

Notes

[1]He has become known for what many take to be outrageous positions (like being pro-choice for infanticide), but his entry on the academic scene was a very influential article on duties to the poor: "Famine, Affluence, and Morality," *Philosophy and Public Affairs* 1, no. 1 (Spring 1972). His first major book played a leading role in vitalizing the movement for considering non-human animals members of the moral community (*Animal Liberation* [New York: HarperCollins, 1975]). His main systematic work, about to be released in a third edition, is used in ethics courses all over the world: Peter Singer, *Practical Ethics* (New York: Cambridge University Press, 1993).

[2]Peter Singer, *Practical Ethics* (New York: Cambridge University Press, 1993), 169.

[3]Ibid., 89.

[4]As described helpfully by David Hollenbach, S.J., intellectual solidarity involves "an orientation of mind that regards differences among traditions as stimuli to intellectual engagement across religious and cultural boundaries. It is an orientation that leads one to view differences positively rather than with a mindset marked by suspicion or fear" (David Hollenbach, *The Common Good and Christian Ethics* [New York: Cambridge University Press, 2002], 138).

[5]See especially David Tracy, "God, Dialogue, and Society: A Theologian's Refrain," *Christian Century* (October 10, 1990). Several works of feminist theologians like Mary Catherine Hilkert and Elizabeth Johnson also employ this method.

[6]Indeed, in a monograph forthcoming from Cambridge University Press I also deal with these issues in far more detail.

[7]Because of the central place of these two concerns, *Caritas in Veritate* is perhaps a more natural conversation partner for Singer than some other papal documents.

[8]Using the "two-level" theory of his Oxford mentor and Christian philosopher, R. M. Hare, he believes that people should generally live by a well-chosen set of principles—not because rules have some kind of metaphysical standing, but because they produce the best consequences.

[9]For a nice summary of the discussion surrounding this issue, see Bernard Hoose, *Proportionalism: The American Debate and Its European Roots* (Washington, DC: Georgetown University Press, 1987).

[10]Such an argument would involve taking *Veritatis Splendor* seriously on the concept of an intrinsically evil act—but also attempt a different understanding of the relationship of an act's object to its circumstances.

[11]Charles C. Camosy, "Common Ground on Surgical Abortion?—Engaging Peter Singer on the Moral Status of Potential Persons," *The Journal of Medicine and Philosophy* 33, no. 6 (January 2009).

[12]This kind of disagreement also finds its way into debate about moral status at the end of life or for those with a mental disability. For instance, the church is going to want to say that a human being with severe brain damage or with late-stage Alzheimer's counts as a person in light of their active potential for morally significant traits—because of the "kind of thing" he or she is. But Singer will reject these claims and argue that these are "human non-persons" because they aren't actually rational and self-aware creatures.

[13]Peter Singer, *The Life You Can Save: Acting Now to End World Poverty* (New York: Random House, 2009), 3.

[14]Here is just one of many examples: "The more we strive to secure a common good corresponding to the real needs of our neighbours, the more effectively we love them" (*Caritas in Veritate*, 7).

[15]Singer, *The Life You Can Save*, 16.

[16]Ibid.

[17]Pope Benedict XVI, *Encyclical Letter, Caritas in Veritate* (Washington: United States Catholic Conference, 2009).

[18]Peter Singer, *One World: The Ethics of Globalization* (New Haven: Yale University Press, 2002), 170.

[19]Ibid., 171.

[20]Ibid., 180.

[21]For these concerns see chap. 2 of the encyclical *Human Development in Our Time*.

[22]Singer, *One World*, 161.

[23]Ibid., 162.

[24]Ibid., 163.

[25]Peter Singer, *The Expanding Circle: Ethics and Social Biology* (New York: Farrar, Straus and Giroux, 1981), 8.

[26]Singer, *The Life You Can Save*, 164.

[27]For an excellent discussion of this see Steven Pope's *The Evolution of Altruism and the Ordering of Love* (Washington, DC: Georgetown University Press, 1994), 63-64.

[28]*Caritas in Veritate* is quoting Paul VI in *Populorum Progressio* at this point.

[29]For a helpful summary of the pope's ecological thought see Woodeene Koenig-Bricker, *Ten Commandments for the Environment: Pope Benedict Speaks Out for Creation and Justice* (Notre Dame: Ave Maria Press, 2009).

[30]Singer, *Practical Ethics*, 273.

[31]Ibid., 268.

[32]Ibid., 269.

[33]Ibid., 270.

[34]And though it goes beyond the scope of this paper to make the argument, I believe that the church actually has a moral tradition that shares this conclusion.

[35]Singer, *Practical Ethics*, 274.

[36]Ibid., 276.

[37]Ibid., 277.

[38]Ibid., 278-79.

[39]Ibid., 270.

[40]Ibid., 272.

[41]Ibid., 286-87.

[42]Ibid.

[43]For instance, Peter Singer and I executed a major national conference at Princeton University in October 2010 designed to find new ways to think and speak about abortion. It will not only attempt to better demarcate areas of disagreement, but also highlight previously undiscovered areas of common ground.

An Anglican Middle-Axioms Reading
of *Caritas in Veritate*

Christine M. Fletcher

At a time when questions of who shall be ordained and what is a church have strained ecumenical relations between the Anglican Communion and the Roman Catholic Church, it may be helpful to seek common ground in social ethics. During Pope Benedict's recent visit to the United Kingdom he met with the archbishop of Canterbury, Rowan Williams, and the Anglican and Roman Catholic bishops. At that gathering he called for Christians to explore "together with members of other religious traditions, ways of bearing witness to the transcendent dimension of the human person and the universal call to holiness, leading to the practice of virtue in our personal and social lives."[1]

One common ground for the two communions may be the method of middle axioms, a distinctively Anglican approach to social ethics. This approach embodies respect for the autonomy of the social sciences, subsidiarity, participation, and the historically conditioned nature of moral theology on social questions—the principles and perspectives promoted in *Caritas in Veritate*, the most recent addition to Roman Catholic social teaching. It is not surprising that reading a papal document through an unexpected lens can lift up unexpected elements in it. Reading the encyclical in light of a different methodology—that of Anglican middle axioms—helps clarify what level of teaching should be reserved to the pope, and how that teaching effectively relates to current situations through dialogue with the laity as secular experts and practitioners.

Anglican Social Ethics and Middle Axioms

A good place to begin is with the primary sources of theology in the Anglican and Roman Catholic churches. For Roman Catholics scripture and tradition are the sources of theological knowledge. Tradition in this sense refers to the liturgy, the Fathers of the church, the creeds and other doctrinal definitions, the evidence of Christian art and archaeology, philosophy, and the witness of ordinary believers seen as an interconnected unity, the life of the church.[2] Anglicans, on the other hand, refer to their theological project as resting on a three-legged stool, the three legs being scripture, tradition, and reason.

While this may seem to be a small semantic difference, it encapsulates a very important difference between the two communions. For Roman Catholics, human reason, both abstract in philosophy and practical in the moral, liturgical, and social life of the church, falls under the category of tradition. Reason is essential, but it is always in dialogue with the other constituents of the full tradition. In contrast, the Anglican Church has elevated human reason—including the claims of secular disciplines, such as the findings of modern science, for example—to an equal place with scripture and tradition when dealing with theological and moral questions. Arthur Ramsey describes the Anglican vocation as one that "risk[s] untidiness and rough edges and apparently insecure fences so that it may be in and through the intellectual turmoil of the time—and not in aloofness from it—that the Church teaches the Catholic faith."[3]

As the Anglican Church is an open communion welcoming those of diverse theological viewpoints, from Anglo-Catholics to Evangelicals, so Anglican social ethics is diverse and has two major streams: one roughly analogous to natural theology and the other to revealed theology. Middle axiom social ethics fall in the natural theology category, which is founded on the belief that God can be found in the world, society, and human nature.

The term "middle axioms" was first used in the proceedings of the Conference on Christian Politics, Economics and Citizenship (COPEC) in 1924. COPEC was the first large ecumenical conference on social ethics in Britain and was attended by 1,500 delegates from almost all denominations, although Roman Catholics withdrew a few weeks before the conference. Alan Suggate tells us that this conference "used the principles of the Christian faith to expose the deficiencies of the current system and passed a veritable cavalcade of middle axioms."[4] J. H. Oldham and others also used the term middle axioms in preparatory work for the Conference on Church, Community and State held at Oxford in 1937. This conference along with the Edinburgh Faith and Order Conference of 1937 proposed that there be a single ecumenical body; once created it evolved into the World Council of Churches.[5]

These middle axioms are not the broad demands of the gospel or a particular decision in a concrete situation. They are "provisional definitions of the type of behavior required of Christians at a given period and in given circumstances."[6]

This approach was used most famously by William Temple, archbishop of Canterbury from 1942 till his death on October 26, 1944.[7] Temple was the son of an archbishop of Canterbury with a wide experience of life. He was a philosophy don, a schoolmaster, the founder of the Workers' Educational Association, a London rector, a canon of Westminster Abbey, the bishop of industrial Manchester, the archbishop of York, and, for two short years, archbishop of Canterbury. Temple was a well-regarded Christian leader in social ethics. In a tribute shortly after Temple's death, Reinhold Niebuhr wrote that Temple "was able to relate the ultimate insights of religion about the human situation to the immediate necessities of political justice and the proximate possibilities of a just social order more vitally and creatively than any other Christian leader."[8]

In preparation for the COPEC conference Temple had identified three possible attitudes of social reformers. The first stressed the organic character of society and viewed any action by the state as able to check evil but able to do little positive good. Temple found this unsatisfactory. The second attitude created an ideal system and sought to realize it. Temple saw the affinities of this approach with the kingdom of God, but he also held that we have no detailed account of how the kingdom would arrive in the context of a social order. The third rested on the belief that there are principles of conduct that are always valid and that should be applied to all aspects of life. This attitude, Temple believed, had the strengths of the other two, yet was realistic and adaptable to changing situations. He wrote:

> The Gospel, being a proclamation of the true nature of God and Man, and of the true relationship between them, necessarily consists of principles from which some others may with perfect security be deduced. . . . [The precepts of the Sermon on the Mount] are explicitly based on the unchanging character of the eternal God and the unchanging relationship of His children towards Him. . . . Our aim therefore must be to work out the primary principles of the Gospel into those *secondary principles* which may make them effective guides to action in the world of our own time, yet without seeking to determine the details to which judgment of practical expediency is always relevant.[9]

These secondary principles became known as "middle axioms." Temple grounded his theological ethics in the incarnation, since for him the central declaration of St. John's gospel, "The Word became flesh," is the affirmation of the sacramental principle, while the atonement completes the incarnation.[10] From these doctrines he moved to what he called "primary principles" that derive necessarily from Christian faith: "the basic importance of each person and of the structures of relationship in and through which each person should grow to his full stature in community with others."[11]

Temple then moved from primary principles to social principles, which he listed as freedom, social fellowship, and the duty of service.[12] These principles, though helpful, are still too vague when discussing a concrete issue, such as unemployment. Christians disagree as to what policy prescriptions are needed with such actual social problems. The middle axiom approach, therefore, tries to find agreement within the Christian community on defining the issue and on a general direction for policy prescriptions.[13]

In his introduction to the proceedings of the Malvern Conference, "The Life of the Church and the Order of Society" (1941), Temple wrote that theologians and Christians [who can appreciate the work of theologians] should think out the general implications of fundamental Christian principles in relation to contemporary needs, so supplying what among the ancients were called "middle axioms"—maxims for conduct which mediate between the fundamental principles and the tangle of particular problems.[14]

Ronald Preston, considered one of the Church of England's leading authorities on social ethics, is another major figure in the middle axiom tradition. Preston's first degree was in economics from the London School of Economics. After working for the Student Christian Movement he studied theology at Oxford and became the study secretary and editor of *The Student Movement*. He was a lecturer on social ethics at Manchester University from 1948 to 1970, and then was appointed to the university's newly created chair of Social and Pastoral Theology, which he held until his retirement in 1980. His career brought him into contact with Temple, and with other great figures of the 1930s such as J. H. Oldham and Reinhold Niebuhr. In the post-war years he worked with the Church of England's Board for Social Responsibility, and with the World Council of Churches. He "made a bridge between theology as practiced in the university and theology as the servant of the church in the world."[15]

Preston's training as an economist and a theologian are reflected in his development of the methodological principle of middle axiom ethics. He notes that "we cannot move directly from basic Christian insights to these areas [social questions] without some kind of empirical investigation, with its inevitable hazards of incomplete information, uncertain interpretation of it and hidden ideological distortions."[16] This approach is open to the contributions of non-Christian thinking and language, and sees the task of social ethics as engaging in dialogue with specialists in economics, sociology, and politics in order to formulate middle axioms. Preston describes the process in three steps: "(1) Identify the problem. . . . (2) Get at the "facts" by searching for the relevant evidence from those involved in the problem, whether as expert witnesses or as experiencing it personally. (3) Try to arrive at a broad consensus on what should be done—first of all at a middle level. This indicates a general direction at which policy should aim."[17]

As a way of doing social ethics in practice, this methodology usually involves convening a group of experts from the secular sciences to dialogue with theologians about a particular issue. This may produce a consensus, or it may produce a list of areas in which committed Christians disagree. In Preston's estimation, both are useful: "If one is led to listen to the criticism of Christians who have different commitments it sharpens one's awareness and diminishes the element of fanaticism to which the political realm is prone. And if this probing leads to further insights which society is tempted to ignore or has not realized, that is a further Christian contribution to the body politic."[18]

A middle axiom should be at the level of providing a direction for policy proposals: a level between generality and specifics. This level is appropriate for church pronouncements because it recognizes that the church has something to say about the secular order, but, at the same time, is appropriately humble about the competence of churchmen to direct secular affairs, and respects the freedom of the laity in their responsibility to and in the world.

One of the great strengths of this method is that it recognizes the autonomy of the secular sciences and puts theology in dialogue with them to the benefit of both. Theology recognizes the limits of its expertise, and respects the contributions of the secular scientists. This process respects the limitedness of human knowing, those hazards of partial knowing and of unacknowledged bias. It is of its essence a communal method that recognizes that no one is wise enough on his or her own to arrive at a conclusion.

However, this approach seems to make theology just one of many approaches, thereby not giving sufficient weight to God's revelation and action in Christ. In our world, the right of churches to comment on public affairs is widely disputed. Malcolm Brown, currently director of the Church of England's Department of Mission and Public Affairs, describes this situation:

> The Church's engagement with the worlds of politics, science, and social affairs generally now takes place in a context where the right of the church to take a seat at the table is not only questioned but often hotly contested. Any

engagement from the perspective of faith in public ethics must have a missiological quality since it cannot be taken for granted that any of the Church's interlocutors have the slightest grounding in, let alone sympathy for, the idea that ethics may look different when God is factored in.[19]

It is from this perspective that I now turn to *Caritas in Veritate*, with particular attention to some recommendations in Chapter V, The Cooperation of the Human Family. The method of middle axioms will clarify the levels of recommendations proposed in the encyclical and also pose the question: Does the encyclical properly respect the principles of autonomy of the secular sciences and subsidiarity?

Basis for Dialogue

As a methodology Anglican middle axioms provide a legitimate partner for a dialogue with Catholic social teaching, particularly as expressed in *Caritas in Veritate*, first because *Caritas in Veritate* itself calls for a dialogue with secular sciences: "[M]oral evaluation and scientific research must go hand in hand, and that charity must animate them in a harmonious interdisciplinary whole. . . . The Church's social doctrine . . . allows faith, theology, metaphysics, and science to come together in a collaborative effort in the service of humanity" (31). An encyclical that addresses the major problems of a global economic system in crisis should highlight the need for input from economists, sociologists, development professionals, and political scientists to propose local policies that embody the principles of Catholic social teaching.

Second, the encyclical and the middle axiom tradition, particularly in Temple's work, share a common philosophical frame of reference in their appeals to natural law, understood as an objective morality, discoverable by reason, that should guide human action. Archbishop Temple had a critical appreciation of and commitment to natural law reasoning. As an active theologian during World War II, "Temple . . . engage[d] with natural law as part of an important search for deeper foundations in the face of world crisis; at the same time many Catholics on the Continent found in natural law a practical defence of the person against totalitarianism."[20]

Temple began working for the Jews in 1933 when Hitler came to power and, through the next years, his interest in natural law grew so that "he planned a personal approach to the Vatican, hoping that Anglican and Roman Catholic theologians might undertake a joint study of natural law."[21] For instance, Temple thought that the incarnation provided insight into the universe as sacramental, and that the practical import of this sacramental principle revealed that the total being of humanity—material and individual, social and historical—falls within God's plan of redemption.[22] Temple would use the words natural law and natural order interchangeably, and he thought natural morality offered a bridge between Christians and non-Christians on moral questions.

Temple critiqued the understanding of natural law in Catholic ethics in a 1944 speech to the London Aquinas Society, suggesting that natural law reasoning should take greater account of the historical context, recognize that revelation is given in events and not propositions, appreciate individual personality more, and give a greater place to sin as distinct from sins.[23]

He seems to have arrived at the post-Vatican II understanding of natural law held by many modern Roman Catholic ethicists, with a notable exception in the area of application. Temple was the leader of a church that had, in the Lambeth Conference of 1931, approved of contraceptive use by married couples.

Despite the differences in the understanding of natural law and therefore the differences in sexual ethics between the Anglican and Roman Catholic social ethicists, the common commitment to a natural moral order and to the Christian narrative of creation and redemption establishes a ground for dialogue between the Anglican middle axiom tradition and Catholic social teaching. Benedict XVI's understanding of natural law as presented in *Caritas in Veritate* appears to satisfy Temple's criticisms:

> In all cultures there are examples of ethical convergence, some isolated, some interrelated, as an expression of the one human nature, willed by the Creator; the tradition of

ethical wisdom knows this as the natural law. This universal moral law provides a sound basis for all cultural, religious and political dialogue, and it ensures that the multi-faceted pluralism of cultural diversity does not detach itself from the common quest for truth, goodness and God. Thus adherence to the law etched on human hearts is the precondition for all constructive social cooperation. Every culture has burdens from which it must be freed and shadows from which it must emerge (59).

This provides a nuanced view of natural law in human cultures, each of which has its shadows. This is part of the theological foundation of *Caritas in Veritate*, and is a concept shared with Anglicans in the Temple tradition, although they would wish to dialogue about its interpretation in relation to human sexuality in particular. This shared tradition of moral reasoning leads to a closer analysis of *Caritas in Veritate*, particularly Chapter V, The Cooperation of the Human Family.

What Level of Teaching Principle?

Analyzing the encyclical text to determine what level of teaching is given—foundational principle, intermediate principle, middle axiom, or policy prescription—will demonstrate that all these levels are in the encyclical. This essay, however, contends that the encyclical's teaching should remain at the level of foundational and intermediate principles. The middle axioms and policy prescriptions should be formulated by the local churches with the help of experts in economics, politics, and other secular sciences.

Caritas in Veritate clearly makes Catholic theological anthropology its foundational principle for evaluating true human development. Human beings are understood as free (17), relational (53), made for love (1-3), living in different cultural and historical contexts (4), and directed to their ultimate good in God (1, 78). Chapter V examines human cooperation and expands the relational characteristics of human beings: "*The development of peoples depends, above all, on a recognition that the human race is a single family* working together in true communion, not simply a group of subjects who happen to live side by side" (53).

The model for the human family is the Trinity itself (54). This foundation is similar to Temple's primary principle of the basic importance of each person within a community.

From this foundation, Benedict gives a definition of the individual and the community that indicates a fuller appreciation of the individual, also a point made by Temple:

> reason finds inspiration and direction in Christian revelation, according to which the human community does not absorb the individual annihilating his autonomy . . . but values him all the more because the relation between individual and community is a relation between one totality and another. Just as a family does not submerge the identities of its individual members . . . so too the unity of the human family does not submerge the identities of individuals, peoples and cultures, but makes them more transparent to each other and links them more closely in their legitimate diversity (53).

This encyclical also values the diversity of religion and culture, defending the place of religions in the public realm, in culture, society, economics, and politics. A corollary of this is that neither the exclusion of religion from the public square nor religious fundamentalism will lead to true development; reason needs faith and faith needs reason (56). The encyclical recognizes that the social order is no longer static, which was Temple's first point.

Solidarity and Subsidiarity

Subsidiarity and solidarity, two basic principles of Catholic social teaching, are used throughout this chapter. Subsidiarity is linked to solidarity: "*The principle of subsidiarity must remain closely linked to the principle of solidarity and vice versa*, since the former without the latter gives way to social privatism, while the latter without the former gives way to paternalist social assistance that is demeaning to those in need" (58).

Benedict defines the principle of subsidiarity in the context of human development as "an expression of inalienable human freedom. Subsidiarity is first and foremost a form of assistance to the human person via the autonomy of intermediate bodies" (57). He links subsidiarity to the theology of relation: "By considering reciprocity as the heart of what it is to be a human being, subsidiarity is the most effective antidote against any form of an all-encompassing welfare state" (57). It fosters participation, and the assumption of responsibility. As a principle it protects individuals: "In order not to produce a dangerous universal power of a tyrannical nature, *the governance of globalization must be marked by subsidiarity*" (57). These two basic principles of Catholic social teaching begin to define what responsible citizenship requires.

The foundations of theological anthropology, natural law, and the principles of subsidiarity, solidarity, participation, human dignity, and the common good are applied to a series of current economic problems: international development aid, migration, poverty and unemployment, labor unions, finance, consumption, and world governance.

In these paragraphs, as indeed earlier in the encyclical, the text moves between principles, observations about the current situation, and recommendations. Recommendations seem to be at various levels: intermediate principles, middle axioms, and policy prescriptions. For example, the encyclical calls for the establishment of a greater degree of international ordering, marked by subsidiarity, to manage globalization. This could be classified as an intermediate principle. The recommendation that policies on migration should result from close collaboration between countries that balance the needs of migrants and the host country seems to be a middle axiom; it is more specific than an intermediate principle but it does not specify a particular policy. The "urgent need for a world political authority" (67), on the other hand, is a policy prescription. The result can be somewhat muddled. A close examination of the pope's treatment of international aid from the perspective of middle axioms reveals changes in the levels of recommendations found in the encyclical: foundational principles, secondary principles, middle axioms, and policy prescriptions.

International Aid

As the encyclical focuses on human development, a discussion of international aid forms a significant portion of the chapter. The principles of solidarity and subsidiarity are equally important when evaluating aid: aid should not be paternalistic or lead to social privatism (58). This seems to be a secondary principle derived from the primary principles of solidarity and subsidiarity. International aid is criticized because it can lock people into a state of dependence and foster situations of localized oppression and exploitation. This recognition of the unintended consequences of aid is helpful to frame the discussion and follows from the principles of solidarity and subsidiarity.

Applying the principle of participation, the distribution of aid must involve not only governments but also citizens, again a clear secondary principle. The aid should develop the human resources of the receiving country as developing human capital is necessary to "guarantee a truly autonomous future for the poorest countries" (58). This is a secondary principle derived from the basic principle of human dignity. Aid should not be a handout but should develop the productivity of local or national economies so that they can participate in the international economy. The products developed should compete in the global market and not simply in fringe markets. This requires a system of fair-trade regulations for agricultural and manufactured products (58). These statements seem to be, in effect, middle axioms, moving from the primary and secondary principles to a middle axiom that can be used for discussion with secular experts to derive policy prescriptions.

The encyclical asks, "What aid programme is there than can hold out such sufficient growth prospects—even from the point of view of the world economy—as the support of populations that are still in the initial or early phases of economic development?" (60). This question seems to preempt discussion on whether economic growth or economic sustainability should be the goal of international aid. Such a discussion by experts in dialogue with theologians is needed in the developing countries to arrive at policy proposals. These statements seemingly accept uncritically the international market institutions, offering no criticism of unlimited consumption, or of the option to protect a developing economy. A further discussion is necessary with contributions by experts to determine how to link development and trade and what is truly "fair."

Turning to donor countries, the encyclical recommends that they give more aid to developing countries and that they find this money by reforming their welfare systems by "applying the principle of subsidiarity and creating better integrated welfare systems with the active participation of private individuals and civil society" (60). Reform that would eliminate waste and fraud and reduce bureaucracy would improve social services and foster solidarity. The encyclical recommends fiscal subsidiarity, allowing citizens to decide how to allocate a portion of the taxes they pay to the state, provided that this does not promote special interests.

These statements are policy proposals rather than middle axioms. They oversimplify a complex reality and ignore important political and economic debates. The fault is not with the desired result, but with the glossing over of the considerable complexities of the modern welfare state and the difficulty of having a political discussion of these alternatives, as we can see with the pension crisis in the European Union and in the United States. The reference to special interests gestures toward the "fallen world," where self-interest comes first, but it does not include a theological perspective on fallen human nature, its effect on political realities, or the reality of structural sin. Deriving proper middle axioms and then policy proposals requires a more nuanced theological approach to the reality of human self-seeking that limits the acceptance of solidarity with all humanity. This should occur before the dialogue with secular experts can begin.

Analysis via Middle Axioms

This exercise in reading *Caritas in Veritate* from the Anglican perspective of middle axioms illuminates the contrasts between the ecclesiology of the two communions and their methodologies in applying social ethics. This papal encyclical is presented as the work of the authoritative teacher of Catholic doctrine; it is addressed to the world, both the church and all people of good will. Anglican social documents such as *Faith in the City*,[24] produced by a commission that included churchmen and secular experts to examine the inequities in British society during the Thatcher years, are equally directed to all people of good will, however they are the products of and are directed to the local church, the Church of England, and so would be comparable to *The Challenge of Peace* or *Economic Justice for All* of the U.S. Catholic bishops.

The archbishop of Canterbury, like the pope, is the leader of a global communion. The theological diversity within the Anglican Communion as well as the independence of the local churches is a markedly different ecclesial reality than Roman Catholicism. In such a communion, any work of social ethics proposed—even by the archbishop of Canterbury—is understood to be open for debate. The preparation of social documents involves theologians and secular experts. *Unemployment and the Future of Work*, for example, is an ecumenical effort of the churches and secular experts.[25]

Archbishop Temple's principles—freedom, social fellowship, and service—are of a higher level of generality than the core principles of Catholic social teaching. In *Christianity and Social Order*, Archbishop Temple puts his policy recommendations into an appendix, using the text to develop his moral arguments from the principles he espoused.[26] To move from those principles to a public statement about a particular social problem requires the input of experts from the secular sciences. Social questions are addressed in documents prepared by a group of theologians and secular experts convened to address them in the name of the church, often the local church. As an example, the Church of England was part of the Council of Churches of Britain and Ireland group that produced *Unemployment and the Future of Work* with a working group that included economists, social scientists, the long-term unemployed, church workers, and theologians.

In Roman Catholicism, however, social ethics as expressed in papal encyclicals are viewed as *authoritative (nondefinitive)* doctrine.[27] It would be impossible for the pope to issue encyclicals on the level produced by the middle axiom methodology: he speaks to a global church, and so would need to consult with experts not only in various disciplines, but experts in different areas of the world. Yet, the generality of the encyclicals is their strength: they guide the work of theologians, politicians, ethicists, and economists who examine problems within their specific area to formulate true middle axioms. Further, the guiding principles of Catholic social teaching—human dignity, solidarity, subsidiarity, participation, and the common good—are more specific than Temple's principles of freedom, social fellowship, and service.

Catholic social teaching is known as the best kept secret of the church, partly because of this methodology. The business slogan of

"No involvement, no commitment" captures the problem. We have specialists who know the tradition and many ethicists and theologians working in it, but the tradition has a difficult time entering the world of practical politics and of economic decision-making. If, however, the encyclicals stayed on the general level of principles to guide the local churches, and the local churches adopted the methodology of middle axioms, Catholic social teaching would benefit by better crafting its interventions in the secular realm and by becoming a lived ecclesial reality for the lay faithful.

Caritas in Veritate speaks of the problems of international tourism based on hedonism and consumerism, a topic that the local churches in both the country of origin and the destination of tourists could address effectively. In the country of origin, a local discussion on the ethics of tourism with input from experts in economics and the psychology of marketing could awaken the laity to their responsibilities as tourists. In the destination country, such a local discussion by secular experts could empower the local population to ensure that the development of tourist destinations is socially as well as economically positive for their society.

This is not an unrealistic option as can be seen in the history of the social encyclicals. Catholic social teaching has undergone a transformation from the early encyclicals produced prior to Vatican II when "The papacy rather uncritically presupposed that it already possessed, within the deposit of the faith, all the answers to the problems of the age."[28] *Gaudium et Spes* recognized that church teaching needed to learn from the world. In *Octogesima Adveniens* Pope Paul VI was even more specific: "In the face of such widely varying situations it is difficult for us to utter a unified message and to put forward a solution which has universal validity. It is up to the Christian communities to analyze with objectivity the situation which is proper to their own country" (4). This approach is more respectful of the basic principles of subsidiarity and participation. The American bishops fulfilled the pope's call in their pastorals *The Challenge of Peace* and *Economic Justice for All*, pastorals that made use of a methodology of open listening, which closely parallels the development of middle axioms.

This methodology, however, was criticized in *Libertatis Conscientia* (Instruction on Christian Freedom and Liberation, 1986), which specified that it was the task of Christians not to formulate church teaching but only to apply that which has already been formulated.[29] Nevertheless *Caritas in Veritate,* like *Populorum Progressio,* seems to revert to the earlier, consultative model. It recognizes that true human development and social ethics require an interdisciplinary approach (30-31): "Faced with the phenomena that lie before us, charity in truth requires first of all that we know and understand, acknowledging and respecting the specific compe-tence of every level of knowledge" (30). The encyclical reiterates Pope Paul IV's recognition that in dealing with the secular sciences, "all social action involves a doctrine" (*Populorum Progressio,* 39). *Caritas in Veritate* brings the theological anthropology of person, the theology of relation, and the idea of gift "unrecognized because of a purely consumerist and utilitarian view of life" (34) to the discussion of the current crisis.

This encyclical is at its best and most authoritative when it ex-plains the links between the principles of Catholic social teaching, which is founded on revelation and natural law, and the current situation. Such teaching does not violate the autonomy of the secular sciences, or the consciences and moral responsibility of lay Catholics in their vocation in the world.

However, when the encyclical leaves this level of principle and writes policy prescriptions such as we find in Chapter V, problems arise. First, the variety of empirical contexts combined with the constraints of space imposed by the form of the letter means that the formulations read either as pious aspirations or as judgments that pre-empt debate on a given problem, such as aid.

Second, the encyclical's own declared methodology of interdis-ciplinarity is not apparent. There are reports that the encyclical is an uneasy hybrid between the Congregation for Justice and Peace and Pope Benedict XVI, and that several drafts were rejected by the pope.[30] We know the encyclical was delayed from its original expected date of 2007 and was finally released by the Vatican to coincide with the G8 summit in 2009.[31] We do not know who was consulted in the document's preparation. This gives the ap-pearance of undervaluing secular knowledge and of glossing over the complexity of social issues.

It also seems to move prudential judgments to a higher level of authority than they are entitled to have. Christians of good will can agree on principles and on ends and yet disagree on the means to attain those ends. Theologically, the greatest weakness in the encyclical's recommendations is that they seem to ignore the reality of original sin, which makes politics such an interesting and frustrating process. A document that handled the theology of the fallen world could make a significant contribution to understanding not only the social problems of today's world but also the unintended consequences of many reform efforts and social programs.

Conclusion

The Anglican method of interdisciplinary consultations, with theologians from various theological schools in dialogue with secular experts, would not work as a way of producing papal encyclicals. However, it is an excellent model for making the encyclicals of Catholic social teaching live in the world. *Economic Justice for All* used this approach and was a stronger statement with a bigger public impact because of it. Charles Curran writes:

> The pastoral letters of the U.S. bishops in the 1980s on nuclear war and deterrence and the economy had a greater effect on the American public in general and the Catholic Church in the United States than any other documents coming from the U.S. Bishops. The primary reason comes from the unique and public way in which these letters were written and discussed.[32]

The model of interdisciplinary discussions within parishes, Catholic colleges and universities, dioceses, and national bishops' conferences should be an essential part of the new evangelization to help Catholics see their faith as requiring action in the world. Such a method would ensure that the encyclicals do not remain the preserve of the academic who specializes in Catholic social teaching.

Such a method would not violate the prohibition expressed in *Liberatis Conscientia*. It would require that the encyclical authors be more respectful of the difference between fundamental and secondary principles and their application, and avoid putting their own policy prescriptions into the authoritative documents. This would also show that the church respected the lay vocation and gave more than lip service to the autonomy of the secular sciences. The dialogue between the principles of Catholic social teaching and the secular sciences would offer a critique, as we find in *Caritas in Veritate*, of secular methodologies that are based on a radically different anthropology.

Finally, using this method would mean that the church is living the principle of participation, bringing the insights of lay Christians into a dialogue, for the church to undertake true, effective social action. We might seek the courage, like our Anglican brothers and sisters, "to risk untidiness and rough edges and apparently insecure fences so that it may be in and through the intellectual turmoil of the time—and not in aloofness from it—that the Church teaches the Catholic faith."[33]

Notes

[1] Pope Benedict XVI, "Culture Is Growing Ever More Distant from Its Christian Roots," Address at Lambeth Palace, September 17, 2010, http://www.zenit.org/article-30381?l=english (accessed 9/30/10).

[2] Aidan Nichols, O.P., *The Shape of Catholic Theology: An Introduction to Its Sources, Principles and History* (Edinburgh: T & T Clark, 1991), 34.

[3] Arthur Michael Ramsey, *From Gore to Temple: The Development of Anglican Theology between* Lux Mundi *and the Second World War: 1889-1939, The Hale Memorial Lectures of Seabury-Western Theological Seminary, 1959* (London: Longmans, 1960), 89.

[4] Alan M. Suggate, *William Temple and Christian Social Ethics Today* (Edinburgh: T & T Clark, 1987), 35.

[5] Ibid., 39.

[6] Joseph H. Oldham, "The Function of the Church in Society," in *The Church and Its Function in Society*, ed. W. A. Visser't Hooft and Joseph H. Oldham (Chicago: Willett, Clark and Company, 1937), 193-94.

[7] Temple's own work, *Christianity and Social Order* (Harmondsworth: Penguin Books, 1942) is a summary of his positions on social ethics and an excellent example of middle axiom methodology in that he puts his policy proposals into an appendix, rather than into the body of the text. His organization of the COPEC conference and his contributions to the 1937 Oxford Conference on Church, Community and the State (he contributed a paper and drafted the final message of the Conference) show his commitment to this way of doing social ethics. He also organized the Malvern Conference of 1941, which invited specialists to dialogue with theologians on social issues.

[8] Reinhold Niebuhr, *The Nation*, 11 November 1944, quoted in Ronald H. Preston, *The Future of Christian Ethics* (London: SCM Press Ltd. 1987), 100.

[9] William Temple, "Principles or Ideals?" *The Pilgrim*, January 1923, 218-

25, quoted in Suggate, *William Temple and Christian Social Ethics Today* 34, emphasis mine.

[10]Suggate, *William Temple and Christian Social Ethics Today*, 57-58.

[11]Oldham, "The Function of the Church in Society," 106.

[12]Suggate, *William Temple and Christian Social Ethics Today*, 34.

[13]Ibid., 109.

[14]William Temple, "Introduction" in *Malvern, 1941: The Life of the Church and the Order of Society* (London: Longmans, Green and Co., 1941), vii.

[15]Malcolm Brown, "An Anglican Gene? The Lineage of This Book," in *God, Ethics and the Human Genome: Theological, Legal and Scientific Perspectives*, ed. Mark Bratton (London: Church House Publishing, 2009), i.

[16]Preston, *The Future of Christian Ethics*, 1.

[17]Ronald Preston, "A Comment on Method," in *Putting Theology to Work*, ed. Malcolm Brown and Peter Sedgwick (London and Manchester: CCBI and The William Temple Foundation, 1998), 36-37.

[18]Preston, *The Future of Christian Ethics*, 110.

[19]Brown, "An Anglican Gene?" vii.

[20]Suggate, *William Temple and Christian Social Ethics Today*, 106.

[21]Ibid., 70.

[22]Owen C. Thomas, "William Temple," in *The Spirit of Anglicanism: Hooker, Maurice, Temple*, ed. William J. Wolf (Edinburgh: T & T Clark, 1982), 119.

[23]William Temple, "Thomism and Modern Needs," *Blackfriars* (March 1944): 92.

[24]Church of England Archbishop's Commission on Urban Priority Areas, *Faith in the City* (London: Church House Publishing, 1985).

[25]Council of Churches for Britain and Ireland (CBBI), *Unemployment and the Future of Work: An Enquiry for the Churches* (London: CCBI, 1997).

[26]William Temple, *Christianity and Social Order* (New York: Penguin Books, 1942).

[27]Richard R. Gaillardetz, "The Ecclesiological Foundations of Modern Catholic Social Teaching," in *Modern Catholic Social Teaching: Commentaries and Interpretations*, ed. Kenneth R. Himes, O.F.M. (Washington, DC: Georgetown University Press, 2004), 85.

[28]Ibid., 81.

[29]Ibid., 85.

[30]George Weigel, "*Caritas in Veritate* in Gold and Red: The Revenge of Justice and Peace (or So They May Think)," *National Review Online* July 7, 2009, http://www.nationalreview.com/articles/227839/i-caritas-veritate-i-gold-and-red/george-weigel?page=1 (accessed September 30, 2010).

[31]Guy Dinmore, "Pope Condemns Capitalism's 'Failures,'" *Financial Times*, July 7, 2009, http://www.ft.com/cms/s/0/cc9150d0-6af4-11de-861d-00144feabdc0.html.

[32]Charles Curran, "The Reception of Catholic Social and Economic Teaching in the United States," in *Modern Catholic Social Teaching: Commentaries and Interpretations*, ed. Kenneth R. Himes, O.F.M. (Washington, DC: Georgetown University Press, 2004), 483.

[33]Ramsey, *From Gore to Temple*, 89.

Christianity as Closed Monotheism?

A Contemporary Catholic Approach to Interreligious Dialogue

Karen Teel

Effective interreligious dialogue, or civil discussion among adherents of various faith traditions about the similarities and differences of their religious beliefs and practices, is a vital component of life in today's globalized world, yet it remains largely an elusive goal. Christians in particular, not only ordinary Christians but also sometimes prominent leaders, often seem to lack the delicacy required to engage in it. As a case in point, Pope Benedict XVI's mention of a medieval emperor's critique of Islam in his Regensburg address of September 2006 touched off a firestorm of criticism and apology.[1] This tactical error typifies the clumsiness with which Christians sometimes speak, whether critically or uncritically, of religious traditions other than our own. In the face of increasing global mobility and social diversity, and despite numerous exhortations to dialogue in official church documents, many lay Catholics do not have the sensitivity, the confidence, or even the motivation to engage in productive dialogue.

This lack may simply reflect the fact that many of us know very little about religions, or that we have never encountered models of successful dialogue that might inspire imitation. But perhaps the root of the problem runs deeper: it may be a deficiency not only in our knowledge but also in our theological understanding of the uniqueness of our relationship to God, and indeed of God.

In her book *What's Faith Got to Do with It?*, published the same year as Benedict's address, Kelly Brown Douglas names as "closed monotheism" the idea that the Christian God is the only god and that, for those who know this to be true, refusing to worship this god is a grave sin that prevents their salvation. This belief has sometimes been used to justify violence in God's name; Douglas considers this pernicious effect to be a flaw at the heart of Christianity.[2] Indeed, Laurel C. Schneider asserts that if we take seriously certain signs and trajectories within Christianity, as well as diverse experiences of divinity reported in many cultures and religions, Christians may need to move "beyond monotheism."[3] Schneider's "theology of multiplicity" does not renounce God, or Jesus as savior, nor posit that either is simply one of many. Rather, Schneider argues that divinity *happens* in the world in countless ways, and these happenings finally elude all efforts to systematize them as exclusively One.

What theological grounds are needed to enable ordinary Christians to engage in productive interreligious dialogue? And what would such dialogue produce? In the Regensburg address, when Benedict argues that the Christian god is rational and therefore true in a way that is unique among the world's religions, he upholds the consistent Catholic teaching that dialogue is part of the church's mission of evangelization. As Pope John Paul II stated, dialogue can never be completely separated from the mandate to proclaim Jesus as Lord, which is "the permanent priority of mission" and which actively seeks conversions (*Redemptoris Missio*, 44). Elsewhere, Benedict confirms that the ultimate goal of dialogue is to seek the truth that leads to peace.[4] For him, of course, truth has its source in the Christian God. Yet many people today believe that peace is more important than agreement or conversion. Indeed, attempts at proselytization, as proclamation is often interpreted, are sometimes taken as signs of personal, cultural, and religious disrespect, even violence. Theologians and non-theologians alike need to know how to navigate this frequently occurring tension between proclamation and peace.

While Benedict denounces the violence that has often attended the idea of closed monotheism, he never appears to consider whether moving beyond this belief might eliminate it. In this essay, I ask whether the Vatican's insistence on closed monotheism, combined with Benedict's emphasis on reason, provides an adequate foundation for Catholics to enter into productive interreligious dialogue. First, I explore the early Christian development and articulation of closed monotheism, questioning its inevitability and suggesting that, by today's standards, we can judge its effects on dialogue, if not the idea itself, as primarily negative. Second, I survey the church's recent posture toward dialogue, tracing it through documents including *Nostra Aetate*, *Dialogue and Proclamation*, and Pope Benedict's Regensburg address. Third, I present alternatives to the emphasis on an exclusive understanding of monotheism and reason that may prove more compatible with dialogue. In conclusion, I return to the need to involve more Catholics in interreligious dialogue. Proposing a theology of humility, I contend that emphasizing peace, rather than conversions, as the goal of dialogue could both equip and encourage more Catholics to participate.

The Development of Closed Monotheism and Early Modes of Dialogue

Laurel C. Schneider extensively treats the development of closed monotheism (or exclusive or universal or absolute monotheism) in *Beyond Monotheism: A Theology of Multiplicity*. A summary of relevant portions of this book highlights several early articulations and deployments of the idea of closed monotheism, and analyzes the inadequacy of these "dialogue methods" for today. This overview of closed monotheism's origins and initial articulation will position us to examine the Vatican's contemporary approach to dialogue.

Schneider explores how the belief that the Christian god is the only god, now taken for granted by most Christians, was generated and refined over the course of centuries. According to her analysis, exclusive monotheism of the Christian variety developed primarily out of three distinct sources that coalesced in Christian thought: the theology of ancient Israel; Greek philosophy, especially Platonism; and African thought, as represented, for example, by Tertullian.[5] Schneider demonstrates how logical it is that peoples inundated by changes and challenges on all sides would come to understand the divine as a force that favored them out of all peoples on the earth (the Israelites), a force that did not change (the Greeks), and that was relational (Africa). Today, the Catholic Church views the belief in one eternal, unchanging, rational God, which was the outcome of this long evolution, as true and guided by the Holy Spirit. Yet the very human impulses toward feeling secure and special that also doubtless guided this development highlight the fact that this coming-to-understand-the-divine *was* a process. As such, Schneider suggests, it might not be complete.[6]

Before elaborating on her specific proposal, it may be helpful to hear how prominent early Christians articulated their belief in God. Such expressions demonstrate that what we now call monotheism has ancient roots, though it received that name much later.[7] Many ancient thinkers declared their belief in one and only one God not by simple assertion, but by referring to people who disagreed with their beliefs, often other Christians, with disparaging terms such as *idolater* or *enemy*. These thinkers exhibit a clear us-vs.-them mentality: we know the truth, they don't.

Very early on, Justin Martyr proclaimed that those who lived before Christ could be saved if they lived according to "reason." He argued that Christ, as the word (*logos*), is in everyone who is reasonable: "Those who have lived reasonably, and still do, are Christians, and are fearless and untroubled."[8] This generosity is limited to those who lived before Christ; immediately following this passage, for example, Justin condemned Jews, acknowledging favorably the law that any Jew who entered Jerusalem would be executed. It is difficult to imagine a more violent response to difference.

Fourth-century thinkers, who were instrumental in the development of the doctrine of the Trinity, commonly employed a rhetorical style that condemned those who lacked the "truth." Discussing the mind and how it knows truth, Basil the Great stated that lack of faith is the result of devil-inflicted injury, and results in either idolatry or impiety: "If the mind has been injured by devils it will be guilty of idolatry, or will be perverted to some other form of impiety. But if it has yielded to the aid of the Spirit, it will have understanding of the truth, and will know God."[9] Likewise, Ambrose wrote: "We say, then, that there is one God, not two or three Gods, this being the error into which the impious heresy of the Arians doth run with its blasphemies."[10] Here truth is opposed to idolatry, and error equated with blasphemy.

This way of speaking about one's opponents is quite disrespect-ful. Consider the clever segue of Gregory of Nazianzus: "What is their next objection, how full of contentiousness and impu-dence?"[11] Mocking one's interlocutor may be an effective rhetori-cal device, but today this strategy would be useless in dialogue. In addition, confusing the objection with the person is virtually inevitable; indeed, for the ancients not just the objection but the person was impudent, idolatrous, and needed to be brought into line. Gregory distinguished between "rebuking others," which is so easy anyone can do it, and "substituting one's own belief for theirs," which is the goal of a "pious and intelligent man."[12] Persuasion and conversion were of utmost importance, *the* reason for engaging in dialogue in the first place.

Such dialogue was not seen as offering any benefit for the one who was "right." Gregory of Nyssa framed his treaty rebutting the ideas of Eunomius as an effort to save Eunomius from him-self. Gregory sought to learn nothing from Eunomius, but hoped only to perform the charitable act of "drag[ging] him from the abyss of misbelief." Moreover, Gregory violently described the not inconsiderable intellectual effort in Eunomius's treatise as a "poor little abortion, quite prematurely born"; it had to be dashed on the rock of Christ's truth, as the psalm condones the smashing of the children of Babylon against a rock.[13] Augustine, though his language is far more restrained, also said that the goal of rhetoric was to move the audience to understanding, pleasure, and obedience.[14]

During these foundational centuries of Christianity, truth de-manded assent and dissent called for punitive measures. In this context it is perhaps easy to see how, post-Constantine, many Christians thought it right to persecute non-Christians as well as Christians deemed "misbelieving," just as they themselves had recently been persecuted.

In *Salvation Outside the Church?* Francis A. Sullivan, S.J., notes that these thinkers believed that virtually everyone in the world had a genuine opportunity to embrace Christianity. Only with colonial expansion did European Christians realize that huge numbers of people had lived and died never having heard of Christ, and begin to really wrestle with the question of their salvation. Much later still, a more compassionate understanding of the complex psychological and spiritual factors involved in conversion to a new religion began to develop, along with increasing appreciation for the merits of the various religions. Thus Sullivan argues that Christian thinkers have always hoped that God's mercy would prevail for non-Christians, although the Catholic Church has only recently begun to express optimism about this possibility.[15]

Given this history of how those who developed the idea of the Trinity and enshrined it in the Creed understood dialogue with those who disagreed with them, including fellow Christians, we see that they had little or no concept of dialogue as a means to gain true or useful information from interlocutors. It is difficult to see how such dismissive or vitriolic attitudes toward different ideas could fail to influence one's attitude toward the person holding the ideas. In fact, the Christian tendency has been to elide the two: church authorities not only declared ideas judged heretical to be anathema, but also commonly excommunicated persons judged to be heretics. Sometimes they went so far as to execute them, not only in ancient times but continuing at least through the Middle Ages.

Today most Christians have no qualms about declaring that this goes too far. Douglas, for one, examines this early history and concludes that "the closed nature of Christian monotheism precludes an appreciation for religio-cultural difference"; while violent applications of this belief were not inevitable, the fact that they have occurred should prod us to question the belief itself.[16]

Although Douglas does not develop a specific proposal, the long history of violence associated with "the logic of the One"[17] also motivates Schneider's extended critique of exclusive monotheism and her argument to transform it. Attending to the Christian claim that Jesus is the incarnation of God in a particular body and to the religious experiences of people everywhere, Schneider deduces that divinity appears, or is incarnated, in all sorts of ways.[18] It is illogical, she contends, to maintain that a God who has been known to take flesh would do so only once. Rather than a static, absolute, singular or self-contained God, divinity is better described as multiplicity: dynamic, engaged, springing up newly everywhere, fluidly adapting and responding to its surroundings, like the myriad forms of water.[19] With this move "beyond monotheism," Schneider aims neither to deny nor to diminish Christianity but to push it toward greater honesty about its metaphorical exemption, a move she characterizes as a theological "growing up."[20] Rigorously reasoned, theologically and biblically grounded, Schneider's proposal demands careful consideration by Catholic thinkers.[21]

Interreligious dialogue scholar Catherine Cornille would likely call such consideration an exercise in "doctrinal humility," allowing that (some of) our beliefs may be flawed or incomplete.[22] Doctrinal humility is distinct from spiritual humility, a much-cultivated Christian virtue that entails recognizing that we are finite and may err in understanding our beliefs. Cornille believes that although doctrinal humility has not been a hallmark of Christian faith, it is a necessary condition for dialogue that leads to growth and change in individuals and traditions. Indeed, Schneider's theory of divinity-as-multiplicity renders interreligious dialogue a necessity: if divinity can never be contained within one idea or set of experiences, then in inquiring into others' encounters with divinity, we will surely learn more than we already knew.

Even without considering closed monotheism problematic, many Catholics no longer see people of other faiths or no faith as impious, impudent, or heretical, but rather presume their goodwill. Some might find that Schneider's expansive portrayal of divinity resonates better with their sense of the religions than the traditional teaching of closed monotheism. Yet the Catholic Church, while promoting a positive perception of peoples of faith, still teaches that dialogue's primary purpose is to bring people to Christ, the very goal that fueled the ancients' disrespectful methods. In witnessing to what we believe is truth, must we also proselytize? Or might a shift in our assumptions about those with whom we engage, as well as our method for engagement, lead us to re-evaluate our goal?

The Catholic Church's Current Approach to Dialogue

Today many Christians, including Catholics, seeing goodness in most people and religions, do not think non-Christians should be condemned. Again, Sullivan shows that the Catholic Church has become far more optimistic about the likelihood of the salvation of non-Christians; it, too, perceives "rays of truth" in the world's great religions.[23] This raises the possibility that dialogue may engender learning. Over the last half-century, the Vatican's position on dialogue has been developing in documents including *Nostra Aetate*, *Dialogue and Proclamation*, *Dominus Iesus*, and the Regensburg address. Examining this position and the way it is articulated may shed light on why more Catholics today are not involved in serious dialogue.

As is well known, the current position, which can be traced back to ideas of Karl Rahner and others leading up to Vatican II, begins to be articulated in the council documents.[24] *Lumen Gentium* could not be clearer that salvation occurs through Jesus: "Present to us in his body which is the church, Christ alone is mediator and the way of salvation" (par. 14). Having declared that Christians lacking charity cannot be saved and that all those who seek God, especially Jews and Muslims but also others, are included in the "plan of salvation," *Lumen Gentium* states that "Those who, through no fault of their own, do not know the Gospel of Christ or his church, but who nevertheless seek God with a sincere heart, and moved by grace, try in their actions to do his will as they know it through the dictates of their conscience— these too may attain eternal salvation" (16).

Likewise, *Nostra Aetate* lists positive attributes of various religions, asserting that "The Catholic Church rejects nothing of what is true and holy in these religions. It has a high regard for the manner of life and conduct, the precepts and doctrines which, although differing in many ways from its own teaching, nevertheless often reflect a ray of that truth which enlightens all men and women" (2). Following Vatican II, the church made good on these acknowledgments of the worth of non-Catholic traditions by initiating significant endeavors in ecumenical and interreligious dialogue.[25] Meanwhile, it maintained the superiority of Christianity to all other religions and Catholicism to all other forms of Christianity, and the goal of unity among churches and conversion of non-Christians.

These two trajectories have sometimes clashed. As Cornille has recently documented, some Catholic theologians have apparently taken the *Nostra Aetate* clause "although differing in many ways from its own teaching" to mean that other religions contain distinctive truth. This has led them to develop theories of hospitality toward religious difference, based on the doctrine of the Trinity.[26] We should note, however, that the Vatican has responded less than favorably, disciplining some of these thinkers.

Documents such as *Dialogue and Proclamation* discuss dialogue approvingly, acknowledging that its goals include mutual learning and increased respect. Yet, at least for Christians, dialogue remains part of the church's evangelizing mission, the primary aim of which is to proclaim Christ to all people. Thus, interreligious dialogue is called a "dialogue of salvation" (see *Dialogue and Proclamation*, 38, 47-50). Overall, Catholic leadership appears to be seeking a middle approach to dialogue, insisting on the importance of truth as revealed definitively and most fully in Christianity, while also respecting the religious beliefs of non-Catholics. The success of this strategy for encouraging dialogue, as gauged by reactions to recent declarations, has been limited at best. *Dominus Iesus* and the Regensburg address illustrate this well.

Dominus Iesus,[27] authored by the Congregation for the Doctrine of the Faith under the leadership of Joseph Cardinal Ratzinger (now Pope Benedict XVI), appeared in 2000. Framed as a clarification of Christ's universal significance for salvation and the Catholic Church's corresponding mission to evangelize, the document was deemed necessary because some Catholics were confused on this point. *Dominus Iesus* states clearly that interreligious dialogue, at least sometimes, serves the central goal of proclamation: "the Church's proclamation of Jesus Christ . . . today . . . makes use of the practice of inter-religious dialogue" (2). The document's insistence on the unicity and universality of Christ and his church, and its view of truth in other religions as preparation for the Gospel, leave little room to discover truth that is not already present in Christianity. Though dialogue was not the focus, *Dominus Iesus* can hardly be said to encourage it; it may even discourage it, since if all truth is revealed in Christ, it is hardly necessary to seek it elsewhere.

Reactions varied widely. Catholics came down on both sides of the question of whether *Dominus Iesus* was needed, well-timed, and sufficiently tactful. Responses from non-Catholic Christians expressed disappointment in the document's failure to account in a meaningful way for the forty years of ecumenical dialogue that preceded it. One Jewish commentator affirmed the church's right to consider itself superior to other religions but objected to the emphasis on mission/conversion as the goal of dialogue.[28] Apparently the document did not frame its main point, which was that only Christ saves and that the Catholic Church mediates that salvation, sensitively enough to elicit a positive response from its various audiences.

The Regensburg address also failed to anticipate its wide audience, sparking mass protests and possibly violence. In it Pope Benedict XVI argued that the Christian God is inherently rational, while other religions, most notably Islam, do not assume that God is rational. This is why he selected the medieval emperor's quotation that elicited such strong reactions: " 'Show me just what Mohammed brought that was new, and there you will find things only evil and inhuman, such as his command to spread by the sword the faith he preached' " (3). Later, Benedict appeared bemused by the fiercely negative reactions and clarified that the quotation did not represent his own view:

> I am deeply sorry for the reactions in some countries to a few passages of my address at the University of Regensburg, which were considered offensive to the sensibility of Muslims. These in fact were a quotation from a medieval text, which do not in any way express my personal thought. Yesterday, the Cardinal Secretary of State published a statement in this regard in which he explained the true meaning of my words. I hope that this serves to appease hearts and to clarify the true meaning of my address, which in its totality was and is an invitation to frank and sincere dialogue, with great mutual respect.[29]

The Cardinal Secretary of State had announced that Benedict "sincerely regrets that certain passages of his address could have sounded offensive to the sensitivities of the Muslim faithful."[30] In these statements, Benedict regrets that offense was taken, but does not admit the possibility that utilizing the passage without expressing disapproval of the insult was itself a mistake. The later interjection into the official text of a phrase describing the emperor's brusqueness as "startling" and "unacceptable" (3) may indicate that Benedict eventually approached such a realization.[31]

Should the history of how Christians have articulated their belief in closed monotheism make us more or less willing to excuse such an error? It may be an unfortunate slip back into an outdated habit of speaking; or it may reveal that the ancient method is alive and well, albeit well- (or not so well-) disguised in the new (or perhaps not so new) rhetoric of Christian love. In any case, Benedict appears to agree that the God of Islam is not bound by rationality and therefore cannot reliably prevent violence among his followers. Benedict argues that violent conversion should be unnecessary if God and God's followers are rational: "The decisive statement in this argument against violent conversion is this: not to act in accordance with reason is contrary to God's nature" (Regensburg address, par. 4). Christianity, he claims, is the best proponent of this argument because of its Greek heritage; and he continues to insist, echoing *Dominus Iesus*, that "inter-religious dialogue . . . [is] part of [the church's] evangelizing mission" (*Dominus Iesus*, 22). Thus, Benedict's argument that violence is not inherent in Christianity turns on his understanding of Greek philosophy's role in Christian thought.

What exactly is the nature of this role? It's not entirely clear. On the one hand, the Regensburg address describes Greek thought and the Gospel as intimately connected, but not identical. Benedict uses terms such as "correlation" (par. 1), "rapprochement" (pars. 5-8), "mutual enrichment" or "profound harmony" (par. 5); the Greek idea of truth and rationality is a useful "analogy" to God (pars. 6-7). But this is a "real" analogy (par. 7), meaning, perhaps, that it says something literally true about God. On the other hand, then, Benedict describes the Greek concept of reason as essential to Christianity. He says that "the critically purified Greek heritage forms an integral part of Christian faith" (par. 9); that with the Greek word and concept of *logos*, "John . . . spoke the final word on the biblical concept of God, and in this word all the often toilsome and tortuous threads of biblical faith find their culmination and synthesis" (par. 5); that "the truly divine God is the God who has revealed himself as *logos*" (par. 7); that, in short, Christianity is European and Europe is Christian (par. 8). In Benedict's analysis, the Greek spirit *does* "have to be integrated into all cultures" (par. 14) in which people wish to embrace Christian faith, for the Greek articulation of the concept of reason is intrinsic to knowing truth and understanding Christ. For Benedict, these are the same thing.

What are we to make of this claim that the Christian God is the *most reasonable* of divinities, and therefore the *most true?* Benedict insists on this even while acknowledging that members of all religions are reasonable and become offended if it is suggested that their divinities are excluded from the "universality of reason" (Regensburg address, par. 16). While Christianity may be the only religion so intimately intertwined with the Greek articulation of the concept of reason, this does not prove that it is the only one that values reason highly.

Further, in light of Schneider's comprehensive description of the development of Christian monotheism, Benedict's reliance on Greek thought as by far the most important source for Christian truth appears reductive. We know reason only through our human exercise of it. Like all descriptors of the divine, it remains a metaphor, and while Christianity may know something about God, it does not necessarily follow that no other religion knows it. Yet Benedict seems to assume that if traditions do not use the same language to describe the divine, they cannot mean the same thing. His preference, in the Regensburg address, for the phrase "dialogue of cultures" over "interreligious dialogue" (see par. 16) may indicate, perhaps unintentionally, that he sees Christian revelation as true religion and other religions as mere cultures, à la Karl Barth.[32]

Official documents of the Catholic Church over the last half-century, then, recognize that dialogue is an essential aspect of life in today's world. They maintain that the fullness of salvation comes solely through Christ and subsists fully only in the Catholic Church, and they teach that because dialogue is part of evangelization, it is always related to proclamation. In particular, Benedict preemptively rules out the possibility that non-Christian religions may possess truth that is not already revealed in Christianity. As globalization progresses, most of these emphases are increasingly unhelpful for encouraging Catholics to participate in dialogue.

Alternative Frameworks for Contemporary Dialogue

Despite good intentions, emphasizing closed monotheism and taking proclamation as the starting point has rendered the approach exemplified in *Dominus Iesus* and the Regensburg address more a hindrance to dialogue than an encouragement. Non-Catholics are naturally warned off by this strong presumptive claim to truth. Likewise, Catholics, some of whom, despite the church's continued insistence on the importance of spreading the Gospel, are already notoriously weak evangelizers (compared to some other Christians at least), may decide they stand to gain nothing through dialogue. If Catholics can learn nothing essential from anyone else, then dialogue becomes for us, as for the ancients, an act of generosity. It would be particularly unfortunate if this emphasis dissuaded from dialogue Catholics who want to learn about other religions but are reluctant to try to convert their members. Is there another way?

At least two possibilities may be gleaned from the thinkers already discussed. First, as Schneider argues, the recognition that closed monotheism is not serving us as well as it once did may lead us to push beyond it.[33] Schneider's intention to understand divinity better is similar to that of a Catholic inclusivist who, following *Nostra Aetate*, engages in dialogue because he wants to attend to the "rays of truth" God shines everywhere. But Schneider does not assume that the Christian will learn nothing new or essential from non-Christians. Again, for her, a God who is known to have become incarnate somewhere must logically be expected to turn up anywhere and everywhere.[34] Reflection upon her account clarifies that the three by now conventional options of a theology of religions (inclusivism, exclusivism, and pluralism) are firmly based in the worldview generated by closed monotheism. If we move beyond this idea, we may also be able to move beyond these options. Careful consideration of divinity-as-multiplicity will, however, take time, even for theologians.

Then again, the problem may not necessarily be closed monotheism itself; it may be that the problem lies in making this aspect of Christian belief the idea with which we must lead, which is incompatible with dialogue. While Schneider's proposal is being considered, then, Benedict's own corpus picks up another strand of the tradition that suggests a second strategy, one that may be able to be implemented more quickly. Notably, while he emphasizes closed monotheism and mission in documents for a Catholic audience, his language is far more diplomatic when he speaks directly to people of various faiths.

To give one example, in an address to representatives of other religions during his apostolic journey to the United States in 2008, he frames his approach to "interreligious dialogue" more invitingly than in the Regensburg address. Using this phrase rather than "dialogue of cultures" (see pars. 6, 9, 11, and 13), he does not privilege proclamation but distinguishes at least three goals for dialogue: first, in its initial stages dialogue generates mutual understanding and ethical common ground, which can produce solidarity among people of varying beliefs (par. 6); second, the "broader" or "higher" purpose of dialogue is to seek truth (par. 9); third, dialogue aims to establish the "peace and security of the human family" (pars. 9, 12). Proclamation fits most properly in the second category, truth. Benedict cautions against avoiding this category, in which he assumes that differences must be discussed and which he fears is neglected because it is difficult. Without agreement here, he believes peace is impossible. He exhorts his hearers to "address . . . these deeper questions" (par. 9), to offer an "exposition of our respective religious tenets" (par. 13), and to "ponder the deeper questions of [our] origin and destiny" (par. 14). Certainly Benedict does not doubt that a sincere search for truth will lead to Christ, but here he coaxes rather than demands.

This approach may temper the unhelpful zeal toward which *Dominus Iesus* and the Regensburg address tend. Leaving aside the question of whether it is accurate to see mutual understanding and ethical common ground as distinct, even separate, from truth, this message contextualizes Benedict's singular emphasis in the "internal" documents by reaffirming the Catholic Church's teaching that dialogue has worthy goals besides proclamation. His ordering of the categories so they begin with understanding could indicate that when engaging in dialogue, Catholics should *not* begin by announcing an evangelical intent, nor see participation as wholly governed by this objective. It might be possible to allow conversion to occur naturally, so to speak, as a result of second-category discussions, if it occurs at all. In addition, these discussions have the further goal of peace. With the categories thus distinguished, it becomes possible to question whether agreeing on truth-questions is necessary to achieve peace; perhaps agreeing to civilly disagree might suffice.

This gentler approach to proclamation as one task of dialogue rather than the only or even the final goal casts it as something to be borne in mind: it should not be forgotten nor ruled out, but it does not need to be emphasized in every dialogue session. Indeed, there is little reason to lead with urgent efforts to convert, since one can trust that God is drawing all people of goodwill toward Godself in God's own time and way. Future "internal" church declarations, then, might do well to contextualize the goal of establishing truth between its companion goals of solidarity and peace. Or at least those reading these declarations should remember this broader context. Far from watering down the effectiveness of dialogue, this shift in emphasis may well attract more participation by Catholics and non-Catholics alike, and may render us more likely to make progress toward the ideal of peace.

The Goal Is Peace: Toward a Dialogical Posture of Humility

In the categories proposed in the 1984 document of the Vatican's Secretariat for Non-Christians (currently the Pontifical Council for Interreligious Dialogue), and as reiterated in *Dialogue and Proclamation* (42-43), the "dialogue of religious experience" among laypersons is no less necessary or important than the "dialogue of theological exchange" among specialists. Ordinary people must be empowered to discuss their beliefs (though, I have argued, not necessarily agree upon them) if we are to move toward peace. Engaging more Catholics to overcome fear, ignorance, and apathy and participate in interreligious dialogue will require both practical and theoretical/theological approaches. The suggestions offered here are intended not as programmatic but as starting points.

Practical measures are quickly identified. It is likely that some Catholics simply do not know that the Vatican considers dialogue important beyond making conversions. The responsibility to learn more rests with individual Catholics, to be sure, but also with the clergy. Anecdotally, but I think not atypically, I can report that when attending church, I am regularly exhorted to invite people to Mass, because (the priest notes) our mission as Catholics is to bring people to Christ. This is well and good. But I am rarely, if ever, reminded from the pulpit that I am called to sincere dialogue with people of faiths that differ from mine. This needs to change. Moreover, clergy who cultivate their own dialogical practices with their counterparts in various religions could serve as a rich resource for parishioners by speaking about these experiences, inviting dialogue partners to speak in their parishes, or collaborating with these partners to bring together members of their respective traditions. These remedies are straightforward, even obvious. Catholics need dynamic models of successful dialogue not only in books but where we live, work, and worship.

Theologically, I maintain that Catholics need the ability to contextualize more carefully and articulate more humbly the Catholic Church's claim to the fullness of truth. The arrogance that has attended Christian expressions of closed monotheism reflects a God who is perhaps stingier with love and self-revelation than the one in whom we profess to believe. To this end, I have proposed that the church would do well to begin to practice doctrinal humility, specifically by entertaining the possibility that it is indeed time to move "beyond monotheism."

Schneider's "deceptively simple" thesis[35] pushes the bounds of what the Vatican considers orthodox, and some Catholics may worry about compromising their Catholicity; at any rate, most lack the time and training to discover all the implications of this move. While the *sensus fidelium* must be a deciding factor, scholars, clergy, and other experts will play a vital role in this cooperative venture into doctrinal humility. Even if it should be determined that now is not the time to move "beyond monotheism," a thorough and self-critical re-evaluation of this belief could precipitate a shift in how we articulate it, which should decrease the likelihood of catastrophic blunders. This is imperative in our contemporary world, for despite the Vatican's frequently successful dialogue efforts, events like the Regensburg fracas get great publicity.

Further, the relationship of proclamation to dialogue needs careful ongoing treatment. The Christian who enters into dialogue intent on the partner's conversion, no matter how lovingly, is experienced by all but the most confident, empathetic dialogue partner as committing an act of violence. It must be clear that agreement on truth-claims is a possible but unnecessary outcome of dialogue; mutual learning naturally precedes it, and peace is the final goal. The church's mission can never cease to be evangelization, bringing Christ to the world. Insofar as dialogue is engaged in by believing Christians, it cannot fall outside the scope of this mission. But Christians believe that the reign of God, the end toward which the Church's mission strains, will be characterized by the absence of pain and sorrow—that is, by perfect peace. If Christ means peace, then to bring peace through dialogue is to fulfill the church's mission, regardless of agreement on truth-claims. Within the conventional framework, these statements might be viewed as either inclusivist or pluralist. I have tried to suggest that Schneider's idea of divinity as multiplicity could propel us beyond these options to a more supple stance.

As a way Christians might begin working toward this theology of humility, consider the position taken by Francis X. Clooney, S.J., in his book *Hindu God, Christian God: How Reason Helps Break Down the Boundaries between Religions*.[36] Clooney presumes that, since religious people are rational and hold that our beliefs make sense, if we discuss them calmly and with genuine curiosity (not assuming that we know what the other is going to say or that we have something better to say), we may find more similarities between our faiths than we might have guessed. Indeed, Clooney finds common ground between Hinduism and Christianity on the level of what Benedict calls "truth" in the beliefs that divinity exists and can be known, at least in part, through reason, that divinity can become incarnate, and that revelation can be known, at least in part, through reason. As we have seen, Benedict begins both *Dominus Iesus* and the Regensburg address by declaring that only his religion can be truest and naming what he believes are irreducible differences among religions. Conversely, Clooney begins by looking for similarities at the very same level of truth-claims.

This difference in method produces vastly different results. Although it is possible that both thinkers ultimately believe Christianity is true (or at least more true) and other religions are false (or at least less true), Benedict's starting point may make it difficult for him to attract dialogue partners, while Clooney's allows him to engage dynamically with members of another tradition. In fact, one Hindu scholar's response to Clooney's book is included as a postscript. Whereas Benedict assumes Christians will learn nothing important about God from another faith, Clooney leaves this possibility open. He does not assume that he will gain new information about God; he simply does not predetermine whether he will do so. Not assuming that others do not know what we know is a first step toward doctrinal humility, and this does not require surrendering the claim that Christianity is true or even unique.[37] But privileging the gathering of information and the increasing of understanding allows real dialogue to take place—dialogue in which both members can learn something they did not already know, and in which the non-Christian need not inevitably be put off by the Christian's *real* goal of converting her. Clooney's effort leads to a peaceful and productive relationship with his interlocutor even though they do not reach complete agreement on all truth-claims. This is a challenging and worthwhile aim for dialogue in our chaotically interconnected world.

Put simply, then, a theology of humility in dialogue means that the realization that we do not know everything, and that others know something as well, remains operative in our thoughts about and conversations with people of varying religious traditions. In comparing beliefs, reason allows us to try to understand one another, but it does not always allow us to pass judgment on competing claims. The ultimately mysterious nature of God requires us to embrace the possibility—and even to expect—that we will learn something new as we seek together the peace that passes all understanding.

The teachings of Jesus can support a theology of humility: the assertion that "the last shall be first," the injunction to love our enemies, the Golden Rule. Moreover, Jesus' description of the last judgment, the parable of the sheep and the goats recounted in Matthew 25, indicates that all who live in solidarity with our neighbors—that is, in authentic peace—will be saved, regardless of whether we profess belief in Christ. Humility as the method and peace as the goal should equip and encourage many more Catholics to engage in the vital work of interreligious dialogue.

Notes

[1]Benedict XVI, "Faith, Reason and the University: Memories and Reflections" (hereafter "Regensburg address"), given at the University of Regensburg, Germany, September 12, 2006. For this and other papal and church documents, unless noted otherwise, I have used the English translations available on the Vatican's website, www.vatican.va. The text of the Regensburg address does not include paragraph numbers; I have assigned them for convenient reference.

[2]Kelly Brown Douglas, *What's Faith Got to Do with It? Black Bodies/Christian Souls* (Maryknoll, NY: Orbis Books, 2006), esp. 10-16, 42-50.

[3]Laurel C. Schneider, *Beyond Monotheism: A Theology of Multiplicity* (London and New York: Routledge, 2008).

[4]The example I use in this essay is Benedict XVI, "Meeting with Representatives of Other Religions: Address of His Holiness Benedict XVI" (hereafter "Meeting with Representatives"), given during the apostolic journey to the United States at the Pope John Paul II Cultural Center, Washington, D.C., April 17, 2008. The text does not include paragraph numbers; I have assigned them for convenient reference.

[5]Schneider, *Beyond Monotheism*, chaps. 2, 3, and 4, respectively.

[6]Ibid., 154-57.

[7]Schneider outlines the history and interrogates the usefulness of the word "monotheism"—which, she reports, first appeared in print about 1680 C.E., shortly after "polytheism" (see chap. 2 of *Beyond Monotheism*). The research that follows here is my own.

[8]Justin Martyr, *First Apology*, trans. Thomas B. Falls (New York: Christian Heritage, 1948), chap. 46.

[9]Basil the Great, "Letter CCXXXIII, To Amphilochius," trans. Blomfield Jackson, in *Nicene and Post-Nicene Fathers, Second Series*, vol. 8, *St. Basil: Letters and Selected Works*, ed. Philip Schaff and Henry Wace (1895; Peabody, MA: Hendrickson, 1994), 273.

[10]Ambrose, *Of the Christian Faith*, trans. H. de Romestin, in *Nicene and Post-Nicene Fathers, Second Series*, vol. 10, *St. Ambrose: Select Works and Letters* (1896; Peabody, MA: Hendrickson, 1994), 203.

[11]Gregory Nazianzen, *The Third Theological Oration: On the Son*, trans. Charles Gordon Browne and James Edward Swallow, in *Nicene and Post-Nicene Fathers, Second Series*, vol. 7, *S. Cyril of Jerusalem, S. Gregory Nazianzen*, ed. Philip Schaff and Henry Wace (1894; Peabody, MA: Hendrickson, 1994), 302.

[12]Gregory Nazianzen, *The Third Theological Oration*, 301.

[13]Gregory of Nyssa, *Against Eunomius*, trans. William Moore and Henry Austin Wilson, in *Nicene and Post-Nicene Fathers, Second Series*, vol. 5, *Gregory of Nyssa: Dogmatic Treatises, etc.*, ed. Philip Schaff and Henry Wace (1893; Peabody, MA: Hendrickson, 1994), 35-36. See also Psalm 137:9 (NAB).

[14]Augustine, *On Christian Teaching*, trans. with an introduction and notes by R. P. H. Green (Oxford: Oxford University Press, 1997), 141.

[15]Francis A. Sullivan, S.J., *Salvation Outside the Church? Tracing the History of the Catholic Response* (New York: Paulist Press, 1992), especially chaps. 4, 5, and the Conclusion.

[16]Douglas, *What's Faith Got to Do with It?* 14.

[17]Schneider, *Beyond Monotheism*, ix.

[18]Ibid., chaps. 11-12.

[19]Ibid., esp. chaps. 7, 11.

[20]Ibid., 156.

[21]See especially Schneider's lyrical rereading of the story of Jesus and the woman at the well in *Beyond Monotheism*, 117-20.

[22]Cornille discusses humility and four other virtues she deems essential to dialogue in *The im-Possibility of Interreligious Dialogue* (New York: Crossroad Publishing, 2008). On humility, see chap. 1 and the Conclusion.

[23]See Sullivan, *Salvation Outside the Church?* esp. chaps. 9-11.

[24]Translations in this paragraph are from Austin Flannery, OP, ed., *Vatican Council II: Constitutions, Decrees, Declarations* (Northport, NY: Costello, 1996).

[25]For a detailed history of many of these efforts, see Edward Idris Cardinal Cassidy, *Ecumenism and Interreligious Dialogue: Unitatis Redintegratio, Nostra Aetate* (New York: Paulist Press, 2005).

[26]Cornille, *The im-Possibility of Interreligious Dialogue*, 198.

[27]Congregation for the Doctrine of the Faith, *Declaration "Dominus Iesus" on the Unicity and Salvific Universality of Jesus Christ and the Church* (hereafter *Dominus Iesus*), August 6, 2000.

[28]See the responses collected in Stephen J. Pope and Charles Hefling, eds., *Sic et Non: Encountering Dominus Iesus* (Maryknoll, NY: Orbis Books, 2002), esp. David Berger's "On *Dominus Iesus* and the Jews," 39-43.

[29]Benedict XVI, "Angelus, Castel Gandolfo, Sunday, 17 September 2006."

[30]"Pope 'sincerely regrets' he offended Muslims," MSNBC, September 17, 2006, available at http://msnbc.com/id/14861689/ (accessed October 20, 2010).

[31]The original text can be found online at http://www.catholicculture.org/news/features/index.cfm?recnum=46474 (accessed October 20, 2010). In the amended (official) text, see also note #4, clearly added or expanded later.

[32]Recall also the distinction put forth in *Dominus Iesus*, par. 7, between "theological faith" (in Christianity) and "belief" (in non-Christian religions). This contrast between religion and culture, or faith and belief, echoes Barth's elevation of Christian "revelation" over "religion" in *Church Dogmatics* I.2, section 17, "The Revelation of God as the Abolition of Religion." For Barth, Christianity is *not* "the true religion, fundamentally superior to all other religions," because God is revealed only in Christianity, whereas "religion is unbelief" (*Church Dogmatics* I.2, ed. G. W. Bromiley and T. F. Torrance, trans. G. T. Thomson and Harold Knight [Edinburgh: T & T Clark, 1956], 298-99).

[33]Schneider, *Beyond Monotheism*, 190-91.

[34]Ibid., chap. 12.

[35]Ibid., 1.

[36]Francis X. Clooney, S.J., *Hindu God, Christian God: How Reason Helps Break Down the Boundaries between Religions* (New York: Oxford University Press, 2001).

[37]Benedict, following the church's inclusivist position, certainly would not surrender this claim. Clooney, whose work focuses on comparing texts, has not definitively declared his position on the theology-of-religions spectrum; he has recently stated, "My comparative theology is in harmony with those inclusivist theologies, in the great tradition of Karl Rahner, SJ, and Jacques Dupuis, SJ, that balance claims to Christian uniqueness with a necessary openness to learning from other religions." He goes on to characterize his as an "including theology" (Francis X. Clooney, *Comparative Theology: Deep Learning across Religious Borders* [Malden, MA: Wiley-Blackwell, 2010], 16).

List of Contributors

Charles C. Camosy is an assistant professor of Christian ethics at Fordham University in New York City, where he also serves on the Ethics Committee of Children's Hospital. In addition to planning a conference with Peter Singer designed to find new ways to think and speak about abortion, he is the author of two forthcoming books: *Too Expensive to Treat?* and *Peter Singer and Christian Ethics*.

Laurie Cassidy is an assistant professor of religious studies at Marywood University in Scranton, Pennsylvania. She is the co-editor, with Alex Mikulich, of *Interrupting White Privilege: Catholic Theologians Break the Silence*, a Catholic Theology Society's book of the year (2007). Her work as a 2009 Luce Faculty Fellow for the Society for the Study of Art in Religion and Theological Studies will be published in *She Who Imagines: A Catholic Feminist Aesthetic*, a volume co-edited with Maureen O'Connell. Cassidy's research draws on the resources of Christian mysticism for individual and social transformation, particularly in responding to contemporary culture.

Christine M. Fletcher is an assistant professor of theology at Benedictine University in Lisle, Illinois. At Benedictine she has designed a new theology program that includes a certificate in Theology in Life. She holds a Master's in politics and philosophy from Oxford University and a Ph.D. in theology with subspecialties in business ethics and literature from Anglia Ruskin University in Cambridge, England.

Timothy R. Gabrielli is a doctoral student in the University of Dayton's theology program in Catholicism in the United States. He holds an M.A. in theology from the University of Dayton.

His primary areas of research and teaching include sacramental theology and ecclesiology.

Roberto S. Goizueta holds the Margaret O'Brien Flatley Chair in Catholic Theology at Boston College. A past president of the Catholic Theological Society of America and the Academy of Catholic Hispanic Theologians of the United States, he is author of many articles and *Caminemos con Jesús: Toward a Hispanic/Latino Theology of Accompaniment* and *Christ Our Companion: Toward a Theological Aesthetics of Liberation*.

Elizabeth Lee recently received her Ph.D. in ethics and social theory at the Graduate Theological Union. Her dissertation, "Made in the Images of God: Towards a Trinitarian Virtue Ethics," explores the ways in which different understandings of God can have different implications for moral anthropology and the kinds of virtues Christians pursue.

Vincent Miller holds the Gudorf Chair in Catholic Theology and Culture at the University of Dayton. He is the author of *Consuming Religion: Christian Faith and Practice in a Consumer Culture* and co-editor, with Robert Schreiter, of a volume of *Theological Studies* on "Theology and Globalization" in June 2008. He is currently working on a book that engages the ethical, cultural, and theological consequences of globalization and new communications and media technologies.

Anselm K. Min is dean and the Maguire Distinguished Professor of Religion, The School of Religion at Claremont Graduate University. He is the author of, among others, *Paths to the Triune God: An Encounter between Aquinas and Recent Theologies*, *The Solidarity of Others: A Postmodern Theology after Postmodernism*, and *The Dialectic of Salvation: Issues in Theology of Liberation*. He has published on Hegel, postmodernism, pluralism, liberation theology, and Asian theology as well as on the usual topics of systematic theology. He is working on a systematic theology of globalization.

María Teresa Morgan is an assistant professor of theology at St. John Vianney College Seminary in Miami where she also coordinates the Humanities and General Education Programs. Her research and praxis focus on local theologies emerging from cultural and ethnic diversity, on the works of Teresa of Avila and John of the Cross, and on theological aesthetics.

Maureen H. O'Connell is an assistant professor of theology at Fordham University. She authored *Compassion: Loving Our Neighbor in an Age of Globalization*, which argues for a revival of the virtue of compassion in light of Hurricane Katrina and global poverty. Currently, she explores the arts as a source of ethical wisdom and a catalyst for moral action in *If These Walls Could Talk: Community Muralism and the Beauty of Justice* (forthcoming). She is a board member of the Society for the Arts in Religious and Theological Studies.

Rebecca Todd Peters is an associate professor and chair of the Religious Studies Department at Elon University. Her book, *In Search of the Good Life: The Ethics of Globalization*, won the 2003 Trinity Book Prize. She is co-editor of *Justice in the Making*; *Justice in a Global Economy: Strategies for Home, Community and World*; and *To Do Justice: A Guide for Progressive Christians*, and is currently working on a book on solidarity ethics. An ordained PC(USA) minister, she is active denominationally and ecumenically and is a member of the Faith and Order Commission of the World Council of Churches.

Andrew Prevot is a doctoral candidate in systematic theology at the University of Notre Dame and is currently writing a dissertation on theology as a prayerful mode of thought. His research highlights connections between contemporary Catholic theology, continental philosophy of religion, modern social theory and praxis, and the history of Christian spirituality.

Daniel P. Scheid is an assistant professor of theology at Duquesne University in Pittsburgh. His publications include the article "Common Good" for the *Encyclopedia of Sustainability* and "Vedānta Deśika and Thomas Aquinas on the Intrinsic Value of Nature" in the *Journal of Vaishnava Studies*. His research interests are in ecological and comparative ethics.

Ryan Stander is currently a graduate student at The University of North Dakota, Grand Forks, pursuing a Master of Fine Arts in mixed media. His focus reflects his interdisciplinary interests of art and theology and, in particular, the cultivation of place and its significance for human life. Approaching place from two disciplines offers a variety of unique conversation points, methodologies, and curious trajectories.

Karen Teel earned her Ph.D. at Boston College and is an assistant professor in the Department of Theology and Religious Studies at the University of San Diego. Her recent research has focused primarily on Christian anthropology, womanist theologies, and theological responses to racism. She is also interested in the theology of religions and interreligious dialogue.

Johann M. Vento is an associate professor and chair of the Department of Religious Studies, Theology and Philosophy and a member of the Women's Studies faculty at Georgian Court University in Lakewood, New Jersey. Her research and published works focus on the interrelationship of political theology and feminist theology and on violence against women. Dr. Vento serves on the think tank of the Elijah Interfaith Institute.

Traci C. West is a professor of ethics and African American studies at Drew University Theological School in Madison, New Jersey. She is the author of *Disruptive Christian Ethics: When Racism and Women's Lives Matter*, *Wounds of the Spirit: Black Women, Violence, and Resistance Ethics*, the editor of *Our Family Values: Religion and Same-sex Marriage*, and the author of several articles on justice issues in church and society. She is an ordained minister in the United Methodist Church.

Mary Ann Zimmer, N.D., is an assistant professor of religious studies at Marywood University in Scranton, Pennsylvania. She is the author of *Mary 101: Tradition and Influence*. Her work has appeared in *Women and the Shaping of Catholicism*, the *Proceedings of the Forum on Religion and Public Life* for the Community of Christ, and *In the Embrace of God: A Feminist Reader in Theological Anthropology*.